CU20871674

The Globalization of Liberalism

Published in association with *Millennium: Journal of International Studies*

Titles include:

Dominique Jacquin-Berdal, Andrew Oros and Marco Verweij (*editors*)
CULTURE IN WORLD POLITICS

Hugh C. Dyer and Leon Mangasarian (*editors*)
THE STUDY OF INTERNATIONAL RELATIONS
The State of the Art

Michi Ebata and Beverly Neufeld (*editors*)
CONFRONTING THE POLITICAL IN INTERNATIONAL RELATIONS

Lorraine Eden and Evan Potter (*editors*)
MULTINATIONALS IN THE GLOBAL POLITICAL ECONOMY

Rick Fawn and Jeremy Larkins (*editors*)
INTERNATIONAL SOCIETY AFTER THE COLD WAR

Eivind Hovden and Edward Keene (*editors*)
THE GLOBALIZATION OF LIBERALISM

Maria Lensu and Jan-Stefan Fritz (*editors*)
VALUE PLURALISM, NORMATIVE THEORY AND INTERNATIONAL RELATIONS

Kathleen Newland (*editor*)
THE INTERNATIONAL RELATIONS OF JAPAN

Hakan Seckinelgin and Hideaki Shinoda (*editors*)
ETHICS AND INTERNATIONAL RELATIONS

Sarah Owen Vandersluis (*editor*)
THE STATE AND IDENTITY CONSTRUCTION IN INTERNATIONAL
RELATIONS

Sarah Owen Vandersluis and Paris Yeros (*editors*)
POVERTY IN WORLD POLITICS
Whose Global Era?

The Globalization of Liberalism

Edited by

Eivind Hovden
Associate Professor
Programme for Research and Documentation
Centre for Development and Environment
University of Oslo
Norway

and

Edward Keene
Formerly Lecturer in International Politics
School of Oriental and African Studies
University of London

in association with
Millennium Journal of
International Studies

First published 2002 by
PALGRAVE
Houndmills, Basingstoke, Hampshire RG21 6XS and
175 Fifth Avenue, New York, N.Y. 10010
Companies and representatives throughout the world

PALGRAVE is the new global academic imprint of
St. Martin's Press LLC Scholarly and Reference Division and
Palgrave Publishers Ltd (formerly Macmillan Press Ltd).

ISBN 0–333–72475–5

This book is printed on paper suitable for recycling and made from fully managed and sustained forest sources.

Cataloguing-in-publication data

A catalogue record for this book is available from the British Library.

A catalogue record for this book is available from the Library of Congress.

10 9 8 7 6 5 4 3 2 1
11 10 09 08 07 06 05 04 03 02

Printed and bound in Great Britain by
Antony Rowe Ltd, Chippenham, Wiltshire

Contents

Acknowledgements

Chapter 2 is based on Robert O. Keohane, 'International Liberalism Reconsidered', in J. Dunn (ed.), *The Economic Limits to Modern Politics* (Cambridge University Press, 1990), and permission from Cambridge University Press to use this material is gratefully acknowledged. The idea behind this book (as well as some of the contributions) originated from a special issue of *Millennium* in 1995. Like most things connected to *Millennium*, it is the product of a collective effort that goes well beyond ourselves. In particular, we would like to acknowledge the enormous contribution of the members of the *Millennium* team who worked on this volume, notably: Amer Al-Baho, Mari Johnson, Bice Maiguashca, Maya Prahbu, Mark Basil Salter, Paris Yeros, Catherine Eschele, Stephen B. Idowu, Sarah Owen and Beverly Neufeld. Without their generous and unstinting dedication to the journal, this book would undoubtedly not have been possible, and we offer our sincere thanks for all they have done. In addition, we would like to express our gratitude for the support that *Millennium* enjoys from the International Relations Department at the London School of Economics, especially from the numerous graduate students and faculty members who generously gave their time to help us put together the special issue on the 'globalization of liberalism'. The Program for Research and Documentation for a Sustainable Society (ProSus) at the University of Oslo, and the Fridtjof Nansen Institute at Lysaker, have both provided us with valuable assistance, for which we are very grateful.

We would also like to thank the contributors for their commitment and hard work. Finally, we owe a great debt to our families and friends for their support, especially to Mala and Molly. Their patience and encouragement have been priceless for both of us.

Notes on the Contributors

Katerina Dalacoura is Lecturer in International Relations at the London School of Economics and Political Science. She has also worked at the University of Essex and the International Institute of Strategic Studies. Her research interests include international relations theory, human rights and the Middle East, and she is the author of *Islam, Liberalism and Human Rights: Implications for International Relations*.

Richard Falk is Albert G. Milbank Professor of International Law and Practice at the Center of International Studies at Princeton University, New Jersey. His main area of interest concerns global governance and international law. He has also written extensively on conflict and peace, foreign policy, world poverty and human rights. His most recent books include *Law in an Emerging Global Village* and *Predatory Globalization: A Critique*.

Mervyn Frost is Professor of International Relations at the University of Kent at Canterbury, UK. His research is in the field of normative international relations theory and he has published extensively in this area, including *Towards a Normative Theory of International Relations* and *Ethics in International Relations*, as well as recent articles in *Political Studies, Review of International Studies* and *Cambridge Review of International Affairs*.

Stephen Gill is Professor of Political Science at the York University, Toronto. He has written extensively on international political economy, international relations theory and historical materialism. He is author of *American Hegemony and the Trilateral Commission*, co-author of *The Global Political Economy* and editor of *Gramsci, Historical Materialism and International Relations* and *Innovation and Transformation in International Studies*. He has published articles in *Millennium, Alternatives, New Political Economy, International Studies Quarterly, Monthly Review* and *Geoforum*.

Eivind Hovden recently completed his PhD on environmentalism and international relations theory. Formerly a Senior Research Fellow at the Fridtjof Nansen Institute, Oslo, where he joined the Institute's European Programme in 1999, he is now Associate Professor in the

Programme for Research and Documentation for Sustainable Society, at the Centre for Development and Environment, University of Oslo. His research interests include EU environmental policy, as well as international relations theory and the environment. He was the editor of *Millennium: Journal of International Studies* (Volume 24).

Christopher Hughes is Lecturer in International Relations at the London School of Economics and Political Science. His publications include *Taiwan and Chinese Nationalism*, as well as articles on Chinese nationalism in *Millennium, China Quarterly* and *Asian Thought and Society*.

Edward Keene recently completed his PhD on the Grotian tradition, the practice of colonialism and modern international society. He was editor of *Millennium: Journal of International Studies* (Volume 24), and is currently living in Georgia and writing a book on the history of international political thought.

Robert O. Keohane is James B. Duke Professor of Political Science at Duke University, North Carolina. His most important publications include *Power and Interdependence* (with Joseph Nye) and *After Hegemony*, and he edited the highly influential volume *Neorealism and its Critics*. A collection of his essays was published as *International Institutions and State Power*. His most recent publications include *Internationalization and Domestic Politics* (with Helen V. Milner), and a new and revised edition of *Power and Interdependence*.

David Long is Associate Professor of International Affairs in the Norman Paterson School of International Affairs at Carleton University and President of the European Community Studies Association of Canada. He is the author of *Towards a New Liberal Internationalism*, and co-editor of *Thinkers of the Twenty Years' Crisis, New Perspectives on International Functionalism*, and a Special Issue of the *Journal of European Integration* on The EU's Common Foreign and Security Policy.

John MacMillan is Lecturer in International Relations at the School of Politics, International Relations and the Environment at Keele University, UK. His research interests include liberalism and international relations, democratic peace and global governance. He is the author of *On Liberal Peace: Democracy, War and the International Order*.

A. K. Ramakrishnan is Reader in the School of International Relations, Mahatma Gandhi University, Kerala, India. He is currently at Bucknell University, Lewisburg, Pennsylvania, as a Distinguished International

Scholar and Visiting Professor. His areas of teaching, writing and interest include international relations theory, postcolonialism, feminism and West Asian area studies.

John Gerard Ruggie is James T. Shortwell Professor of International Relations at Columbia University in New York City. He is currently on leave to work as Assistant Secretary-General at the United Nations. His research interests include international relations theory and political economy, and he has published extensively in these fields. His most recent publications include *Winning the Peace: American and World Order in the New Era* and *Constructing the World Polity: Essays on International Institutionalization.*

Tom Young is Senior Lecturer in Politics at the School of Oriental and African Studies, University of London. He has written extensively on Southern African politics, and is currently working on a book about liberal political thought.

Introduction

Eivind Hovden and Edward Keene

In a typically pithy aside, Karl Marx commented that '[i]t is far too easy to be "liberal" at the expense of the Middle Ages'.[1] His point was that most histories of feudalism are coloured by 'bourgeois prejudices', and ignore the fact that 'although the soil of England, after the Norman conquest, was divided up into gigantic baronies ... it was strewn with small peasant properties, only interspersed here and there with great seigniorial domains'.[2] By not recognizing that such smallholdings existed, the conventional historiography painted an exaggerated picture of the miserable and servile condition of the feudal peasant, so as to extol by comparison the virtues of the system of 'equal' rights and 'free' labour associated with democratic politics and market economics. According to Marx, these historians, and the political economists who deliberately or accidentally repeated their mistake, had thus failed to take account of one of the main processes by which capitalist relations of production were introduced in England: 'the great feudal lords ... created an incomparably larger proletariat by forcibly driving the peasantry from the land, to which the latter had the same feudal title as the lords themselves, and by usurpation of the common lands'.[3]

We are presenting this book on the 'globalization of liberalism' because we believe that a similar, albeit differently framed, problem exists within international relations theory today. To adapt Marx's phrase, it is far too easy to be 'liberal' at the expense of the anarchical states system. What we mean by this is that international relations are typically described in a way that makes them appear fundamentally distinct from the domestic organization of liberal societies, and liberalism is thus insulated from the undesirable features of modern international relations and freed from responsibility for contemporary international problems. Of course, this is usually seen as disadvanta-

1

geous for international liberalism, since it therefore becomes vulnerable to the charge of being utopian. This accusation is often based on the empirical grounds that, as Joseph Nye puts it in a popular textbook, '[s]ome aspects of international politics have not changed since Thucydides, which is chastening for liberals'.[4] The historical point that anarchy is a peculiarly enduring feature of international relations is taken to imply that liberalism, which employs a 'language appropriate to man's control of his social life' to construct a 'theory of the good life', is ill-suited to the kinds of practical problems that continually recur at the international level, such as how to survive in a world that lacks any central political authority and where force is the *ultima ratio* of politics.[5]

However, at the same time this understanding of the division between liberal political theory and the practice of the anarchical states system credits liberalism with an important role as a critical perspective on existing forms of international order, and it allows liberalism to be associated with those aspects of international relations that do not fit with the power-political dynamics that are held to result from anarchy and the division of the world into territorial, sovereign units. Thus, realism becomes a language of stasis, war, competition, security dilemmas, the will of the stronger and survival; liberalism becomes associated with progressive change, peace, cooperative regimes, institutions for global governance, justice and the good life. This is not a particularly bad arrangement for liberals. Their theoretical discourse comes to provide the basic vocabulary for conceptualizing these normatively desirable goals, and the only price they have to pay is being labelled 'utopian', which may easily be overcome when one considers that the accusation of utopianism rests on the dubious claim that anarchy is not merely a persistent feature of international relations in the past, but that it will continue to be the organizing principle of the international system in the future.

It is significant that this comforting picture is undermined when one asks what the relationship is between the political 'utopianism' of liberalism and the actually existing structure of the capitalist world economy.[6] If one accepts that there is some relationship between liberalism and capitalism, then it becomes much harder to insulate liberal political ideals from the more unpleasant realities of modern international economic order. If we broaden our description of modern international relations to include other aspects than simply the political aspects of conflict and competition in the anarchical states system, such as structural violence and inequality in the world economy, we acquire a very different perspective on liberalism's claim that it offers a critical perspective about how to go beyond actually existing patterns of international order. If liberalism is already such an important part of oppressive and exploitative modern international practices through its connection to capitalism, what sense does it make to describe liberalism as a 'utopian' set of ideal-theoretical prescriptions? Liberal ideas may still be defensible, perhaps as a corrective to the worst implications of capitalist economics, but they can no longer be treated as normatively pristine.

Moreover, while international economic relations might present this problem for liberalism in an especially acute and challenging way, there may also be a sense in which liberalism cannot even be insulated from the political structure of the actually existing international society. As Chris Hughes points out in his chapter in this volume, for example, one can see the legal-political framework of the modern international society as founded upon a 'semantic shift that took place in the European tradition [of thought], when states came to be conceived in terms of a macrocosm of the human being, possessing all the attributes of a soul, body, and rights that this entails', and this has created certain 'ambiguities in the language of liberalism' that can be exploited to mount a defence of regimes that may be judged as illiberal by other criteria. What is significant here, for the moment at least, is that these ambiguities are *internal* to the language of liberalism; they are not evidence that the modern international society itself is legally and politically organized in a fundamentally illiberal way, and that liberals are in an antagonistic position towards it. Again, it becomes harder for liberals to present themselves as critics of the existing patterns of international order, since their conceptual vocabulary is so deeply implicated in the structure of the modern international society.

Alternatively, one could argue that if liberal political theory is understood to have a close connection to the kinds of reasoning associated with the Enlightenment, one might reasonably ask whether liberalism is so far removed from many of the problems created by modern international relations. For example, contemporary problems of environmental degradation are sometimes seen as arising from the Enlightenment belief that humans have a right, and should therefore have the capacity, to dominate, control and use nature. Again, as with the shift in focus towards the relationship between liberalism and capitalist economics, if liberal political theory is connected with Enlightenment attitudes towards nature, it can no longer insulate itself from the realities of modern international practice and the problems associated with those modern practices. Liberals can more easily defend themselves against the charge of utopianism, indeed such an accusation becomes faintly ridiculous, but only at the price of losing their political innocence. At the very least, one has to ask a serious question about the actual normative and political content of international liberalism, in the sense that one needs to ask how liberal principles have been developed within the modern international order, and whether we can treat liberal political theory as expressing prescriptions that can be described as idealistic at all.

One reason why this question is ignored by the conventional way of thinking about liberal 'utopianism' is the conceptual vagueness that surrounds the idea of liberalism, and not just in international relations: as a necessary clarification, then, the first chapter in the book, by Robert Keohane, presents a useful survey of different strands within liberal thought about international relations. For our part, in an attempt to provide a yet more general framework than Keohane offers, we would suggest that there are at least three distinct themes contained within liberalism, which all inform the ways in which international liberalism can be understood.

First, liberalism may be associated with a particular doctrine about moral and political philosophy, which seeks to provide a justification for individuals' liberty and rights, usually in terms of their natural characteristics or capacities as human beings. Of course, this moral point of view has many different forms of expression: it may, for example, be traced to the 'possessive individualism' that attended seventeenth-century British notions that individuals have a property right over their own persons and the fruits of their labour; or it may be seen as connected to eighteenth-century French and German ideas about the human capacity for reason.[7] Second, there is a methodological orientation peculiar to liberal social science, which is often expressed in terms of the idea that all social institutions should be understood as aggregations of individuals who have some degree of freedom of choice. Therefore, liberal approaches to social science stress the importance of interpreting individuals' intentions, in the sense of their rational self-interest or subjectively and intersubjectively held ideas, for understanding their behaviour and the outcomes of their collective actions.[8] Third, there is a particular form of liberal social and political organization, associated with the separation of the private and the public spheres from each other, with the institutionalization of a system of market relations in the former and equal, democratic rights and liberties in the latter. While this may or may not be precisely in accordance with the prescriptions of liberal moral and political philosophy, what it suggests is that liberalism is, in Tom Young's phrase, a 'project' that has been progressively realized over the last three hundred years and is still being pursued today, both within and beyond European societies. To the extent that liberal moral doctrines can be seen merely as a rationalization of this state of affairs, they may be criticized as a form of ideology; a quite different objection to the claim that they are utopian.

The criticism that international liberalism is 'utopian' reflects only the first of these themes within liberalism in general, and more or less disregards the others completely. Some scholars, particularly 'neoliberal' institutionalists like Keohane, have neatly responded to this criticism by stressing the second element in liberal thought, its methodological orientation for social science, from which they have developed a positive liberal theory of international relations which can, as Keohane points out, be used to support liberalism's various normative commitments if one so chooses. The strength of this position is that, if it can demonstrate that liberalism offers a useful form of social scientific enquiry, then it is mistaken to dismiss it as 'merely' ideal-theoretical, and Keohane's suggested kind of 'non-utopian' liberalism can actually inform international relations theory in a very profound way. Admittedly, while Keohane's version of international liberalism has undoubtedly been highly influential in contemporary international relations theory, this move is not without its problems or critics: David Long objects to Keohane's move, arguing that it goes too far in its neglect of the first strand of liberal moral and political thought, and 'does violence to liberal political philosophy'.

In Part I, we present Long's argument, in company with Keohane's discussion of the core themes within liberal approaches to social science that might inform international relations theory and his response to the kind of objection that Long raises. We think that this debate is important for a proper understanding of the problems that are created by the oversimplistic treatment of international liberalism as purely ideal-theoretical and potentially utopian. Here, we include John MacMillan's discussion of the relationship between Immanuel Kant's political thought and contemporary thinking about the connection between democracy and peace (which Keohane describes as 'republican liberalism'). MacMillan's argument highlights another awkward feature of international liberalism: the juxtaposition of liberal moral or political philosophical doctrines with liberalism as the definitively modern form of political and social organization.

This enquiry is developed in more detail in Part II. In general, the thrust of the chapters here is that modern international relations have been organized in ways that fundamentally correlate with liberal patterns of social organization, and they try to ascertain how these liberal features of modern international order are changing, developing or even, in John Gerard Ruggie's phrase, becoming 'disembedded' in the contemporary international system. They also, as in the contribution from Richard Falk for example, investigate certain contradictions that exist between different aspects of the modern liberal international order, particularly with respect to the capitalist nature of the world economy and the political principles embodied in projects for institutional development. Despite their very different attitudes towards liberalism – compare, for example, Richard Falk and Mervyn Frost with Stephen Gill and Tom Young – they broadly agree on the proposition that it is a serious mistake to divorce modern international practices from liberalism. On the contrary, they contend that one cannot understand the structure of modern international order without an appreciation of the ways in which it has been informed by liberal organizing principles. The main problem that they pose, then, is how to evaluate this 'really existing' international liberalism,[9] and to ask what is currently happening to these modern patterns of liberal international order.

The final part of this volume looks at the complications that international liberalism encounters when it is put into a truly global context. The underlying theme here concerns the way in which liberalism has been part of the process of the expansion of the modern international society and how it affects contemporary non-European societies. The three chapters in Part III reflect on quite different aspects of this process. Hughes explores the ways in which Chinese statesmen have been able to exploit ambiguities in the language of liberalism for their own purposes; Katerina Dalacoura investigates the impact of liberal ideas about human rights upon political debates about rights within Middle Eastern countries; and A. K. Ramakrishnan analyses the possibilities for the construction of a distinctly non-liberal form of social organization in India. These reflections are highly significant additions to the arguments in Part II because, if the modern international order can be conceived as an expanding liberal political, social and economic order driven by European imperialism and dominance, then it is vital that students of international relations should make the effort to understand what kinds of responses from non-European societies are possible. This is an important way of thinking about the relationship between liberalism and processes of change or 'globalization' in contemporary international relations. Too often, liberalism is seen as a way of evaluating, and perhaps even directing, such processes of transformation, so as to move us beyond the inadequacies of the anarchical states system. Once liberalism is located within its practical modern context, however, it is easier to recognize how some of these current developments may actually be direct challenges to liberalism, or at least serve as evidence of the ways in which non-European societies are capable of developing their own formulations of liberal principles that differ from those traditionally favoured by European thinkers.

It is our hope that this volume will contribute to a better understanding of the intimate relationship between liberalism and modern patterns of international order, so as to work towards a better appreciation of the relevance, implications and normative content of international liberalism today, raising, as Hughes puts it, 'uncomfortable questions about the future of liberalism itself'. Here we should note that the book certainly does not intend to offer a straightforwardly anti-liberal perspective. Obviously, many of the contributors, such as Gill or Young, are indeed hostile towards liberalism. However, the work of scholars like Falk, Frost, Keohane, Long and MacMillan reflects the fact that it would be foolish to suggest that liberalism has no conceivable basis as either a compelling moral doctrine, a useful method for social-scientific enquiry, or a practical form of international political and social organization. Rather, our main concern is that the conventional treatment of liberalism as a utopian alternative to realism is a serious mistake, which obstructs our ability to make sense of a number of different historical and contemporary phenomena. To put it bluntly, the central thrust of this book is that we live in a liberal world, whether we like it or not. The question, then, is not whether liberal principles can be realized, but how they have already been put into practice, how they are being pursued or challenged today, and what their implications are for the future of contemporary international order. In our view, to ignore this dimension of modern and contemporary international relations would simply make it far too easy to be 'liberal'.

Notes

1. Karl Marx, *Capital: A Critique of Political Economy*, Volume 1, trans. B. Fowkes (Harmondsworth: Penguin, 1967), p. 878n.
2. *Ibid.*, p. 878.
3. *Ibid.*

4. Joseph Nye, *Understanding International Conflicts: An Introduction to Theory and History* (New York: HarperCollins, 1993), p. 5.
5. Martin Wight, 'Why Is There No International Theory?', in Herbert Butterfield and Martin Wight (eds.), *Diplomatic Investigations: Essays on the Theory of International Politics* (London: George Allen & Unwin, 1966), pp. 17–34.
6. See especially the chapters by Stephen Gill and Tom Young in this volume.
7. Some contemporary debates within liberal political theory reflect this distinction, which may crudely be conceived in terms of the distinction between Lockean and Kantian variants of liberalism. On the former, see C. B. Macpherson, *The Political Theory of Possessive Individualism: Hobbes to Locke* (Oxford: Oxford University Press, 1962); Robert Nozick, *Anarchy, State and Utopia* (Oxford: Blackwell, 1974); and Hillel Steiner, *An Essay on Rights* (Oxford: Blackwell, 1994). On the latter, Kantian variant of liberal thought, see John Rawls, *A Theory of Justice* (Oxford: Clarendon Press, 1972), and *Political Liberalism* (New York: Columbia University Press, 1993).
8. The classic locus for this interpretative, 'neo-Kantian' approach to social science is the work of Max Weber. See especially the methodological essays where he confronts the question of how to comprehend the meaningful character of social relations: *Roscher and Knies: The Logical Problems of Historical Economics*, trans. G. Oakes (London: Macmillan, 1975); *The Methodology of the Social Sciences*, trans. E. Shils and H. Finch (New York: Free Press, 1949); and *Critique of Stammler*, trans. G. Oakes (New York: Free Press, 1977).
9. This apt phrase is borrowed from a piece in an earlier *Millennium* special issue that conducts a similar kind of enquiry: Chris Brown, '"Really Existing Liberalism" and International Order', *Millennium*, Vol. 21, No. 3 (1992), pp. 313–28. In this article, Brown examines the problem that societies that 'are in some sense "liberal", certainly do exist, but do not function in the manner anticipated by the classics of liberalism' (p. 316). As should be clear, our book investigates a similar problem, but more with respect to the structure of international society than with regard to the patterns of international behaviour that might be expected from states having a certain kind of 'really existing' liberal regime.

Part I
Understanding International Liberalism

1
Moral Commitment and Liberal Approaches to World Politics

Robert O. Keohane

David Long recently wrote a critique in the *Millennium* special issue that forms the back-drop for this edited collection of what he called the 'Harvard School of Liberal International Relations Theory'. His principal objection to arguments made by myself and my former Harvard colleagues was that we had constructed a narrowly focused and uncritical version of liberalism, which virtually subordinates it to realism. He suggested, as an alternative, reflection on 'the development of liberalism as a political tradition or ideology and its application to international relations/world politics'.[1] Since I undertook such a task in a modest way in an essay published in 1990, which he cites, most of my response to Long will simply involve restating the core of that argument.[2]

My conceptualization of liberalism is quite properly a subject for critical discussion. What would be less interesting, indeed tedious, would be a debate over whether my theoretical stance is truly 'liberal', or how it relates to a specific interpretation of realist theory. It is less important what label is attached to an approach to international relations than whether the concepts, analytical frameworks and theories of that approach illuminate the world that we seek to understand. I have presented my essential concepts and theoretical arguments in systematic form elsewhere,[3] and I have attempted more recently to apply them not merely to issues of political economy but to the end of the Cold War and to the operation of international environmental institutions.[4]

Long also raises ethical issues, claiming that I seek to 'absolve' myself from moral judgement in my theoretical work.[5] Nothing could be further from the truth. On the contrary, I believe that scholars, like policy-makers, require moral purpose to make their professional lives meaningful. Why study international relations at all? Ours is not a field in which cumulative advances in our understanding can be confidently anticipated. Nor is much of what we study beautiful, or intrinsic to the joys of human life. I presumably could have decided to study international relations on purely self-interested utilitarian grounds – because I had discovered that I was relatively adept at this activity, found it interesting and could make a living at it. Admittedly, the theory of international relations to which I adhere would regard such behaviour as normal. However, I would find such a calculus ethically empty and therefore profoundly dissatisfying. I see no good reason why the assumptions of my explanatory theory for the behaviour of states and other organizations should provide the basis for the way I live my own life.

Like many of my colleagues in the field, I was drawn to the study of international relations because I thought I could make a contribution to the quality of collective human life by helping to understand the conditions for cooperation and conflict, and by sharing with others any insights that I might derive. War is so terrible for human beings, and so many opportunities for improvement in the human condition are missed due to failure to act together, that nothing seemed more important than trying to understand how mutually beneficial cooperation could replace personally damaging and soul-destroying conflict.

Since scholarship has ethical implications, scholars, like policy-makers, should subject themselves to a moral standard. That standard, however, is not met by preaching to leaders – a notably futile task for those who write in journals read by only a few cloistered academics. Nor is it met by glossing over the tough, self-interested behaviour that has so often characterized world politics, and on which realists over the centuries have commented. I think that moral concerns should be at the heart of our scholarly enterprise, but it should be a morality with as few illusions as possible.

To meet an appropriate ethical standard, in my view, requires having both a sense of moral purpose in one's work and a strategic conception about how one's action serves that moral purpose. Having indicated my moral purpose, let me say a few words about strategy.

I believe that I can make a greater emancipatory contribution by showing how human agency can prevent and ameliorate conflict through international institutions than I could by engaging in moral exhortation. In my view, to be convincing requires sufficient distance and discipline so that other scholars and, ultimately, policy-makers take one's work seriously as social science rather than dismiss it as political pleading. Other scholars have made different choices, but those who preach can be as subject to moral criticism for self-indulgence, as those who analyse can be justly criticized if they lapse into merely technical argument or persuade themselves that they are morally neutral and objective. It is worthwhile, I think, to strive for objectivity, but we should never fool ourselves into believing that we have attained it.

Like any approach to a complex subject, my formulations are incomplete and flawed. They are also subject to misinterpretation. For example, I remain committed to an understanding of world politics that rejects a 'state-centric' paradigm as described (and decried) by Joseph S. Nye and myself 25 years ago.[6] But my perception of the need to contest realist disparaging of international cooperation on its own terrain – by analysing interstate behaviour – has led me to focus in much of my work on the actions of major states, still the organizations in world politics that control the largest resources, both material and symbolic. This emphasis on the actions of states has confused some readers such as Long, who appeal to liberals to 'go beyond the Harvard School's understanding of state-centric international relations to envision a world politics of individuals and groups'.[7] In my conception of world politics states still loom large, but they interact with firms and nongovernmental organizations (NGOs) within the context of institutions shaped by the collective activities of many individuals. There is a double irony in Long's critique: along with Andrew Moravcsik, I represent the 'Harvard School', although I am no longer at Harvard, and I am criticized for 'state-centric' work, although the first work of which I am aware using that phrase was the book that Nye and I edited in 1972.

What, Long asks, is 'the Harvard School of Liberal International Relations Theory struggling against?'[8] Against the notion, common to realists, that world politics is an anarchic realm, whose institutions are insignificant and in which sustained cooperation is chimerical. We seek to open paths to cooperation by showing how it can be fostered, by wise policies but most of all through well-designed institutions, and without requiring the fundamental reform of societies or the transformation of human nature. Better people and more perfect democratic societies might well produce better international relations; but even self-centred human beings in imperfect societies can cooperate to foster prosperity, human rights and ecological sustainability. Traditional realism emphasizes the limits of effective cooperation; and its prudential advice is worth considering seriously. Without being utopians, liberal institutionalists stress the possibilities of cooperative action within institutions that create incentives for such activity.

Liberal institutionalists do not believe that cooperation is always good. The success and complexity of the transnational drug trade suggest that cooperation among drug dealers must be extensive, even under adverse conditions – but such cooperation is not morally praiseworthy. Aggressive alliances and cartels require cooperation as well. But while recognizing that cooperation can have bad effects, we hold that it is a necessary condition for effective management of an interdependent world economy and an even more interdependent world ecology. Unless we know how to cooperate, we have no chance to cooperate well for good ends.

Even the highest motives are subject to distortion, and strategies can be misguided. One needs also to reflect critically, from time to time, on whether one's actions are consistent with that sense of purpose and conception of strategy. Critiques such as that of Long are welcome, in so far as they prompt such reflection. It is all too easy to become a captive of one's environment. We need especially, I think, to guard against two types of capture: *political* and *professional*.

I use 'political capture' to refer to a process by which a scholar accepts the interests and values of her own society, unproblematically, as a basis for understanding and evaluating world politics. Scholars who become very close to the policy process – and therefore have to accept its premises to have any influence – are particularly vulnerable to political capture, but it can happen to any of us, particularly citizens of a large and powerful country such as the United States. It is worthwhile to be reminded of this danger.

A sign of political capture is the scholar 'whispering in the policymaker's ear' rather than speaking to a broader audience. As a liberal and a democrat, I believe that knowledge, widely diffused among a free people, is liberating because it facilitates intelligent collective as well as individual choices. As a democrat, I believe that public purposes that are endorsed by a diverse and knowledgeable electorate are likely to meet normative standards involving equality and justice better than those decided upon by self-appointed élites. I therefore favour the diffusion of knowledge in a democracy. Knowledge held closely by a few members of an élite is not necessarily liberating.

Scholars acquire reputations, which arise from the consensus of their professional peers. Career success is achieved by developing a reputation for a productive line of analysis and by securing its place in the professional 'canon', through one's own work and that of one's students and others. This reputational system creates incentives to criticize the work of others, and may also stimulate creativity, since new ideas and formulations gain more attention than the repetition of old ones. However, it can also generate conservatism, since it may be hazardous to one's reputation to depart too far from the professional consensus. It may also create incentives to borrow from high-status fields – such as economics in the United States – rather than from low-status ones, regardless of the fruitfulness of the insights thereby generated. I use the phrase 'professional capture' to denote a process of succumbing to these incentives, to the detriment of original or critical thought. It is a danger that all of us face.

The following selection constitutes the bulk of the 1990 essay on 'international liberalism reconsidered', where I take issue with

the common denigration of liberalism among professional students of international relations. My argument is that liberalism – or at any rate, a certain strand of liberalism – is more sophisticated than many of its critics have alleged. ... Liberalism makes the positive argument that an open international political economy, with rules and institutions based on state sovereignty, provides incentives for international cooperation. ... It also makes the normative assertion that such a reliance on economic exchange and international institutions has better effects than the major politically-tested alternatives. I do not necessarily subscribe to all of these claims, but I take them seriously.[9]

Liberalism as a theory of international relations

As Michael Doyle points out, 'there is no canonical description of Liberalism'.[10] Some commentators equate liberalism with a belief in the superiority of economic arrangements relying on markets rather than on state control. This conception of liberalism identifies it with the view of Adam Smith, David Ricardo and generations of classical and neoclassical economists. Another version of liberalism associates it more generally with the principle of 'the importance of the freedom of the individual'.[11] From this classic political perspective, liberalism 'begins with the recognition that men, do what we will, are free; that a man's acts are his own, spring from his own personality, and cannot be coerced. But this freedom is not possessed at birth; it is acquired by degrees as a man enters into the self-conscious possession of his personality through a life of discipline and moral progress'.[12]

Neither the view of liberalism as a doctrine of unfettered economic exchange nor its identification with liberty for the individual puts forward an analysis of the constraints and opportunities that face states as a result of the international system in which they are embedded. Instead, the emphasis of liberalism on liberty and rights suggests only a general orientation toward the moral evaluation of world politics.

For the purposes of this chapter, therefore, it is more useful to consider liberalism as an approach to the analysis of social reality rather than as a doctrine of liberty.[13]

I will therefore regard liberalism as an approach to the analysis of social reality that (1) begins with individuals as the relevant actors, (2) seeks to understand how aggregations of individuals make collective decisions and how organizations composed of individuals interact, and (3) embeds this analysis in a world-view that emphasizes individual rights and that adopts an ameliorative view of progress in human affairs. In economics, liberalism's emphasis on the collective results of individual actions leads to the analysis of markets, market failure and institutions to correct such failure; in traditional international relations theory it implies attempts to reconcile state sovereignty with the reality of strategic interdependence.

Liberalism shares with realism the stress on explaining the behaviour of separate and typically self-interested units of action, but from the standpoint of international relations, there are three critical differences between these two schools of thought. First, liberalism focuses not merely on states but on privately organized social groups and firms. The transnational as well as domestic activities of these groups and firms are important for liberal analysts, not in isolation from the actions of states but in conjunction with them. Second, in contrast to realism, liberalism does not emphasize the significance of military force, but rather seeks to discover ways in which separate actors, with distinct interests, can organize themselves to promote economic efficiency and avoid destructive physical conflict, without renouncing either the economic or political freedoms that liberals hold dear.[14] Finally, liberalism believes in at least the possibility of cumulative progress, whereas realism assumes that history is not progressive.

Much contemporary Marxist and neo-Marxist analysis minimizes the significance of individuals and state organizations, focusing instead on class relations or claiming that the identities of individuals and organizations are constituted by the nature of the world capitalist system, and that the system is therefore ontologically prior to the individual. Thus, liberalism is separated from much Marxist thought by a rather wide philosophical gulf. Yet liberalism draws substantially on those aspects of Marxism that analyse relations between discrete groups, such as investigations of multinational corporations or of the political consequences of capital flows. Both schools of thought share the inclination to look behind the state to social groups. Furthermore, both liberals and Marxists believe in the possibility of progress, although the liberals' rights-oriented vision is to emerge incrementally whereas Marxists have often asserted that their collective new world order would be brought about through revolution.

Liberalism does not purport to provide a complete account of international relations. On the contrary, most contemporary liberals seem to accept large portions of both the Marxist and realist explanations. Much of what liberals wish to explain about world politics can be accounted for by the character and dynamics of world capitalism, on the one hand, and by the nature of political–military competition, on the other. The realist and Marxist explanations focus on the underlying structure of world politics, which helps to define the limits of what is feasible and therefore ensures that the intentions of actors are often not matched by the outcomes they achieve. Yet, as noted above, these explanations are incomplete. They fail to pay sufficient attention to the institutions and patterns of interaction created by human beings that help to shape perceptions and expectations, and therefore alter the patterns of behaviour that take place within a given structure. Liberalism's strength is that it takes political processes seriously.

Although liberalism does not have a single theory of international relations, three more specific perspectives on international relations have nevertheless been put forward by writers who share liberalism's analytic emphasis on individual action and normative concern for liberty. I label these arguments republican, commercial and regulatory liberalism. They are not inconsistent with one another. All three variants of international liberalism can be found in Immanuel Kant's essay 'Perpetual Peace', and both commercial and regulatory liberalism presuppose the existence of limited constitutional states, or republics in Kant's sense. Nevertheless, these liberal doctrines are logically distinct from one another. They rest on somewhat different premises, and liberals' interpretations of world politics vary in the degree to which they rely upon each set of casual arguments.

Republican liberalism

Republican liberalism argues that republics are more peacefully inclined than are despotisms. For Kant, a principal spokesman for all three versions of liberalism, republics are constitutional governments based on the principles of freedom of individuals, the rule of law and the equality of citizens. In republics, legislatures can limit the actions of the executive; furthermore, 'the consent of the citizens is required in order to decide whether there should be war or not', and 'nothing is more natural than that those who would have to decide to undergo all the deprivations of war will very much hesitate to start such an evil game'.[15] Yet, as Doyle has pointed out, for Kant, republicanism only produces caution; it does not guarantee peace. To prevent war, action at the international as well as the national level is necessary.[16]

The association of republics with peace has often been criticized or even ridiculed. Citizens in democracies have sometimes greeted war enthusiastically, as indicated by the Crimean and Spanish-American wars and with respect to several belligerent countries, by the onset of the First World War. Furthermore, many of the peoples affected by war have not been enfranchised in the actual republics of the last two centuries.[17] In the twentieth century, it was difficult for legislatures to control actions of the executive that might be tantamount to war. And republics have certainly fought many and bloody wars.

Yet, the historical record provides substantial support for Kant's view, if it is taken to refer to the waging of war between states founded on liberal principles rather than between these states and their illiberal adversaries. Indeed, Doyle has shown on the basis of historical evidence for the years since 1800 that 'constitutionally secure liberal states have yet to engage in war with one another'.[18]

This is an interesting issue that could bear further discussion. But my essay concerns the impact of *international relations* on state behaviour. Republican liberalism explains state behaviour in the international arena on the basis of *domestic* politics and is thus not directly germane to my argument here. Furthermore, as noted above, sophisticated advocates of republican liberalism, such as Kant, acknowledge that even well-constituted republics can be warlike unless international relations are properly organized. Attention to liberalism's arguments about international relations is therefore required.[19]

Commercial liberalism

Commercial liberalism affirms the impact of international relations on the actions of states. Advocates of commercial liberalism have extended the classical economists' benign view of trade into the political realm. From the Enlightenment onward, liberals have argued, in Montesquieu's words, that 'the natural effect of commerce is to lead to peace. Two nations that trade together become mutually dependent only if one has an interest in buying, the other has one in selling; and all unions are based on mutual needs'.[20] Kant clearly agreed: 'It is the *spirit of commerce* that cannot coexist with war, and which sooner or later takes hold of every nation.'[21]

This liberal insistence that commerce leads to peace has led some critical observers to define liberalism in terms of a belief in 'a natural harmony that leads, not to a war of all against all, but to a stable, orderly and progressive society with little need for a governmental intervention'.[22] The utopianism that could be fostered by such a belief is illustrated by a statement of the American industrialist and philanthropist, Andrew Carnegie. In 1910, Carnegie established the Carnegie Endowment for International Peace, stating, as the Endowment's historian says, 'that war could be abolished and that peace was in reach, and that after it was secured his trustees "should consider what is the next most degrading remaining evil or evils whose banishment" would advance the human cause and turn their energies toward eradicating it'.[23]

In its straightforward, naïve form, commercial liberalism is untenable, relying as it does both on an unsubstantiated theory of progress and on a crudely reductionist argument in which politics is determined by economics. The experience of the First World War, in which major trading partners such as Britain and Germany fought each other with unprecedented intensity, discredited simplistic formulations of commercial liberalism. Yet in my judgement too much has been discredited: commentators have identified commercial liberalism with its most extreme formulations and have thus discarded it rather cavalierly. Defensible forms of commercial liberalism have been put forward in this century, most notably in the 1930s.

At the end of that decade, Eugene Staley proposed a particularly lucid statement of commercial liberalism. Staley begins, in effect, with Adam Smith's dictum that 'the division of labour depends on the extent of the market'. Increased productivity depends on an international division of labour, for countries not exceptionally well endowed with a variety of resources. Economic nationalism blocks the division of labour, this leading to a dilemma for populous but resource-poor states, such as Japan: expand or accept decreased living standards:

> The widespread practice of economic nationalism is likely to produce the feeling in a country of rapidly growing population that it is faced with a terrible dilemma: either accept the miserable

prospect of decreased living standards (at least, abandon hope of greatly improved living standards), or seek by conquest to seize control of more territory, more resources, larger markets and supply areas.[24]

This leads to the following general conclusion:

> To the extent, then, that large, important countries controlling substantial portions of the world's resources refuse to carry on economic relations with the rest of the world, they sow the seeds of unrest and war. In particular, they create a powerful dynamic of imperialism. *When economic walls are erected along political boundaries, possession of territory is made to coincide with economic opportunity.* Imperialistic ambitions are given both a partial justification and a splendid basis for propaganda.[25]

Staley's argument does not depend on his assumption about increasing population, since increasing demands for higher living standards could lead to the same pressure for economic growth. The important point here for our purposes is that in Staley's version of commercial liberalism, incentives for peaceful behaviour are provided by an open international environment characterized by regularized patterns of exchange and orderly rules. Commerce by itself does not ensure peace, but commerce on a non-discriminatory basis within an orderly political framework promotes cooperation on the basis of enlightened national conceptions of self-interest that emphasize production over war.

Regulatory liberalism

Advocates of regulatory liberalism emphasize the importance for peace of the rules governing patterns of exchange among countries. Albert O. Hirschman points out that as people began to think about interests in the eighteenth century, they began to realize 'that something was to be gained for both parties (in international politics) by the adherence to certain rules of the game and by the elimination of "passionate" behaviour, which the rational pursuit of interest implied'.[26] Kant regards regulation as a central principle of perpetual peace. He proposes a 'federalism' of free states, although this federation is to fall short of a world republic, since a constitutionally organized world state based on the national principle is not feasible.[27]

Kant does not go into details on how such a federation would be institutionalized, but his vision clearly presages the international organizations of the twentieth century, with their established rules, norms and practices. A major change in the concept of regulatory liberalism, however, has taken place, since relatively few contemporary international organizations limit membership to republics. Indeed, most members of the United Nations would qualify as despotisms by Kant's criteria. Contemporary practice has created different types of international organizations. Some, such as the European Union and the Organization for Economic Cooperation and Development, are at least for the most part limited to republics, but the United Nations, a variety of global economic organizations, and regional organizations outside Europe are not. Contemporary advocates of regulatory liberalism may continue to believe that republics in Kant's sense are the best partners for international cooperation; but for a number of global problems, it would be self-defeating to refuse to seek to collaborate with autocratic states. Even autocracies may have an interest in following international rules and facilitate mutually beneficial agreements on issues such as arms control, nuclear reactor safety and the regulation of international trade.

Kant's argument for a federation is in my view profoundly different from the conception (also found in 'Perpetual Peace') of the gradual emergence of peace through commerce as a natural process, implying a theory of progress. In contrast not only to Marxism and realism, but also to this notion of peace deriving automatically from commerce, regulatory liberalism emphasizes discretionary human action. International rules and institutions play a crucial role in promoting cooperation; yet there is a great variation in their results, depending on the human ingenuity and commitment used to create and maintain them. This emphasis of regulatory liberalism on human choices conforms with experience: the life-histories of international organizations differ dramatically. In some cases, their institutional arrangements, and the actions of their leaders, have encouraged sustained, focused work that accomplishes common purposes and maintains support for the organization: NATO, the European Union, the Association of South East Asian Nations (ASEAN) and the World Health Organization (WHO) are examples. Other organizations, such as UNESCO, have failed to maintain the same level of institutional coherence and political support.[28]

If we keep the insights of regulatory liberalism in mind, along with the experiences of international organizations in the twentieth century, we will be cautious about seeking to predict international behaviour on the basis of 'the effects of commerce'. Such an inference is no more valid than purporting to construct comprehensive analyses of world politics solely on the basis of 'the constraints of capitalism' or the necessary effects of anarchy. 'Commerce', 'capitalism' and 'anarchy' can give us clues about the incentives – constraints and opportunities – facing actors, but without knowing the institutional context, they do not enable us to understand how people or governments will react. Regulatory liberalism argues that we have to specify the institutional features of world politics before inferring expected patterns of behaviour. I believe that this awareness of institutional complexity is a great advantage, that it constitutes an improvement in subtlety. It improves our capacity to account for change, since change is not explained adequately by shifts in patterns of economic transactions (commercial liberalism), fundamental power distributions (realism) or capitalism (Marxism).

Nothing in regulatory liberalism holds that harmony of interest emerges automatically. On the contrary, cooperation has to be constructed by human beings on the basis of a recognition that independent governments both hold predominant power resources and command more legitimacy from human populations than do any conceivable international organizations. Neither peace nor coordinated economic and social policies can be sought on the basis of a hierarchical organizing principle that supersedes governments. Governments must be persuaded; they cannot be bypassed. This means that international institutions need to be constructed both to facilitate the purposes that governments espouse in common and gradually to alter governmental conceptions of self-interest in order to widen the scope for cooperation. International institutions provide information, facilitate communication and furnish certain services that cannot be as easily offered by national governments: they do not enforce rules. Liberals recognize that although it is possible to cooperate on the basis of common interest, such cooperation does not derive from an immanent world community that only has to be appreciated, nor does it occur without sweat and risk.

The accomplishments of regulatory liberalism in our age are substantial. They should not be dismissed because severe dangers and dilemmas continue to face governments or because much that we would like to accomplish is frustrated by state sovereignty and conflicts of interest. The global environment would be in even greater danger in the absence of the United Nations Environmental Programme (UNEP) and agreements reached under its auspices; protectionist trade wars might be rampant were it not for the General Agreement on Tariffs and Trade

(GATT); starvation would have been much worse in Africa in the early 1980s without the World Food Programme and other international cooperative arrangements; smallpox would not have been eradicated without the efforts of WHO. Regulatory liberalism asserts that better arrangements that constructively channel the pursuit of self-interest – or that enrich definitions of self-interest – can realistically be constructed, not that they will appear without effort. History supports both parts of its claim.

Sophisticated liberalism

Commercial liberalism stresses the benign effects of trade; in Staley's version, trade may, under the right conditions, facilitate cooperation but does not automatically produce it. Regulatory liberalism emphasizes the impact of rules and institutions on human behaviour. Both versions are consistent with the premise that states make choices that are, roughly speaking, rational and self-interested; that is, they choose means that appear appropriate to achieve their own ends. Yet this premise misses an important element of liberalism, which does not accept a static view of self-interest, determined by the structure of a situation, but rather holds open the possibility that people will change their attitudes and their loyalties. As students of European political integration have shown, a combination of strengthened commercial ties and new institutions can exert a substantial impact on people's conceptions of their self-interest.[29] People cannot be expected, in general, to cease to act in self-interested ways, but their conceptions of their self-interest can change.

What I call sophisticated liberalism incorporates this sociological perspective on interests into a synthesis of commercial and regulatory liberalism. It does not posit that expanding commerce leads directly to peace but rather agrees with Staley that conditions of economic openness can provide incentives for peaceful rather than aggressive expansion. This is likely to occur, however, only within the framework of rules and institutions that promote and guarantee openness. Not just any set of commercial relationships will lead to peace: the effects of commerce depend on the institutional context – the rules and habits – within which it takes place. Furthermore, the development of commerce cannot be regarded as inevitable, since it depends on a political structure resting on interests and power.

What liberalism prescribes was to a remarkable extent implemented by the United States and its Western European allies after the Second World War. The United States, in conjunction with Western

European governments, set about constructing a framework of rules that would promote commerce and economic growth. Consistent with the expectations of both realism and Marxism, American power was used to ensure that the rules and institutions that emerged satisfied the basic preferences of American élites. What the Europeans established differed considerably from American plans, and the construction of European institutions preceded the implementation of the global economic arrangements that had been outlined at the Bretton Woods Conference and at the negotiations leading to the GATT.[30] Yet, without American prodding, it is unclear whether these European institutions would have been created; and the United States had relatively little difficulty accepting the new European institutions, which promoted basic American goals of security and prosperity within the institutional frameworks of representative government and capitalism.

Even if the European institutions were not entirely devoted to the principles of commercial liberalism – and the European Payments Union, the European Coal and Steel Community and the European Economic Community had many restrictionist elements – they were not sharply inconsistent with the institutions of Bretton Woods and the GATT, which emphasized the value of open markets and non-discriminatory trade. The resulting arrangements, taken as a whole, epitomized a liberalism that was 'embedded' in the postwar interventionist welfare state. That is, liberalism no longer required rejection of state interventionism, but rather efforts to ensure that interventionist practices were limited by joint agreements and rules, in order to maintain their broadly liberal character and to facilitate international exchange.[31] Economic growth, promoted by international trade and investment, was expected to facilitate the growth of democratic institutions within societies, and thus to reshape states in pacific directions as well as to provide incentives for peaceful economic expansion rather than military conquest. The political complications entailed by growing economic interdependence were to be managed by an increasingly complex network of formal and informal institutions, within Europe and among the advanced industrial countries.[32]

This strategy was remarkably successful. Indeed, the benign results foreseen by such writers as Staley ensued, although it might be difficult to prove decisively that they resulted principally from institutionalized patterns of interdependence more than from the looming presence of the Soviet Union. At any rate, war and threats of war were eliminated as means of economic aggrandisement for the advanced parliamentary democracies. Furthermore, as American hegemony began to wane after the mid-1960s, the value of liberalism's emphasis on rules became more evident to those who sought to avoid a return to economic warfare and generalized conflict. International regimes such as those revolving around the GATT or the International Monetary Fund have displayed remarkable staying power, even after the power constellations that brought them into being had eroded.

Liberals have used their positive theory stressing the role of institutions to bolster their normative argument that liberal orders are to be preferred to available alternatives. It is important to note here that the liberal stress on institution building is not based on naïveté about harmony among people, but rather on agreement with realists about what a world without rules or institutions would look like: a jungle in which governments seek to weaken one another economically and militarily, leading to continual strife and frequent warfare. Liberals do not believe in the soothing effects of 'international community'. It is precisely because they have seen the world in terms similar to those of the realists – not because they have worn rose-tinted glasses – that sophisticated liberals from Kant to Staley to Stanley Hoffmann have sought alternatives. Their pessimism about world politics and human conflict makes sophisticated liberals willing to settle for less than that demanded by utopians of whatever stripe.

Evaluating liberalism: doctrine and practice

Regulatory liberalism argues for the construction of institutions to promote exchanges regarded by governments as beneficial. This is to be done without directly challenging either the sovereignty of states or the inequalities of power among them. Liberals who appreciate Marxist and realist insights are careful not to present these exchanges as unconstrained or necessarily equally beneficial to all parties concerned, much less to categories of people (such as the rural poor in less developed countries) that are unrepresented at the bargaining table. As a reformist creed, liberalism does not promise justice or equity in a setting, such as that of international relations, in which inequalities of power are so glaring and means of controlling the exercise of power so weak. It is therefore open to charges of immorality from utopians and of naïveté from cynics; and depending on the context, liberals may be guilty of either charge, or of both. Liberals seek to build on what exists in order to improve it, and run the risk that their policies will either worsen the situation or help to block alternative actions that would radically improve it. Nevertheless, liberals can fairly ask their opponents to propose alternative strategies that are not merely attractive in principle, but seem likely to produce better results in practice.

Yet, even if we accept the liberal argument this far, we may be reluctant to embrace liberalism as a normative theory of international affairs. Before we could do so, we would need to consider the negative as well as the positive aspects of the open international order, with its rules and institutions to guide the actions of states, that liberals favour. In particular, we would need to consider the impact of such an order on two major values: peace and economic welfare. What are the effects of an open, interdependent international order on the constraints facing states, and on the ways in which states are reshaped in world politics? What is the liberal view of these constraints? How do these constraints compare with those imposed by alternative arrangements for the management of international affairs?

Liberalism and peace

As we have seen, liberalism assures states of access, on market or near-market terms, to resources located elsewhere. 'In a liberal economic system', admits a critic of liberalism, 'the costs of using force in pursuit of economic interests are likely to outweigh any gains, because markets and resources are already available on competitive terms'.[33]

This access to markets and resources is assured by complex international political arrangements that would be disrupted by war. If the division of labour is limited by the extent of the market, as Adam Smith taught, the extent of the market is limited by the scope of international order. The more tightly intertwined and interdependent the valued interactions of states, the greater the incentives for long-term cooperation in order to avoid disrupting these ties. In international relations, as in other social relations, incentives for cooperation depend on whether actors are 'involved in a thick enough network of mutual interactions' and on the degree to which they benefit from these ties.[34] This does not mean that commerce necessarily leads to peace, or that entwining the Soviet Union in networks of interdependence stopped the Soviets from fostering revolution in the Third World; but it is reasonable to assert that a calculation of costs and benefits will enter into state decision-making, and that this calculation will be affected by the costs of disrupting beneficial ties. Thus, we can find analytical support for the view, espoused by liberals such as Staley, that an open, rule-oriented international system provides incentives for peaceful behaviour.[35]

The existence of an orderly and open international system may affect the balance of interests and power for societies poised between commercial and belligerent definitions of self-interest. Japan before and after the Second World War provides the outstanding example. Admittedly, the contrast between its behaviour before the Second World War and since is partly accounted for by the restructuring of Japanese government and society during the American Occupation and by the dependence of Japan on the United States for defence against the Soviet Union. Nevertheless, the dominance of peacefully inclined commercial rather than bellicose military élites in postwar Japanese policy-making has surely been encouraged by the opportunities provided for Japanese business by relatively open markets abroad, particularly in the United States.[36]

Yet the picture for liberalism is not as rosy as the previous paragraphs might seem to suggest. Liberalism may indeed inhibit the use of force, but it may also have the opposite effect. Whether American liberalism was in any way responsible for the massive use of violence by the United States in Southeast Asia is still unclear: liberal moralism may have justified the use of force, although it seems from *The Pentagon Papers* that a skewed conception of geopolitics provided a more powerful motivation for action.[37] Furthermore, liberal values were crucial in providing the moral basis for the popular protests against United States military involvement in Vietnam, which eventually brought the war to an end.

Yet, even if liberalism tends to be peacefully oriented and was not responsible for the war in Vietnam, the effects of liberalism on peace may not necessarily be benign. The extension of economic interests worldwide under liberalism in search of wider markets requires the extension of political order: in so far as that order is threatened, protection of one's own economic interests may entail the use of force. Thus, a global political economy may make it difficult for leaders of a peacefully oriented liberal state not to use force, precisely by making it vulnerable to the use of force against it by non-liberal states or movements. Three examples illustrate this point:

Direct foreign investment

The United States in recent decades has intervened directly or indirectly in a number of countries in which it had substantial direct foreign investments, including Guatemala (1954), Cuba (1961) and

Chile (1973). Fear of the extension of Soviet influence to the Western
Hemisphere seems to have been a principal motivation for American
action, but in all three cases, intergovernmental conflicts were generated by the presence of US-owned companies in societies undergoing
revolutionary change. In the absence of the extension of American
economic interests to these countries, such interventions would, it
seems, have been less likely to occur.

Control over resources

The Carter Doctrine, which raised the possibility of American intervention in the Persian Gulf, was clearly motivated by US government
concern for access to oil resources in that area. So was the movement
of a large US naval task-force into the Gulf in the spring and summer
of 1987. Such military action in defence of far-flung economic interests
– of the United States' allies even more than of itself – has obviously
contributed to military conflict involving the United States. The
general point is that the global economic interests of liberal states
make them vulnerable to threats to their access to raw materials and to
markets. Liberal states may use violence to defend access to distant
resources that more autarkic states would not have sought in the first
place.

Air transport

Liberal societies not only extend their economic interests worldwide,
they also believe in individual freedom to travel. This means that at
any given time, thousands of citizens of such societies are in aero-
planes around the world – potential hostages or victims of terrorists.
Since socialist or mercantilist governments not only have limited
foreign economic interests but often restrict travel by their own people,
they are not so vulnerable. Reacting to their vulnerability, powerful
republics may escalate the use of force, as the United States did in April
1986 against Libya. The global extension of international activity fostered by liberalism's stress on economic openness and political rights
not only creates opportunities for terrorists but also provides incentives
for powerful republics to use force – even if its use is justified as
defensive and protective rather than aggressive.

How do incentives for the use of force balance out against incentives
against such use? The peaceful behaviour of liberal governments
towards one another, and their reluctance to resort to force against
non-liberal states in the oil crisis of the 1970s, suggest that the current

interdependent international political economy may have inhibited –
or, at least, has not encouraged – widespread resort to force. Barry
Buzan argues that, despite this success, liberalism will lead in the long
run to the use of force because it is unstable and will deteriorate.[38] The
upsurge of terrorism in the 1980s reminded us that this caution is well
founded. A degenerating liberal system, in which commitments and
vulnerabilities exceed the capacities of liberal states to deal with them,
could be exceedingly dangerous – perhaps even more so than a decaying system of self-reliant mercantilist states. But this observation could
just as well be taken as a justification for committing ourselves more
strongly to underpinning a liberal economic system with multilateral
institutions supported by power, than as an argument against a liberal
international system. To regard the dangers of a decay of liberalism as
an argument against an open international system is reminiscent of
Woody Allen's character in *Hannah and Her Sisters* who attempts to
commit suicide out of fear of death!

Liberalism and economic welfare

Conservative economists find the international order favoured by liberalism congenial. The international market serves as a 'reality test' for
governments' economic strategies. Inefficient policies such as those
overemphasizing provision of welfare and state bureaucracy will do
badly.[39] Eventually, the failure of these policies will become evident in
slow and distorted growth and balance-of-payments problems. From
this standpoint, the constraints imposed by the world economy are not
properly seen as malign constraints on autonomy, but rather as
beneficial limits on governments' abilities to damage their own
economies and people through foolish policies. International liberalism fosters a world economy that gives timely early warning of economic disaster, rather than enabling states to conceal crises by using
controls that in the long run only make matters worse. As John Locke
said about law, 'That ill deserves the Name of Confinement which
hedges us in only from Bogs and Precipices'.[40]

  The international political economy of modern capitalism is viewed
more critically, however, by liberals who empathize strongly with
ordinary people in the Third World and by First World supporters of
social democracy. It is evident to many liberals as well as Marxists that
the modern capitalist world economy exerts a bias against poor,
immobile people as well as against generous welfare states. Conservative
economists point this out with some glee: the McCracken Report
argues that 'countries pursuing equality strenuously with an inadequate

growth rate' may suffer 'capital flight and brain drain'.[41] The existence of international capitalism improves the bargaining power of investors *vis-à-vis* left-wing governments. The ease with which funds can flow across national boundaries makes it difficult for any country with a market-oriented economy to institute measures that change the distribution of income against capital.

Capital flight can have catastrophic effects on the debt-ridden nations of the Third World. As Marxists emphasize, it also constrains attempts to promote equity or nibble away at the privileges of business in the advanced industrialized countries of Europe, North America and the Pacific. When Margaret Thatcher or Ronald Reagan sought to help business and improve profits, capital flowed into their countries – at least temporarily. When François Mitterrand sought to expand the welfare state, stimulate demand and nationalize selected industries, by contrast, capital flowed out, the franc declined and his social democratic policy was eventually exchanged for austerity. An open capitalist world financial system therefore tends to reinforce itself. Ironically, states with strong but flexible public institutions, able to manipulate the world economy when possible and to correct for its effects when necessary, seem to thrive best in an open world political economy. For countries not blessed with such institutions, the international economic order of modern capitalism manifests a pronounced bias against policies promoting equality.[42]

International liberalism: an evaluation

The international order proposed by liberalism has a number of appealing features, particularly when a substantial number of powerful states are republics. Orderly exchange, within a framework of rules and institutions, provides incentives for peaceful expansion and productive specialization. International institutions facilitate cooperation and foster habits of working together. Therefore, a realistic liberalism, premised not on automatic harmony but on prudential calculation, has a great deal to commend it as a philosophy of international relations.

Yet liberalism has several major limitations, both as a framework for analysis and as a guide for policy. It is incomplete as an explanation, it can become normatively myopic and it can backfire as a policy prescription.

Liberalism makes sense only as an explanatory theory within the constraints pointed out by Marxism and realism. Viewed as an explanation of state action, sophisticated liberalism emphasizes the difference that international rules and institutions can make, even when neither the anarchic system nor world capitalism can be transformed or eliminated. If major powers come into violent conflict with one another or capitalism disintegrates, the institutions on which liberalism relies will also collapse. International liberalism is therefore only a partial theory of international relations: it does not stand up on its own.

Normatively, liberalism is, as John Dunn has put it, 'distressingly plastic'.[43] It accommodates easily to dominant interests, seeking to use its institutional skills to improve situations rather than fundamentally to restructure them. Liberalism is also relatively insensitive to exploitation resulting from gross asymmetries of wealth and power. Liberals may be inclined to play down values such as equality when emphasis on such values would bring them into fundamental conflict with powerful élites on whose acquiescence their institutional reformism depends. Liberalism is sometimes myopic as a normative theory, since it focuses principally on moderating 'economic constraints on modern polities' in a way that facilitates governments' purposes, rather than directly on the condition of disadvantaged groups. To satisfied modern élites and the middle classes, liberalism seems eminently reasonable, but it is not likely to be as appealing to the oppressed or disgruntled.

As policy advice, liberalism can backfire under at least two different sets of conditions. First, if only a few governments seek to promote social equity and welfare in an open economy, they may find their policies constrained by the more benighted policies of others. 'Embedded liberalism' represents an attempt to render a liberal international order compatible with domestic interventionism and the welfare state. As we have seen, this is a difficult synthesis to maintain. Second, liberalism may have perverse effects if the global extension of interests that it fosters cannot be defended. Decaying liberal systems may be the most dangerous of all. One way to deal with this problem of decay is to use military power to uphold the liberal order. But we may also want to consider how to make ourselves less vulnerable by trimming back some of these interests, in so far as we can do so without threatening the rule-based structure of exchange that is the essence of a liberal order. It would be foolish for liberalism to commit suicide for fear of death. But perhaps we could go on a diet, reducing some of the excess weight that may make us vulnerable to disaster.

The appeal of liberalism clearly depends in part on where you sit. Liberalism can become a doctrine of the status quo; indeed, this danger is probably greater for the non-utopian liberalism that I advocate than for the utopian liberalism that E. H. Carr criticized almost half a century ago. But realism has an even greater tendency to be morally complacent, since it lacks the external standards of human rights that liberalism can use to criticize governments in power. Realism lacks the 'imaginative flexibility' of liberalism about human possibilities, and is therefore missing an ethical dimension that liberals possess.[44] Marxism is anything but complacent about the capitalist status quo, although as a moral theory the weakness of orthodox Marxism is its inability to show that the alternatives it proposes *as they are likely actually to operate in practice* are morally superior to feasible reformist alternatives. Soviet Marxists, of course, traditionally supported the status quo in socialist states within the Soviet sphere of influence, regardless of how repressive their governments actually were.

The strength of liberalism as moral theory lies in its attention to how alternative governing arrangements will operate in practice, and in particular how institutions can protect human rights against the malign intentions of powerholders. Unlike realism, liberalism strives for improvement; but unlike Marxism, it subjects proffered 'new orders' to sceptical examination. 'No liberal ever forgets that governments are coercive.'[45] A liberalism that remains faithful to its emphasis on individual rights and individual welfare as the normative basis for international institutions and exchange, can never become too wedded to the status quo, which never protects these rights adequately.

In the end, I return to the emphasis of liberalism on human action and choice. Liberalism incorporates a belief in the possibility of ameliorative change facilitated by multilateral arrangements. It emphasizes the moral value of prudence.[46] For all its faults and weaknesses, liberalism helps us to see the importance of international cooperation and institution building, even within the fundamental constraints set by world capitalism and the international political system. Liberalism holds out the prospect that we can affect, if not control, our fate, and thus encourages both better theory and improved practice. It constitutes an antidote to fatalism and a source of hope for the human race.

Notes

1. David Long, 'The Harvard School of Liberal International Relations Theory: A Case for Closure', *Millennium: Journal of International Studies*, Vol. 24, No. 3 (Winter 1995), p. 502.
2. Part of what follows is reprinted, with the consent of Cambridge University Press, from Robert O. Keohane, 'International Liberalism Reconsidered', in John Dunn (ed.), *The Economic Limits to Modern Politics*

(Cambridge: Cambridge University Press, 1990), pp. 165–94. This article was written over ten years ago, and was published in 1990. It appears here as published, with the exception of two examples of then-current situations that have now changed, and no longer illustrate the general point being made.

3. Most systematically, in *After Hegemony: Cooperation and Discord in the World Political Economy* (Princeton, NJ: Princeton University Press, 1984).

4. Robert O. Keohane, Joseph S. Nye and Stanley Hoffman (eds.), *After the Cold War: International Institutions and State Strategies in Europe, 1989–1991* (Cambridge, MA: Harvard University Press, 1993); Peter M. Haas, Robert O. Keohane and Marc A. Levy (eds.), *Institutions for the Earth: Sources of Effective Environmental Protection* (Cambridge, MA: MIT Press, 1993); and Robert O. Keohane and Marc A. Levy (eds.), *Institutions for Environmental Aid* (Cambridge, MA: MIT Press, 1996).

5. Long, 'The Harvard School of Liberal International Relations Theory', p. 494.

6. Robert O. Keohane and Joseph S. Nye (eds.), *Transnational Relations and World Politics* (Cambridge, MA: Harvard University Press, 1972), introduction and conclusion by the editors.

7. Long, 'The Harvard School of Liberal International Relations Theory', p. 502.

8. *Ibid.*, p. 503.

9. Keohane, 'International Liberalism Reconsidered', pp. 166–7.

10. Michael W. Doyle, 'Liberalism and World Politics', *American Political Science Review*, Vol. 80, No. 4 (1986), p. 1152.

11. Michael W. Doyle, 'Kant, Liberal Legacies, and Foreign Affairs', Part I, *Philosophy and Public Affairs*, Vol. 12, No. 3 (1983), p. 206. A parallel definition, focusing on political freedom, is offered by Stanley Hoffman, 'Liberalism and International Affairs', in Hoffman, *Janus and Minerva* (Boulder, CO: Westview Press, 1986).

12. R. G. Collingwood, 'Preface', in Guido de Ruggiero, *The History of European Liberalism*, trans. Collingwood (Boston, MA: Beacon Press, 1959), pp. vii–viii, and quoted by John Dunn, *Rethinking Modern Political Theory* (Cambridge: Cambridge University Press, 1985), p. 158. The use of the word, 'man', rather than 'person', in this quotation reflects a limitation of the thinking of classical liberalism, with the notable exception of John Stuart Mill, as well as of other schools of political thought before the late twentieth century: women are not regarded as the political equals of men, and labour and nurturing by women, which have traditionally been instrumental in the development of children's personality, are ignored.

13. For this suggestion I am indebted to Andrew Moravcsik.

14. As a large critical literature emphasizes, of course, liberalism is not power-free: as E. H. Carr emphasized, liberal economic institutions have typically been undergirded by structures of power, which may be hidden by the veil of economics and therefore more or less invisible.

15. Immanuel Kant, 'Eternal Peace' (1795), in Carl J. Friedrich (ed.), *The Philosophy of Kant* (New York: Modern Library, 1949), pp. 437–9.

16. Doyle, 'Liberalism and World Politics', p. 1160.

17. Susan Okin has pointed out to me that Kant excluded from citizenship women and day labourers. Many republics excluded people without

property from voting until late in the last century, and women until early in this one.
18. Doyle, 'Kant, Liberal Legacies, and World Affairs', p. 213. Doyle defines liberal states in a manner consistent with Kant's specifications.
19. Another reason for this emphasis is that recent work on liberalism and international affairs, especially that by Doyle, has discussed republican liberalism with great sophistication, but has paid less attention to commercial and regulatory liberalism.
20. Albert O. Hirschman, *The Passions and the Interests: Political Arguments for Capitalism Before its Triumph* (Princeton, NJ: Princeton University Press, 1977), p. 80.
21. Kant, 'Eternal Peace', p. 455, emphasis original.
22. Kenneth N. Waltz, *Man, the State and War: A Theoretical Analysis* (New York: Columbia University Press, 1954), p. 86. Twenty years before Waltz's book, E. H. Carr argued that liberalism was essentially utopian in character, and that the liberal engaged in 'clothing his own interest in the guise of a universal interest for the purpose of imposing it on the rest of the world'. Carr, *The Twenty Years Crisis, 1919–1939*, 2nd edn. (London: Macmillan, 1946), pp. 27 and 75.
23. Larry L. Fabian, *Andrew Carnegie's Peace Endowment* (New York: Carnegie Endowment for International Peace, 1985), p. 43.
24. Eugene Staley, *The World Economy in Transition* (New York: Council on Foreign Relations, 1939), p. 103.
25. *Ibid.*
26. Hirschman, *The Passions and the Interests*, p. 51.
27. Kant, 'Eternal Peace', pp. 441 and 445.
28. For a comparative analysis of eight international organizations that substantiates the importance of institutional histories and choices, see Robert W. Cox and Harold K. Jacobson (eds.), *The Anatomy of Influence: Decision Making in International Organization* (New Haven, CT: Yale University Press, 1973).
29. The pioneering works are: Karl W. Deutsch *et al.*, *Political Community and the North Atlantic Area: International Organization in the Light of Historical Experience* (Princeton, NJ: Princeton University Press, 1957), and Ernst B. Haas, *The Uniting of Europe: Political, Social and Economic Forces, 1950–1957* (Stanford, CA: Stanford University Press, 1958).
30. For an impressive work of scholarship that emphasizes the European ability to obstruct American plans and implement their own, see Alan Milward, *The Reconstruction of Western Europe, 1945–1951* (Berkeley and Los Angeles, CA: University of California Press, 1984).
31. John Gerard Ruggie, 'International Regimes, Transactions and Change: Embedded Liberalism in the Post-War Economic Order', *International Organization*, Vol. 36, No. 2 (1982), pp. 379–415.
32. For a discussion, see Robert O. Keohane and Joseph S. Nye, Jr., *Power and Interdependence: World Politics in Transition* (Boston, MA: Little, Brown, 1977).
33. Barry Buzan, 'Economic Structure and International Security: The Limits of the Liberal Case', *International Organization*, Vol. 38, No. 4 (1984), p. 603.

34. Russell Hardin, *Collective Action* (Baltimore, MD: Johns Hopkins University Press, 1982), p. 228.
35. For a book that revives this thesis, in a not entirely consistent or persuasive form, see Richard N. Rosecrance, *The Rise of the Trading State* (New York: Basic Books, 1985). Rosecrance drifts too much, in my view, into seeing the 'rise of the trading state' as a more or less inevitable trend, ignoring some of the qualifications that must be made to the thesis, as observed above.
36. It is hard to be more specific than this about the effects of the international system without detailed empirical investigation. In general, we must guard against the temptation to overestimate the effects of international arrangements on the propensity of governments to use force. Even sophisticated international liberalism is a systemic theory which does not probe deeply into the nature of domestic political and social coalitions. The impact of the international system is only one of many factors – even if an important one – affecting the behaviour of states.
37. For an analysis of policy-making in the Vietnam War, based principally on *The Pentagon Papers*, see Leslie H. Gelb, with Richard K. Betts, *The Irony of Vietnam: The System Worked* (Washington, DC: The Brookings Institution, 1979).
38. Buzan, 'Economic Structure and International Security'.
39. See, for instance, Paul McCracken *et al.*, *Towards Full Employment and Price Stability* (Paris: OECD, 1977), for an analysis along these lines by a 'blue-ribbon panel' of economists.
40. John Locke, *Second Treatise of Government* (1690), para. 57, in Locke, *Two Treatises of Government*, ed. P. Laslett, 2nd edition (Cambridge: Cambridge University Press, 1967), p. 323.
41. McCracken *et al.*, *Towards Full Employment*, pp. 136–7.
42. For an elaboration of this argument, see Robert O. Keohane, 'The World Political Economy and the Crisis of Embedded Liberalism', in John H. Goldthorpe (ed.), *Order and Conflict in Contemporary Capitalism* (Oxford: Clarendon Press, 1984), pp. 22–6.
43. Dunn, *Rethinking Modern Political Theory*, p. 169.
44. The phrase, 'imaginative flexibility', I owe to John Dunn.
45. Judith Shklar, *Ordinary Vices* (Cambridge, MA: Harvard University Press, 1984), p. 244.
46. Dunn, *Rethinking Modern Political Theory*, p. 169.

2
The Harvard School of Liberal International Theory: A Case for Closure*

David Long

This chapter advances a critique of an increasingly dominant school in international relations: the Harvard School of Liberal International Theory.[1] The academics who make up this school are joined in a common project of creating an alternative to realism and neorealism in international theory, and draw explicitly or silently on liberal premises, theories and/or ideas to advance this project. The focus of this chapter is on two authors, Robert O. Keohane and Andrew Moravcsik, who exemplify the Harvard School of Liberal International Theory.

Several recent publications have endeavoured to summarize or promote the primacy in international relations of the debate between realism and neoliberalism.[2] This work reflects a general rise in interest in the definition of liberal international theory, which has been prompted by both a concern to develop a coherent alternative or supplement to an apparently fading realist paradigm,[3] and a recognition that liberalism in international relations has itself remained inchoate. Keohane and Moravcsik have the most theoretically developed conceptions of liberal international theory and attempt to frame liberalism in international relations as explanatory theory, thus going beyond the taxonomies of liberal international theories.

The echo with the title of Roy Jones's seminal article, 'The English School of International Relations: A Case for Closure,[4] is quite deliberate. Jones sought not only to label a school of international thought; in setting out the themes underlying the approach of the English School, he sought also to critique it.[5] The existence of a school in the case of the Harvard School is indicated by the shared sense of purpose in developing a social scientific approach to international relations that comprehends the totality of the international system. The members of the School share a commitment to the sovereign state as the central actor in international relations. Their style is usually recognizable by its deployment of the economics-inspired fields of game theory and rational choice theory, though these techniques are as often referred to as used explicitly. They eschew traditional political theory and political philosophy, maintaining that these concerns are questions of individual conscience, and should therefore be distinct from social scientific analysis. Finally, as the name suggests, Harvard University has been home to more than a few of the international theorists of this School.[6]

The aim of this chapter is to show that, while the Harvard School's aim to develop a more coherent and rigorous liberal theory is well intentioned, they wittingly or unwittingly share a number of normative, ontological and methodological premises with their supposed opponents, the realists.[7] Furthermore, this squeezing of liberalism into contemporary categories of international relations does violence to liberal political philosophy and its international dimension, liberal internationalism. It flattens out some of the contradictions in liberal theory, but also stifles the prospects for change in liberalism and a renewal of its emancipatory project. Indeed, the attempt to create a *liberal* theory in this way must fail and is a threat to critical thinking in liberal international theory. One of the primary reasons for this failure and this threat is that, in focusing on international relations as a field, the Harvard School, for the most part knowingly, re-creates the centrality and primacy of state-centric power-oriented realism. Additionally, a narrow methodological commitment excludes much of the creative political (and economic) theorizing that has, in the past, advanced liberalism and liberal international thought.

I have drawn my inspiration for the alternative visions of liberalism that inform the critique that is advanced here from my reading of turn-of-the-century social (or new) liberals: such as J. A. Hobson and L. T. Hobhouse, among others. An alternative view of liberalism can be derived from a reading of the liberal internationalism that emerged from the changes in liberalism wrought by these writers. This new liberal/social democratic internationalism crystallized (initially, at least) in the writings of David Mitrany, and is oriented towards the global common good and human welfare.[8]

The two approaches within the Harvard School manifested in the work of Keohane and Moravcsik are closely complementary. While Keohane has recently dropped the moniker 'liberal' or 'neoliberal' from his institutionalism, both his and Moravcsik's orientation can plausibly be labelled as liberal on the basis of two analogies: the analogy to liberal economics in the US pluralism-inspired approach taken by Moravcsik, and the analogy of liberalism applied to states in the international system in the case of Keohane. Yet, a significant narrowing of the liberal tradition is involved here. It is this narrowing that I wish to expose as the primary flaw in the Harvard School's approach: in attempting to forge a liberal theory of international relations, realism is restored or retained and liberalism reduced.

The first section outlines and critiques Robert Keohane's neoliberal institutionalism. I then turn my attention to Andrew Moravcsik's positive liberal international theory. The third section summarizes the case for closure, emphasizing the dangers of the project to construct a realist-liberal synthesis. I conclude with a brief discussion of alternative visions of liberalism in international relations.

Robert Keohane's neoliberal institutionalism

If anyone represents the Harvard School of Liberal International Theory it is Robert Keohane, especially in the parts of his work where he has elaborated the approach to international relations he has called neoliberal institutionalism, or simply institutionalism. Keohane argues for a sophisticated liberalism that marries the best of commercial and regulatory liberal approaches. This idea is summed up in his description of neoliberal institutionalism.[9]

Keohane begins by describing the similarities and contrasts of the neoliberal institutionalist perspective with neorealism. He notes that realism and neoliberal institutionalism share conceptions of the international system and the goals and methods of social scientific study: '[l]ike neorealists, neoliberal institutionalists seek to explain behavioral regularities by examining the nature of the decentralised international system.' Both accept the salience of anarchy in international relations and 'take state power seriously'.[10]

However, neoliberal institutionalism regards neorealism's conception of, and focus on, international structure as too narrow. For Keohane, relative shifts in capabilities are not the only determinants of state behaviour. According to the neoliberal institutionalist position, the use of force is of declining utility in a world of 'complex interdependence', because expectations and relations between states become stable, predictable and routinized. Neoliberal institutionalism believes that international institutions, from conventions to formal international organizations, make a difference in the anarchic world of states, by stabilizing expectations and reducing transactions costs.[11]

Keohane has been the subject of attacks for the neorealist and utilitarian tendencies in his thinking, as well as his suggestion that certain feminist thinking could be incorporated into neoliberal institutionalism.[12] A rather larger number of criticisms of Keohane's argument, specifically with regard to the persistence and durability of international regimes 'after hegemony', have emerged in the context of the debate with realism. David Baldwin has demarcated the lines of the debate in his introduction to *Neorealism and Neoliberalism*.[13] The main bones of contention between the two approaches listed by Baldwin involve the nature and consequences of international anarchy, the significance of international cooperation, whether states seek relative or absolute gains, whether economic benefit or security is the principal goal of states, whether intentions or capabilities better explain international outcomes, and the significance of institutions and regimes.[14] This is very much a limited debate, where issues of methodology and substantive focus are shared by the protagonists: the explanatory role of theory, the existence of international anarchy and the primacy of states are common features to both approaches. Indeed, the restricted focus of the debate between neorealism and neoliberalism is celebrated as an achievement and an advantage.[15]

Whatever can be said regarding realist critiques, Keohane acknowledges that neoliberal institutionalism differs from previous articulations of liberalism in international relations. The most notable difference concerns the possibilities for international cooperation. Keohane argues that many, rather naïve, liberals see cooperation as nearly automatic, while he regards it as conditional.[16] Here, we see an important shift in the meaning of a central concept of liberalism. In refining the meaning of cooperation, Keohane adopts a position close to a game-theoretical understanding, where so-called rational individuals pursue their self-interested objectives: 'intergovernmental cooperation takes place when the policies actually followed by one government are regarded by its partners as facilitating realization of their own objectives, as a result of a process of policy coordination'.[17] For Keohane, this refinement allows him to distinguish between a condition of harmony, where cooperation is unnecessary, and cases where cooperation is required. Keohane's meaning of cooperation, however, also entails the fulfilment of individual, separate interests, rather than allowing for common interests. The obvious implication is that, in practice, harmonies of interests rarely occur and are, furthermore, theoretically uninteresting. This view contrasts starkly with the older liberal view as presented by Hobhouse, for example, in his *Liberalism*.[18] Hobhouse argues that the heart of liberalism is cooperation, by which he means revealing and realizing the underlying common interest of all in society.

For Keohane, liberals offer an overarching set of guiding principles for contemporary social science through their belief in the possibility of human progress. This metatheoretical status of liberalism is reinforced by Keohane's suggestion that liberalism is the belief in the value of individual freedom. He goes on to subjectivize this basic element of liberalism in a discussion of his own liberal sentiments: 'this commitment of mine is not particularly relevant to my analysis of international relations. One could believe in the value of individual liberty and remain either a realist or neorealist in one's analysis of world politics.'[19] He thus renders the 'doctrine of liberty' a non-issue in social science, distances it from liberal international theory, and simultaneously absolves himself from moral judgement in his theoretical work.

However, the differences between neoliberalism and liberal international theory go much deeper than Keohane admits. As Grieco puts it, neoliberal institutionalists are

> at once more cautious and more daring. They claim to accept realism's view that anarchy inhibits cooperation, but they argue that institutions can alleviate the inhibitory effects of anarchy on the willingness of states to work together when they share common interests.[20]

The concession to neorealism of state-centrism and the primacy of an international anarchy of states is entirely alien to liberalism, where the state is conceived as sitting astride a society whose interests it is supposed to represent. As Moravcsik notes, 'Judged by their analytical assumptions … such arguments are more properly termed "modified structural realism", not "neo-liberal institutionalism".'[21] They are realist because international anarchy and the absence of common interests are emphasized and because states are the actors. Keohane himself has withdrawn the term neoliberal from the self-description of his theory and now prefers merely 'institutionalism'.

Even so, Moravcsik is only partly correct; Keohane's institutionalism remains a form of liberal international theory. Indeed, an assumption of state-centrism in one context actually enhances the prospects for a superficially liberal theory of international relations. By treating states as agents in international relations, neoliberal institutionalism is liberalism by analogy. Neoliberal institutionalism's holism at the level of the state creates the possibility of liberal prescriptions by analogy for states in the international system. Rejecting the Hobbesian analogy to a state of nature, neoliberal institutionalism embraces a more Lockean view of states entering contracts while pursuing their self-interest. At one level, the Lockean domestic analogy renders Keohane's neoliberalism very close to Hedley Bull's understanding of the Grotian conception of international society.[22] However, the similarity demonstrates all the more clearly that 'liberalism by analogy' lacks the liberal focus and/or commitment to liberty and to individuals and social groups, as it renders the individuals and groups invisible in the analogical world of state-persons. Rather, individuals, groups and their preferences, values, and so on are aggregated into the preferences of the state just as they are with realism.

Keohane's justification for international institutions also deviates from the liberal advocacy of such organizations or arrangements. There are many different cases made by various liberals in support of international institutions. The case for institutions is made by some in terms of market failure, and by others in terms of developing the institutions that preserve the rule of law that constitutes the rules of the game. For yet other liberals, such as Hobson and Hobhouse, there is a need to ensure that formal rights can in practice be exercised, and this leads to measures associated with the welfare state and social democracy. All these liberal proposals share a desire for the growth of individual freedom and the development of community, seen as the aggregation of individual need-fulfilment through the rule of law and the market.[23] The analogue, welfare internationalism, has appeared in formulations first by David Mitrany and then Ernst Haas, in their functionalism and neofunctionalism respectively.[24]

All these liberal defences of institutions, domestic or international, ultimately rest on the ability of institutions to improve the conditions for the individual or social group. In contrast to previous liberal approaches, neoliberal institutionalism is again revealed as liberalism by analogy. While neoliberal institutionalism argues for international institutions as a response to market failure, it does not see institutions as aiming to improve the conditions of people. Rather, they address the situations of the agents in the international system as conceived by neoliberal institutionalism: that is, states. Keohane has recently acknowledged that liberal international theory only conditionally endorses international institutions.[25]

The emphasis in neoliberal institutionalism on market failure as the source for international institutions points to a further limitation of the approach as a form of liberalism. Economic factors are only a part of liberalism, indeed, arguably a subsidiary part, subordinate to individual liberty and well-being. Nevertheless, for neoliberal institutionalism, economic factors are central. Substantively, international institutions are created to control or manage economic dislocation and problems in the global economy. While recent discussions of institutions have turned to security matters as well as international political economy,[26] the approach still rests on economic methodology, especially that drawn from neoclassical economics. Thus, the discourse revolves around the supply and demand for regimes, the provision of collective goods, the determination of a state's preference structure and the deployment of cost-benefit analysis to assess a state's foreign policy performance. This utilitarian, or 'rational',[27] approach is liberalism once removed: that is, taking economic science as the basis for a liberal approach to international relations is again liberalism by analogy, this time the analogy being of states to firms in the market.

In sum, Keohane's neoliberal institutionalism is an emasculated liberalism, shorn of its normative concerns with the liberty and well-being of individuals, focusing on economic variables and using the utilitarian discourses and theories of liberal economics, and making states the agents in international relations. In the process, Keohane creates something of a utilitarian calculus of modified realism: a scientized version of English School institutionalism.[28] Liberalism's goals of individual emancipation and personal development, the ethical values that are central to liberalism, disappear.

The positive liberal theory of international relations

Andrew Moravcsik spells out what he expressly claims is a social scientific liberal theory of international relations. The three tenets of his avowedly non-utopian, non-normative liberal theory are (a) that individuals and privately constituted groups are the fundamental actors in world politics; (b) that governments represent a subset of domestic social actors; and (c) that inter-state behaviour is shaped by preferences rather than, as realists assert, power.[29] Moravcsik then uses these assumptions to derive various strands of liberal international theory, such as republican, pluralist and commercial liberalism. In another work, he has also used this approach to explain patterns of behaviour in the European Union.[30]

Moravcsik suggests that his liberal theory is a systemic theory of international relations, because international outcomes are determined by the convergence and divergence of state preferences, rather than simply by relative capabilities as is suggested by realism and neorealism. 'While Liberalism is, in the first instance, a theory of preference formation, Liberals maintain that preferences themselves are a key determinant of interstate bargaining outcomes,' he argues.[31] However, he compromises this 'maximalist' liberal position (that liberalism is a systemic theory of international relations in its own right) in his attempt to carve out a division of labour between his positive liberal theory on the one hand, and neorealism and Keohane's institutionalism on the other. While insisting that 'Liberalism must be the prior part of any synthesis between the two theories', Moravcsik contrasts the systemic approach of his so-called 'Maximalist Liberalism' with a more limited position. He suggests that 'Minimalist Liberals agree that Liberalism provides an accurate theory of preferences, but concede that Realism is often useful as a theory of bargaining'.[32] In addition, he distances his version of liberal theory from an explanation or rationalization of international institutions, such as Keohane's, which he argues can be liberal or realist inspired.

Moravcsik's project is not without its problems, however. I will take the three tenets in turn. While Moravcsik argues for a removal of the normative elements in liberal international theory, the position he takes on liberalism is in fact deeply ideological. For instance, in developing the ideas behind the first tenet of his liberal theory, Moravcsik claims that the 'remaining elements in Liberal theory ... assume a core of rational behaviour by self-interested individuals'.[33] He affirms this as liberalism through reference to classical liberal writers. This is certainly a defensible articulation of *a* liberal position. However, Moravcsik is asking us to accept more than this; his is a formulation of *the* liberal international theory. Yet, self-interest, individualism and rationality defined in terms of individual behaviour are only part of liberalism. They require the complement of the rule of law, equality of opportunity and freedom of expression and association, to name but a few possible additions.

Individualism and instrumental rationality constitute the core of economic or minimalist liberalism, rather than liberalism as a whole. The consonance of this so-called scientific position with one strand of liberalism is not without political significance. While Moravcsik is correct to draw our attention to the importance of individuals and private groups for liberalism, one should not lose sight of the tension in liberalism between individual interest and the common good. The tension for liberals is in the notion of community and common interest. For most liberals, this is more than an aggregation of individual interests, as Moravcsik goes on to suggest in his second tenet. There is an assumption in liberalism that, ultimately, the free pursuit of individual interest constrained by the rule of law will produce the greatest common good. Without the notion of common good, the defence of individual or group interests is not recognisably liberal.[34]

In his second premise, Moravcsik makes the analytical claim that liberals believe that governments represent a subset of domestic social actors. He then shows how liberal theories suggest that foreign policies result from particular configurations of state representation of societal interests, be they benign, as in the case of the Kantian liberal peace argument, or malign, as in the Hobson-inspired critique of imperialism.[35] Moravcsik is correct that liberal international theory identifies domestic political representativeness as an important variable in international relations. The problem here is that the analytical and normative are inextricably linked in liberalism. Simply suggesting that governments represent a section of society is hardly descriptive of liberal ideas on the role of government at all. Indeed, the travails of liberalism as an emancipatory project were to *remove* certain sections of the population from their privileged positions of power, and to install the people at large as the source of power in government. In so far as sectional interests dominate over the general interest, we are outside the realm of liberal political philosophy. The normative aim of liberalism has been popular government, not by some of the people but (in principle) by all.

Of course, Moravcsik's statement represents a pluralist analysis of the state rather than a liberal one. Again we see one fraction (a US fraction at that) of liberalism taken to represent the whole of liberalism. Even were we to concede that pluralist ideas reflect a variety of liberalism, we should note the influence of the analogy of the market. In this case, the analogy is the competition of groups in society to that of firms in a market economy. Alternatively, Moravcsik could defend his second premise by arguing that it offers a liberal *analysis*, from which liberal prescription follows. The problem with this defence is that what is distinctively liberal is the prescription rather than Moravcsik's analysis. That is, it is not simply that the state represents a section of society, but that the state *should* adequately and fairly represent the interests of society at large, whether or not this be interpreted as equivalent to the result of group interests competing for influence.

Moravcsik appears to be on stronger ground with the third premise, where he argues that, '[f]or Liberals, state purpose, not state power, is the most essential element of world politics'.[36] He goes on to argue that this emphasis on preferences does not mean that liberalism is a reductionist theory, as defined by Waltz. Liberal international theory is a systemic theory, since liberals are interested not in one state's preferences, but in the sum total of the aggregated preferences of any relationship of two or more states and in the international system as a whole. As with the second premise, one problem here is the level of generality at which Moravcsik conducts his discussion. An emphasis on preferences is enough to distinguish Moravcsik's approach from realism and neorealism, which are concerned with the constraints on state action and the limits of power in the international system. However, is it enough to justify the label liberal? I would argue that it is not. Instead, what we have is liberalism by analogy once again. Though individuals are supposedly the fundamental actors in world politics, at this point, Moravcsik argues that uppermost in our thoughts should be 'state purpose' and 'state preferences'. Individuals and their preferences are aggregated together and, following Moravcsik's second tenet, represented by the state.

For Moravcsik, because societal interests are represented by states, liberalism's primary concern with individuals and groups becomes an analytical focus in international relations on state preferences. In other words, Moravcsik's first and third tenets can be reconciled only if this second tenet is adopted. Yet, the way Moravcsik interprets representation in the second premise effectively relegates the importance of individuals and groups in liberal international theory. Thus, his approach is actually similar to Keohane's in its emphasis on state preferences as the mode of expression for individual and group interests. In fact, it is hardly coincidental that Moravcsik's approach, which collapses the importance of the individual into the collective agency of the state, is so similar to the approach taken by Keohane. Indeed, it is a staple of the mainstream of neorealist/neoliberal (institutionalist) international relations.

The disappearance of individuals into the state marginalizes another liberal approach to world politics: liberal internationalism, which stresses the interaction of individuals and groups below, beyond and around the nation-state. Moravcsik's formulation leaves precious little room for a nascent global civil society, which could convincingly be claimed as part of the liberal heritage.[37] Furthermore, through this acceptance of the centrality of the state for liberal international theory, Moravcsik has transformed an ideology of individual liberty and the rule of law into a generator of state preferences, which can then be input into realist analyses of international relations. Moreover, it is hard to escape the conclusion that Moravcsik's aim was to outline a perspective for international relations highlighting the importance of the domestic context in state preference formation, rather than to describe a liberal theory of international relations. As valuable as Moravcsik's analysis is, these projects are not identical.

Therefore, each of Moravcsik's propositions involves a significant narrowing (though in different ways) of liberal political thought. On the one hand, there is a reduction to a minimalist classical liberalism. On the other, there is a bald positivism that dispenses with liberal political philosophy. The approach is state-centric and presents a liberal theory of international relations based at most on state preferences, but more likely on a compromise with realism. The result is a distortion of liberalism and a misnaming of a theory of international relations.

The Harvard School, liberalism and realism

Thus far I have attempted to show that, as propounded by Moravcsik and Keohane, the Harvard School of Liberal International Theory suffers numerous flaws, especially as a form of liberalism in international relations. Here, I want to suggest that the approach of the Harvard School is fundamentally misguided. First, I will discuss the academic context of the School, noting that, to its detriment, this latest variant of liberal theory has been influenced by currents in US academic international relations. Despite the fact that there is much valuable work being conducted within Harvard School parameters, there are important limitations being placed on liberal theorizing in international relations by the approach. These limitations are in the first place analytical, but their implications are political.

Academic context has been all important in the development of the Harvard School of Liberal International Theory. Indeed, the Harvard School is an exemplar of what Stanley Hoffmann has described as 'American Social Science'.[38] Neoliberal institutionalism and the positive liberal theory of international relations both primarily engage with the discourses of US international relations and political science. This academic context has directed the school's understanding of liberal international theory towards orthodox international relations approaches based on the assumption of state centricism. It might be argued that there has always been a state-oriented element in liberalism, and a degree of statism is certainly evident in the writings of

Immanuel Kant and Woodrow Wilson, to take just a couple of examples. Moravcsik states that, '[f]or most Liberals, states remain the basic units of international public political organization; all competitors lack both legitimacy and power'.[39]

However, earlier forms of liberal internationalism did not simply assume the form of the state as given, as is the case with the Harvard School. In earlier liberal theory the state is the subject of historical development, and it is characterized increasingly (according to liberals) by popular self-government and national self-determination.[40] Furthermore, at least since David Mitrany and his development of the functional approach, liberal international theory has posed the question of what sort of institutional form might be required, if individual and group interests cannot be represented by national territorial states.[41] By contrast, for Keohane and Moravcsik, the state is an unquestioned given, a seemingly timeless axiom of theorizing about international relations. Once reduced to this axiomatic level, the state fits neatly into the economics-inspired fields of rational choice and game theory, which, as noted above, influence the Harvard School. This methodological move is significant because the stress on US variants of social science has increasingly marginalized historical, or what Keohane has called 'reflective', approaches to international relations.[42]

There is also a significant theoretical tension in liberalism and liberal internationalism regarding the centrality of international anarchy and the provision of governance by international institutions. The Harvard School reflects this tension, and then rationalizes it. For the Harvard School, as for many liberals and liberal internationalists before them, though freedom is a good, anarchy is feared for its consequences. Yet, the creation of international institutions is not affirmed unconditionally by liberals, as Moravcsik notes, since they view institutions as potentially oppressive.[43] This ambiguity is evident in earlier liberal writings, for example, during and shortly after the First World War, when the term 'international anarchy' was invented by the liberal G. L. Dickinson, and when liberals placed great faith in international law and the institution of the League.[44] The dynamic of individual liberty and social control is one that has been ceaselessly played out in liberalism. Unfortunately, the Harvard School variant, liberalism by analogy (the search for micro-foundations through pluralist market analogies or the analogy to states in international relations), defines the core of these problems out of existence. It reduces them to coordination problems only, the ordering or expression of preferences, rather than issues surrounding the creation and maintenance of a just order that reflects a liberal understanding of the common good. In short, the Harvard School approach reduces substance to process.[45]

Finally, the academic context is important in the development of the Harvard School approach because a fundamental tenet of the Harvard School is that their version of liberal international theory subsumes or can supersede realism or neorealism. Thus, the so-called debate between neorealism and neoliberalism all too quickly becomes an attempt to reconcile a modified liberal international theory with realism in international relations. Moravcsik, for instance, claims to have outlined a liberal theory that fits within the mainstream of academic scholarship on international relations. He then goes on to attempt a reconciliation of his liberal theory with neorealism.[46]

Outside the US academic international relations community such a project might appear obscure. The liberal heritage of the Harvard School seems to be less important than an ulterior motive: the creation of a new hegemonic paradigm in international relations, which will presumably to a certain extent reflect liberal precepts. The basis for the reconciliation, however, is the transformation of both realism and liberalism into utilitarian theories, wherein the focus is on game-theoretic models, micro-foundations and other economics-inspired tools of analysis. This is, as I have noted above, an emasculation of liberalism and liberal internationalism (as it is, indeed, of realism).

Liberal internationalism's alternative futures

Where does this leave liberal international theory? The Harvard School's search for a set of axioms on which to base liberal international theory is not the only possible liberal approach to international relations. Rather than try to develop a positive (as opposed to normative and/or utopian) theory of international relations, one alternative is to reflect on the development of liberalism as a political tradition or ideology and its application to international relations/world politics. While such an approach may seem to fall into the trap of looking backward, or even of appearing to be academic navel-gazing, the value of looking at the history of liberalism and liberal internationalism is that one can step outside the narrow confines of a particular debate, and see instead the wider view of continuity and change in such paradigms or debates in liberal theory. Liberalism and liberal internationalism have developed in part as responses to crises and criticisms as a result of political, economic, social, ideological and technological change, as well as a response to internal divisions and disputes. Liberals have consciously modified their doctrine to account for recent developments in world politics, and to respond to theoretical challenges from other perspectives.

Liberalism is above all a political project. The aim of liberalism has been the greater freedom of individuals in society.[47] As such, liberalism has in the past, as we know, been at the forefront of the opposition to privilege and arbitrary power. Liberalism initially emerged in the West as a creed and a movement against the continued domination of the landed classes. The so-called 'new liberalism' turned, at the end of the nineteenth century, against the newly powerful forces of monopoly capitalism. It advocated a renovated liberalism, which embraced the role of the state as part of the project of economic liberation, in order to permit greater freedom for the large majority of Western populations.[48] This contrasts with the more recent neoliberal attacks on the inefficiencies, lack of democratic accountability and arbitrariness of the modern state. In the international realm, liberal internationalism has attacked the privileged role of ruling classes and state elites in the making of state policy, which has had perverse international outcomes in forms such as imperialism and aggressive interventions. More recently, there has been renewed liberal advocacy of international agreements for freer trade.

In spite of the self-image, liberals have not always been anti-privilege, nor has liberalism been an emancipatory creed throughout its varied history. There have been many disputes within liberalism concerning its critical faculties and cooptation by powerful interests. For example, many turn-of-the-century new liberals reckoned that what they regarded as old liberalism had been captured by those in power, and that liberal principles had been perverted to serve privilege and the wealthier sections of society. Similarly, those supporting and opposing more recent neoliberal ideas and policies suggest ulterior motives in the pronouncement of liberal ideals: for example, in international relations, with regard to the debates about free trade.

Despite these lapses, liberal theories have, nevertheless, usually been constructed in opposition to a variety of bastions of privilege and power. So what is the Harvard School of Liberal International Theory struggling against? In the academic context, the answer is contained in the sham debate between neorealism and neoliberalism, as we have seen. However, neoliberalism and the positive liberal theory of international relations also engage a discourse about the future of liberalism and liberal internationalism, as much as they do that of international relations.

Liberalism as a political project encompasses an approach to international relations but also, of course, ranges far wider. Squeezing an ideology such as liberalism into a category of international relations theory is not without its difficulties, as we have seen in Moravcsik's and Keohane's work. In particular, many strands of liberalism go beyond the Harvard School's understanding of state-centric international relations to envisage a world politics of individuals and groups, as has been suggested by James Rosenau in his *Turbulence in World Politics*. This is hardly novel, as we can see from Keohane and Nye's *Transnational Relations and World Politics*, although there is a much longer heritage than that.[49]

Many forms of internationalism drawing their inspiration directly or indirectly from liberalism have dispensed with a focus on the nation-state. The universalizing drive of liberalism, as an emancipatory project aiming at the realization of personal individual liberty, makes liberalism more at home with concepts such as world politics and world society than international relations, except in so far as international relations can be shown to reflect liberal precepts such as the rule of law, recognition of the rights of individuals and popular sovereignty. In this sense, many (though not all, by any means) of the theories of new social movements and global civil society are intrinsically liberal and need to be recognized as such.[50] This is important to liberal internationalism, as it supplements a narrow understanding that too often associates liberalism simply with the forwarding of individual material interests. It is also important for thinking about new social and global forms. We need to be able to see the linkages between liberal internationalism and thinking on new social movements and the like before we affirm or deny them all *en masse*.

By categorizing liberal internationalism within the mainstream international relations discourse, the Harvard School restricts the prospects for liberal internationalism's progressive renewal, by narrowing its horizons to a limited discourse of international relations precisely at the time when world politics appears to be breaking the bounds of the sovereign territorial state. The result is political conservatism, in terms of the focus on the state and in terms of method, as a positivistic social scientific approach works with the *status quo ante* without questioning its origins or development.[51] An historical approach to liberalism and liberal internationalism demonstrates, by contrast, the various ways that liberalism is a critical project. Additionally, attention to the diversity of opinion in liberalism, and particularly to the silenced voices of social liberalism, makes way for alternative visions, and grounds them in contemporary and past political practice. Just as Cox suggests that the realist Carr can make contributions to a critical international theory,[52] so can liberal internationalists.

Conclusion

In closing, some scepticism should be voiced regarding the liberal project as a whole. The changes after the Cold War appear to bode well for liberalism, notwithstanding the warning signals of the collapse into barbarism in Bosnia, ethnic strife increasing worldwide and the potential proliferation of nuclear weapons, materials or expertise. The collapse of communism and the rise of technologically and economically driven globalism apparently reinforce the lessons of universalist liberalism and undermine the assumptions of old-style realism.

At this moment of apparent triumph, we must step back and wonder at the assumptions of liberalism regarding individual liberty, private property, the bases of community and the sanctity of law and constitutionality. The way in which to do this, it seems to me, is not to develop a systematized form of liberalism in terms of units of analysis, methodology, and so on, but to reflect on the development of liberalism and liberal internationalism. If we look at liberalism this way, we do not merely celebrate its victories or memorialize it; we can also reveal its limitations. Prescribing liberal and institutionalist remedies, for example, for transforming Eastern Europe and the adjusting poorer societies of the South is only a start.[53] Such proposed remedies have to be advanced self-consciously and with a sense of self-criticism, especially given our own democratic dilemmas. Centrally, liberal international theory must confront head on issues such as cultural relations and hegemony, as well as questions of identity and political legitimacy. It must also appreciate the difficulties of realizing on a truly global scale the personal freedoms about which liberalism talks so proudly. In short, the limits of liberalism and liberal internationalism need to be recognized, as does the fact that their promises have not been kept.

These reflections suggest that there are three main reasons to believe that the approach advanced by the Harvard School is fundamentally misguided. First, a malleable meaning of liberal international theory is appropriate to an era of rapid change and transformation, rather than the adoption of a set of scientific axioms. This is especially true in light of the challenges facing the territorial state in the late twentieth century. The adoption of an axiomatic liberalism that reflects a variant of liberal thinking therefore has political as well as analytical implications.

Second, with regard to liberal international theory, the Harvard School is harmful because it demotes the emphasis in the liberal internationalist tradition on sub-state, transnational and global entities. Where transnational factors are considered, these are as the objects of state policy rather than as self-constituting subjects in their own right.

Third, liberalism is a political project. As such it has normative goals and is constantly in motion. Any set of social scientific concepts associated with liberalism will always be contingent. Liberalism is grounded in a social and political philosophy which cannot simply be parcelled out into the academic disciplines. The lessons of liberalism regarding openness and tolerance are ideally an important aspect of the *milieu* of academic life in general. Further, in order to maintain what might be called the critical faculties of liberalism, its universalizing emancipatory project has to come first. Thus, a sophisticated analysis of liberal international theory has to consider the role that it plays in the liberal project of increasing individual freedom. The ideological content and influence of liberalism is hotly contested, of course, but the description of liberal international theory is certainly part of that contest. The Harvard School of Liberal International Theory offers only one path for the development of liberal internationalism, and effectively closes off other promising routes. Because it is a case of closure, the Harvard School of Liberal International Theory is also a case for closure.

Notes

*   This is an amended version of a paper presented at the British International Studies Association Annual Meeting, University of York, December 1994, and under the title, 'New Liberalisms, Old and New: Institutionalism, Positive Theory and the Liberal Political Tradition', at the International Studies Association Annual Convention, Washington, DC, March 1994. I have benefited from comments by Luke Ashworth, Max Cameron, Tobi Davidge, Robert Latham, James Mittleman, Andrew Moravcsik, Hidemi Suganami and Peter Wilson.

1. A couple of caveats regarding this name are in order. Some might ask why I have not called it, for instance, the 'American School of Liberal Internationalism'. This could engender confusion with the type of (liberal) internationalism of Woodrow Wilson and others. Part of the aim of this chapter is to show that, in important respects, the Harvard School

is different from these, hence the specific coining of the term 'Harvard School'.

2. David Baldwin (ed.), *Neorealism and Neoliberalism: The Contemporary Debate* (New York: Columbia University Press, 1993), and Charles Kegley, Jr (ed.), *Controversies in International Relations Theory: Realism and the Neoliberal Challenge* (New York: St. Martin's Press, 1995).

3. Andrew Moravcsik, 'Liberalism and International Relations Theory', Center for International Affairs, Harvard University, Working Paper No. 92-6, 1992; Mark W. Zacher and Richard A. Matthew, 'Liberal International Theory: Common Threads, Divergent Strands', in Kegley, *Controversies*, pp. 107–50; Robert O. Keohane, 'International Liberalism Reconsidered', in John Dunn (ed.), *The Economic Limits to Modern Politics* (Cambridge: Cambridge University Press, 1990), pp. 165–94; Joseph S. Nye, Jr., 'Neorealism and Neoliberalism', *World Politics*, Vol. 40, No. 2 (1988), pp. 235–51; and Robert Latham, 'Liberalism's Order/Liberalism's Other: A Genealogy of Threat', *Alternatives*, Vol. 20, No. 1 (1995), pp. 111–46.

4. Roy E. Jones, 'The English School of International Relations: A Case for Closure', *Review of International Studies*, Vol. 7, No. 1 (1981), pp. 1–13.

5. It is ironic that while the title of Jones' article has reached such currency, the analysis of the article has received relatively little attention. Jones' attack is essentially a classical liberal, constitutionalist critique on the holistic conservatism and statism of Bull, Wight and the rest. Though the subjects of this article and of Jones' critique are different, there are similarities between the English School of International Relations and the Harvard School of Liberal International Theory. Still, it is worth noting that Tony Evans and Peter Wilson have compared the English School with primarily US-based regime theory and found notable similarities as well as important points of difference. See Evans and Wilson, 'Regime Theory and the English School of International Relations: A Comparison', *Millennium: Journal of International Studies*, Vol. 21, No. 3 (1992), pp. 329–51. See also Barry Buzan, 'From International System to International Society: Structural Realism and Regime Theory Meet the English School', *International Organization*, Vol. 47, No. 3 (1993), pp. 327–52.

6. For example, Lisa Martin, *Coercive Cooperation: Explaining Multilateral Economic Sanctions* (Princeton, NJ: Princeton University Press, 1992).

7. Robert O. Keohane, 'Neoliberal Institutionalism: A Perspective on World Politics', in his *International Institutions and State Power* (Boulder, CO: Westview Press, 1989), pp. 1–20. See also Joseph M. Grieco, 'Anarchy and the Limits of Cooperation: A Realist Critique of the Newest Liberal Institutionalism', in Baldwin (ed.), *Neorealism and Neoliberalism*, note 2, pp. 116–40.

8. J. A. Hobson's principal works are *The Social Problem* (London: Nisbet, 1901); *Imperialism*, 3rd edition (London: Allen and Unwin, 1938); *Towards International Government* (London: Allen and Unwin, 1915); *The Morals of Economic Internationalism* (New York: Houghton, 1920); and *Free Thought in the Social Sciences* (London: Allen and Unwin, 1925). For L. T. Hobhouse's liberalism, see *Democracy and Reaction* (London: Fischer Unwin, 1904), and *Liberalism* (London: Williams and Norgate, 1911). Finally, David Mitrany's most important ideas can be found in *The Progress of International*

54 *David Long*

Government (London: Allen and Unwin, 1933), and *A Working Peace System* (London: Royal Institute of International Affairs, 1943). I have discussed Hobson's liberal theory of international relations at length in my *Towards a New Liberal Internationalism: The International Theory of J. A. Hobson* (Cambridge University Press, 1996).
9. Robert O. Keohane, *After Hegemony: Cooperation and Discord in the World Political Economy* (Princeton, NJ: Princeton University Press, 1984), Chapter 1, and Keohane, 'Neoliberal Institutionalism'.
10. Keohane, 'Neoliberal Institutionalism', pp. 7–8.
11. Robert Axelrod and Robert O. Keohane, 'Achieving Cooperation under Anarchy: Strategies and Institutions', in Baldwin (ed.), *Neorealism and Neoliberalism*, pp. 85–115, and Robert O. Keohane and Lisa L. Martin, 'The Promise of Institutionalist Theory', *International Security*, Vol. 20, No. 1 (1995), pp. 39–51.
12. James Der Derian, 'The (S)pace of International Relations: Simulation, Surveillance and Speed', *International Studies Quarterly*, Vol. 34, No. 3 (1990), pp. 295–310; R. B. J. Walker, 'History and Structure in the Theory of International Relations', *Millennium*, Vol. 18, No. 2 (1989), pp. 163–83; and Cynthia Weber, 'Good Girls, Little Girls and Bad Girls: Male Paranoia in Robert Keohane's Critique of Feminist International Relations', *Millennium*, Vol. 23, No. 2 (1994), pp. 337–48.
13. 'Neoliberalism, Neorealism, and World Politics', in Baldwin (ed.), *Neorealism and Neoliberalism*, pp. 3–25.
14. *Ibid.*, pp. 4–8.
15. *Ibid.*, p. 3.
16. Keohane, 'Neoliberal Institutionalism', p. 11.
17. Keohane, *After Hegemony*, pp. 51–2.
18. Hobhouse, *Liberalism*, Chapter 6.
19. Keohane, 'Neoliberal Institutionalism', p. 10.
20. Grieco, 'Anarchy and the Limits of Cooperation', p. 303.
21. Moravcsik, 'Liberalism', p. 34.
22. Hedley Bull, 'The Grotian Conception of International Society', in Herbert Butterfield and Martin Wight (eds.), *Diplomatic Investigations: Essays in the Theory of International Politics* (London: Allen and Unwin, 1966), pp. 51–73.
23. In international economic relations, the range of opinion from Hayek to Keynes in support of, admittedly different, conceptions of international institutions is indicative. See Friedrich A. Hayek, *The Road to Serfdom* (London: Arc, 1986), and D. J. Markwell, 'J. M. Keynes, Idealism and the Economic Bases of Peace', in David Long and Peter Wilson (eds.), *Thinkers of the Twenty Years' Crisis: Inter-War Idealism Reassessed* (Oxford: Oxford University Press, 1995), pp. 189–213.
24. For a discussion of Mitrany and Haas in the context of welfare internationalism, see Hidemi Suganami, *The Domestic Analogy and World Order Proposals* (Cambridge: Cambridge University Press, 1989).
25. Robert O. Keohane, 'Institutional Theory and the Realist Challenge After the Cold War', in Baldwin (ed.), *Neorealism and Neoliberalism*, p. 298 n. 3. See also Moravcsik, 'Liberalism'.
26. Kenneth A. Oye, 'Explaining Cooperation under Anarchy: Hypotheses and Strategies', in Oye (ed.), *Cooperation under Anarchy* (Princeton, NJ: Princeton

University Press, 1986), p. 2, and Keohane and Martin, 'The Promise of Institutionalist Theory', p. 43.

27. Keohane, 'Institutional Theory', p. 298.
28. Hidemi Suganami, 'The Structure of Institutionalism: An Anatomy of British Mainstream International Relations', *International Relations*, Vol. 7, No. 5 (1983), pp. 2363–81.
29. Moravcsik, 'Liberalism', pp. 2–13. Since this paper was originally written, Moravcsik has published a revised version of his argument in 'Taking Preferences Seriously: A Liberal Theory of International Politics', *International Organization*, Vol. 51, No. 4 (1997), pp. 513–53. However, the fundamentals of his argument remain the same, and their theoretical implications were more clearly stated in the 1992 Harvard Working Paper.
30. Andrew Moravcsik, 'Preferences and Power in the European Community: A Liberal Intergovernmentalist Approach', *Journal of Common Market Studies*, Vol. 31, No. 4 (1993), pp. 473–524.
31. Moravcsik, 'Liberalism and International Relations Theory', p. 13.
32. *Ibid.*, pp. 15–16.
33. *Ibid.*, p. 5.
34. Hobhouse, *Liberalism*, is an extended defence of this proposition. See also Josi-Guilherme Merquior, *Liberalism, Old and New* (Boston, MA: Twayne, 1991), Chapters 1 and 2.
35. Moravcsik, 'Liberalism and International Relations Theory', pp. 17–29.
36. *Ibid.*, p. 11.
37. See, for example, Ronnie D. Lipschutz, 'Reconstructing World Politics: The Emergence of Global Civil Society', and M. J. Peterson, 'Transnational Activity, International Society and World Politics', both in *Millennium*, Vol. 21, No. 3 (1992), pp. 389–420 and 371–88 respectively.
38. Stanley Hoffmann, 'An American Social Science: International Relations', *Daedalus*, Vol. 106, No. 3 (1977), pp. 41–60.
39. Moravcsik, 'Liberalism and International Relations Theory', p. 31.
40. See, for example, John Stuart Mill, 'Considerations in Representative Government', in Mill, *Collected Works*, Vol. 19: *Essays on Politics and Society* (London: Routledge & Kegan Paul, 1977), pp. 371–577.
41. Mitrany, *A Working Peace System*.
42. Robert O. Keohane, 'International Institutions: Two Approaches', *International Studies Quarterly*, Vol. 32, No. 3 (1988), pp. 379–96.
43. For a discussion of Kant's views of world government, see Moravcsik, 'Liberalism and International Relations Theory', pp. 30–1.
44. For a discussion of liberal arguments around the turn of the century and during the First World War see Suganami, *The Domestic Analogy and World Order Proposals*, Chapters 4 and 5.
45. See, for example, many of the contributions in Oye (ed.), *Cooperation under Anarchy*.
46. Moravcsik, 'Liberalism and International Relations Theory', pp. 36–8.
47. Merquior, *Liberalism, Old and New*, p. 5.
48. Michael Freeden, *The New Liberalism: An Ideology of Social Reform* (Oxford: Clarendon Press, 1978), Chapter 1. See also Long, *Towards a New Liberal Internationalism*.

49. James N. Rosenau, *Turbulence in World Politics: A Theory of Change and Continuity* (Princeton, NJ: Princeton University Press, 1990), and Robert O. Keohane and Joseph S. Nye, Jr. (eds.), *Transnational Relations and World Politics* (Cambridge, MA: Harvard University Press, 1971).

50. See Lipschutz, 'Reconstructing World Politics'; and Peterson, 'Transnational Activity'.

51. Robert Cox, 'Social Forces, States and World Orders: Beyond International Relations Theory', *Millennium*, Vol. 10, No. 2 (1991), pp. 126–55.

52. *Ibid.*, p. 127.

53. Robert O. Keohane, Joseph S. Nye, Jr. and Stanley Hoffmann (eds.), *After the Cold War: International Institutions and State Strategies in Europe, 1989–1991* (Cambridge, MA: Harvard University Press, 1993).

3
A Kantian Protest against the Peculiar Discourse of Inter-Liberal State Peace

John MacMillan

Immanuel Kant has featured prominently in recent debates about the relationship between liberal states and peace. In particular, he is widely held to be the political philosopher best suited to explain why liberal states appear to be able to maintain peace among themselves, but not in relations with non-liberal states. In this chapter, I will contest the predominant interpretation of Kant's political writings in this debate, and argue that his unique authority as a liberal philosopher has been exploited to establish a new series of exclusionary practices by liberal against non-liberal states. I begin by identifying the main features of the predominant interpretation of Kant's political writings. Then, I will discuss particularly problematic points of interpretation. Throughout, I seek to offer a more inclusive interpretation of Kant's writings and recall the importance he attached to justice as a necessary condition of an enduring peace.

Kant was introduced into the current literature upon liberal states and peace by Michael Doyle in 1983, and was further discussed in Doyle's 1986 and 1993 works.[1] Since then, there has been no alternative interpretation of Kant's legacy from within the literature on the relationship between liberal states and peace.[2] David Forsythe, Francis Fukuyama, Jack Levy, Bruce Russett and Georg Sørensen have all accepted Doyle's reading of Kant.[3] Elsewhere, Kant's association with the liberal peace debate is readily observable in the titles of journal articles, such as 'Kant or Cant: The Myth of the Democratic Peace' and 'Neorealism and Kant: No Pacific Union'.[4] Kant's authority has even extended beyond the academic world.[5] Given the special authority Kant commands as a representative of the liberal tradition in international relations, and especially given the influence he wields in current debates, a careful examination of his writings and the way they are being (ab)used, is urgently required.

The predominant interpretation of Kant's writings

Doyle identifies three features of the political relations of liberal states which, when combined, purport to explain the absence of war between liberal states and the persistence of war between liberal and non-liberal states. At the domestic level, liberalism introduces caution into the affairs of states, since the consent of that same citizenry which will bear the costs of war is required before military action can be undertaken. At the international level, a consensus among liberals upon the rights of states leads to their mutual relations being marked by respect, especially for the principle of non-intervention. At the transnational level, relations are marked by the 'spirit of commerce', which leads states to have a mutual interest in the welfare of other states as trading partners.[6]

It is the international level in particular that holds the key to explaining why liberal pacifism is limited to inter-liberal state relations: the 'separate peace'.[7] In a liberal state, relations between the government and populace are assumed to be characterized by consent; whereas, in a non-liberal state, relations between the government and populace are assumed to be characterized by coercion. Liberals will presume other liberal states to be just, and therefore deserving of accommodation; but presume non-liberal states to be unjust, and therefore regard them with deep suspicion. Hence, while 'fellow liberals benefit from a presumption of amity; non-liberals suffer from a presumption of enmity'.[8]

This prevalent interpretation of Kant's political writings has four significant characteristics. First, the current literature tends to emphasize the differences and, indeed, the opposition between liberal and non-liberal states. These observations have created a potentially dangerous climate of assumptions and expectations regarding future patterns of international relations. As Russett notes, 'social scientists sometimes create reality as well as analyze it. ... Repeating the proposition that democracies [read liberal states[9]] should not fight each other helps reinforce the proposition that democracies will not fight each other.'[10] The converse, however, is less heartening: by inference, repetition of the claim that Kant explains why liberal states *do* fight non-liberal states serves to establish an intellectual climate, in which war between liberal and non-liberal states is made to appear 'normal'.

Second, calls for reform are projected onto non-liberal states, inhibiting criticism of liberal states themselves. As such, the ideological context of the research implicitly accords both 'responsibility' and 'absolution' for that violence that does occur between liberal and non-liberal states. Regardless of the specific causes of any particular war, the underlying 'problem' is the persistence of non-liberal states, and the 'solution' is the replication of the liberal democratic political model.[11] The literature rarely considers that existing liberal states might be in need of critical self-examination, despite being replete with calls for change on the part of others. Questions of social justice, the proper domestic civil–military relationship, the establishment of accountability over the activities of transnational corporations, the concentration of ownership of the media and the preservation of civil liberties within liberal democracies do not appear to have a place.[12] Democracy, in this literature, is sparsely conceptualized and solely for export.

Third, according to the 'separate peace' school, until the liberal model is universalized the prospects for peace are poor. Russett's view is that 'an international system composed of both democratic and authoritarian states will include both zones of peace (... among the democracies) and zones of war or at best deterrence between democratic and authoritarian states'.[13] Netanyahu projects this claim onto his own political purview: 'here, in a nutshell, is the main problem of achieving peace in the Middle East: except for Israel, there *are no democracies*'.[14] These writers ignore crucial questions regarding cooperation between liberal and non-liberal states *prior* to the homogenization of political forms. Such questions, however, were of crucial importance to Kant.

A fourth feature of the current literature is that, while Kant advocated a confederation of states in order to establish a secure international environment within which states would be better placed to perfect their civil constitutions, membership of this confederation should be restricted to liberal states. Fukuyama, for instance, claims that 'if one wanted to create a league of nations according to Kant's own precepts ... it would have to be a league of truly free states brought together by their common commitment to liberal principles'.[15] Similarly, Netanyahu asserts that Kant advocated a world federation of democracies 'strong enough to compel the arbitration of disputes', and blames the earlier failure of the League and United Nations on the inclusion of 'dictators'.[16]

This academic interpretation of Kant's political thought arose first and foremost as an attempt to explain a particular set of empirical phenomena: the removal of 'the occasion of wars among liberal states and not wars between liberal and non-liberal states'.[17] A corollary of this, however, was that the discussion of Kant stressed the significance of the distinction between liberal and non-liberal states, rather than duties to develop global relations as a whole. While both Doyle and Russett are clearly sympathetic to this latter theme,[18] it remains overshadowed in the bulk of their work by the emphasis upon homogenization of domestic political systems. This has led to the neglect of other central elements of Kant's political philosophy which would turn the spotlight of responsibilities and reform upon existing liberal states. In this way, the discourse benefits the strong and disadvantages the weak who might benefit from a richer reading of Kantian notions of global justice.

Kant and the relationship between liberal and non-liberal states

Certainly, Kant posited a link between republics and peace. However, and crucially for Kant, those agents concerned to develop his perpetual peace project ought to focus upon the gradual and pacific evolution of global relations according to principles of right, rather than the homogenization of domestic political forms. To focus upon the replication of a particular domestic political system greatly underestimates the scale of Kant's project, and serves to keep from the political agenda serious questions of global justice which Kant and the liberal tradition have long recognized as central to the establishment of peace.

In this section, I will try to show that Kant did not sanction a rigid dichotomization of the world between (peaceful) inter-liberal and (warring) liberal/non-liberal zones. For Kant, the distinction between republic and non-republic was frequently a matter of degree rather than kind. Following from this, and contrary to orthodox interpretations, Kant intended that the confederation of states would include non-republics as well as republics. By way of perspective, I share with Lynch the position that 'Kant's understanding of historical development and change cannot be considered apart from his emphasis on ethical action and moral purpose', and that a focus upon the creation of specific kinds of political structures should be avoided.[19] Of those aspects of Kant's thought that have been neglected, his attitudes towards the attainment of perpetual peace and the consequent guidelines for politics and policy are fundamental.

Kant was sceptical about the prospects for the realization of his scheme of perpetual peace. In any case, he was well aware that, even if it were to eventuate, its realization would be a long and difficult task.[20]

For this very reason, Kant was primarily concerned to theorize for contemporary conditions rather than for some, possibly unattainable, future point. He recognized that international society comprised states that are ethically and politically diverse, and was concerned to prescribe guidelines for behaviour *prior* to the establishment of perpetual peace. Accordingly, the burden of Kant's political philosophy is as a guide to the *process* of the evolution of international society. In this respect, the one course of action Kant urged above all else was to recognize international law and avoid recourse to the instrument of war: 'war is not the way in which anyone should pursue his rights', even when in the state of nature.[21] In this vein, Brown has shown the importance of Kant's six preliminary articles of perpetual peace as a code for state behaviour, while still in the state of nature, to facilitate the evolutionary development of perpetual peace.[22]

Recalling these fundamental aspects of Kant's writings shows that the current concentration upon securing a world in which the liberal state form is the norm is misplaced. Certainly, there is little question that Kant, like most liberals, would prefer other states also to be liberal: it is the only form of constitutional and institutional framework which would permit individuals to exercise full moral choice, and is a necessary condition of Kant's ultimate vision of perpetual peace.[23] For Kant, however, the significant point is that, prior to the attainment of a world of liberal states, states must act according to principles of right. Foremost is to act in accordance with the categorical imperative (that is, that practices should be universalizable and persons regarded as ends in themselves) in order to perfect the improvement of one's civil constitution. Due to the anarchic nature of the international system, Kant was at pains to point out that, for the sake of the full realization of moral principles in all states (including those regarded as actually existing republics), it was important to recognize one's obligations to non-republics and to cooperate with them in order to mitigate the detrimental consequences of a lawless international environment.

Although such obligations are incumbent even in the absence of reciprocity, Kant did urge the surrender of sovereign rights and the establishment of contractual relations, in order to foster the development of mutual confidence. In 'Perpetual Peace', for instance, Kant writes that 'it is impossible to understand what justification I can have for placing any confidence in my rights, unless I can rely on some substitute for the union of civil society, i.e. on a free federation'.[24] This combination of non-reciprocal and contractual obligations results in a dual structure of ethics. On the one hand, they oblige the establishment of contractual relations with others; whilst on the other, they maintain an obligation to act morally (according to the categorical imperative) not only in relations with fellow contractors, but with all states, and in the absence of the condition of reciprocity. It would be in keeping with Kant's philosophy of history to regard non-liberal states not as non-contractors, but rather as potential contractors. The current literature on the separate liberal peace emphasizes only those obligations that arise between liberal states, and is virtually silent on the nature and implications of the obligations liberal states hold towards non-liberal states.[25] Uppermost are the duties not to wage war to advance one's rights (as distinct from seeking redress), not to intervene, and not to force commerce upon a state.[26] States, for Kant, whether liberal or non-liberal, are subject to obligations arising from moral-practical reason, whether in or out of the state of nature and whether or not others recognize their own obligations.[27]

This interpretation of Kant's political writings can be defended most forcefully through an examination of the three 'definitive articles' of a metaphorical peace treaty, which are the main pillars of Kant's plan for a perpetual peace. The first article states that the civil constitution of every state shall be republican, the second that the right of nations shall be based on a federation of free states, and the third that cosmopolitan right shall be limited to conditions of universal hospitality.[28] It is important at the outset to clarify the nature of the relationship of these three articles to one another.

The importance of the three should not be ranked as in order of presentation, or depicted as forming three concentric circles with the domestic constitution being primary, an international confederation secondary, and then a tertiary notion of cosmopolitan rights and duties. Rather, they should be regarded as of equal status, designed to enshrine the rule of law in their particular realms of jurisdiction. Kant, in the First Supplement of 'Perpetual Peace', identifies the political, international and cosmopolitan as three distinct 'areas of public right'.[29] In writing of them, he acknowledges their own autonomous dynamics which, taken together, will promote the greater agreement over principles that leads in turn to mutual understanding and peace. This interpretation of the relationship of the three fields, marked by contemporaneous and complementary progression rather than a series of three distinct stages, reflects Kant's awareness of the anarchic nature of the international system as an impediment to domestic constitutional development.

In his discussion of the first definitive article, Kant outlines one of the mechanisms which is intended to make republics more pacific than non-republics.[30] In a famous passage Kant writes that because in a republic the consent of those citizens who will bear the costs of war in blood and money is required before war can be declared, such action will not be undertaken lightly. By contrast, in a non-republic the head of state will not have to make the slightest sacrifice and hence 'it is the simplest thing in the world to go to war'.[31] However, in practice there is a long record of liberal states circumventing this direct and immediate link between the political classes and war either through the use of a professional army or conscription policies which privilege those groups closest to the centres of power. Hence, claims that this mechanism in practice differentiates liberal from non-liberal states ought to be treated with caution.[32] While this is not evidence of Doyle misrepresenting Kant, it nevertheless suggests that it may be inappropriate to base claims about a Kantian distinction between liberal and non-liberal states solely on the first definitive article.

Kant's second definitive article of a 'Perpetual Peace' will be considered in more detail, since it is crucial for establishing whether there is Kantian authority for a confederation comprised solely of liberal states, or whether membership should extend beyond such an exclusive grouping. The second article proclaims that 'the Right of Nations shall be based on a Federation of *Free* States'.[33] Doyle's paraphrase of this article runs 'liberal republics will progressively establish peace among themselves by means of the "pacific union"'.[34] Thus, he appears to interpret 'free' as synonymous with a republican constitution. As such, Doyle's interpretation of the criterion for membership of Kant's confederation is one in which a liberal domestic constitution is a necessary requirement. Implicit in Doyle's view is the assumption that, since republics are likely to be more pacific than other forms of state, only they are able to qualify for what Kant did, after all, say ought to be a 'pacific [con]federation'.[35] However, it is possible to show that Kant intended membership of this confederation to be open to non-liberal as well as other liberal states on two grounds.

First, Kant used the term 'free' to refer to status rather than form: that is, states that are independent or sovereign rather than of a certain regime type. According to Kant, 'freedom' is but one of three principles upon which a republican constitution is founded: therefore, the terms cannot logically be synonymous.[36] Further, Kant's definition of 'external and rightful *freedom*' as 'a warrant to obey no external laws except those to which I have been able to give my own consent'[37] clearly signifies the meaning of sovereignty. This meaning is fundamental to the broader Kantian project of maximizing the opportunity for the autonomous *self*-development of each individual or state in accordance with the rights of all.

Second, Kant's illustration of the type of confederation he had in mind clearly indicates the inclusion of non-liberal states. Kant writes that if

> one powerful and enlightened nation can form a republic ... this will provide a focal point for federal association among other states. These will join up with the first one, thus securing the freedom of each state in accordance with the idea of international right.[38]

It is significant that Kant does not stipulate that the 'other states' ought necessarily also to be republican. Moreover, in illustrating such a confederation in the 'Metaphysics of Morals', Kant explicitly refers to states with diverse forms of government. He makes a favourable reference to an assembly of the States General at the Hague in the first half of the eighteenth century, to which 'the ministers of most European *courts* and even of the smallest republics brought their complaints about any aggression suffered by one of their number at the hands of another', and which '*all* neighbouring states' were free to join.[39] Clearly, this was not sufficient to prevent the use of force between states, but it does illustrate that, contrary to Doyle's interpretation, Kant approved of membership in such a confederation extending beyond states with a liberal domestic political system.

When one takes Kant's understanding of the relationship between the nature of the international system and the form of domestic political system into account, it becomes readily apparent that Kant believed republics had a duty to establish a confederation not only with other republics, but also with non-republics. Kant was acutely aware of how the anarchic nature of the international states system not only jeopardized peace by leaving states in the state of nature in relation to one another, but that the system itself also served to limit domestic social and political development. Kant's seventh proposition in 'Idea for a Universal History' explicitly states that 'the problem of establishing a perfect civil constitution is subordinate to the problem of a law-governed *external relationship* with other states, and cannot be solved unless the latter is also solved'.[40] Thus, not only does Kant recognize that states have obligations to subject their external relations to the rule of law, regardless of their form of civil constitution, but he also acknowledges that a fully developed republican constitution is unattainable outside of such a framework. Consequently, it would be not merely immoral, but self-defeating to restrict the membership of a confederation to republican states. It is a point worth emphasizing that, for Kant, given anarchy, no civic constitution can be perfect, and the quality of existing constitutions can be considered as a matter of degree. With reference to the 'separate peace' approach, this aspect of Kant's analysis of international relations renders absurd the notion that 'peace' can wait until the world comprises liberal states. It is only through a delicate process of, on the one hand, mitigating the circumstances of international anarchy and, on the other, constitutional development, that peace *and* republics (in the full Kantian sense) will emerge.

Of course, Kant was also interested in the agencies of political development. While it is true that Kant did identify the long-term mechanism of 'asocial sociability', he also held out hope that states were capable of self-conscious reform. He argues that, even if autocracy and aristocracy, the two constitutional alternatives to democracy, 'are always defective in as much as they leave room for a despotic form of government, it is at least possible that they will be associated with a form of government which accords with the *spirit* of a representative system'.[41] Thus, although it is correct that Kant 'never tires of denouncing the bellicosity of despots',[42] he did not consider all non-republics to be equally despotic. He argues that 'the smaller the number of ruling persons in a state and the greater their powers of representation, the more the constitution will approximate to its republican potentiality, which it may hope to realise eventually by gradual reforms'.[43] Support for the process of gradual reform was developed elsewhere, for in the 'Metaphysics of Morals', he writes that 'it is the only means of continually approaching the supreme political good, perpetual peace'.[44]

Two substantive points reinforce these last two paragraphs. First, while Kant does regard republican constitutional forms as being the type best suited to the avoidance of war, he also recognizes that not all non-republics are bellicose, and that anarchy impedes the constitutional development of all states. Hence, both liberal and non-liberal states are faced with a common plight in the transcendence of anarchy. While there undoubtedly are regimes whose leaders deliberately seek personal aggrandizement and military conquest, the majority are more likely to be concerned with the very difficult, yet conventional, political task of providing for the security and welfare of the populace with limited resources and in difficult conditions. Such states, liberal or otherwise, are, in Barry Buzan's terms, engaged primarily in the struggle for 'security' rather than the struggle for 'power'.[45] For Kant, it would be important for the promotion of security *and* the development of liberalism that such states are offered shelter under a liberal security umbrella.

Second, on the question of intervention, despite his belief that republics are more pacific than non-republics, Kant did not believe that regime type was a criterion for the legitimacy of intervention. First, Kant is, in general, a strong non-interventionist, as is evident in the fifth preliminary article of 'Perpetual Peace'.[46] However, there is an apparent exception to this in the 'Metaphysics of Morals', where Kant writes that an 'unjust enemy' can 'be made to accept a new constitution of a nature that is unlikely to encourage their warlike inclinations'.[47] For Kant, though, an 'unjust enemy' is defined as 'someone whose publicly expressed will [in the field of international right], whether expressed in word or in deed, displays a maxim which would make peace among nations impossible and would lead to a perpetual state of nature if it were made into a general rule'.[48] Hence, such an enemy is defined not by regime type, but by behaviour. As such, Kant's notion of intervention holds similarities to the theory of collective security which penalizes aggression, not regime.

Kant's conception of international right, then, was one in which *all* states, not merely liberal states, were under a duty to confederate. This did not legitimate interference in domestic affairs, but did bind states to observe certain common rules in their relations with one another. Kant did not, however, consider this anything but a compromise. In order to manage the tension between the need to coexist with non-republics whilst maintaining the belief that the republican constitution 'is the only perfectly lawful kind',[49] he introduces (but does not use consistently) the distinction between a *legal* and a *lawful* constitution.[50] The distinction is not a comfortable one, but is consistent with the notion that true law can be founded only on right, though we must respect the current system of legal regulation as the best we have for the time being.[51] 'For any *legal* constitution,' he writes, 'even if it is only in small measure *lawful*, is better than none at all, and the fate of a premature reform would be anarchy.'[52] Kant, then, was acutely sensitive to the fragility of order in political life. He strongly supported the need to respect existing levels of order as representing a better basis for moral and constitutional development than the chaos that would result from their overthrow.

There are, then, certain tensions within Kant's work deriving from the obligation to act according to the categorical imperative in relations with all; to respect the existence of legal arrangements, even if they do not wholly embody principles of *Recht*; and the longer-term project of working towards the submission of the rights of persons and states to *Recht*. Although Kant holds a well-defined notion of the good, it is imperative to respect the notion of right; and thus not to attempt to gain the desired ends by unethical means.[53]

Kant was concerned with international relations as an historical, evolutionary *process*. Moving from a lawless condition in the three areas of public right, civil, international and cosmopolitan, Kant did indeed see a gradual evolution in all three spheres marked by an increasing convergence of principles. Ultimately, if the reign of perpetual peace according to Kantian principles were to commence, then the republican civil constitution would indeed be a necessary (though not sufficient) condition. However, in that Kant was concerned with the processes through which the international system would develop, he emphasized the importance of maintaining peace in order to facilitate this development. In this pursuit, Kant recognized that existing republics were as yet ethically incomplete, and that at least some non-republics were, alongside the deterministic process of asocial sociability, reforming themselves to become republics. In contrast to the 'separate peace' approach, the above reading of Kant stresses his awareness of the moral and political interdependence of liberal and non-liberal states, and his insistence that the strong recognize their obligations and do not abuse their power in relations with the weak.

Conclusion: aspects of the Kantian legacy

The above analysis suggests that the emphasis upon the homogenization of domestic political systems in the literature upon liberal states and peace has misrepresented the burden of Kant's political philosophy. Moreover, the political agenda that has been developed from such an interpretation carries hegemonic implications, through rationalizing and privileging the leadership of that small group of powerful and developed states from where the discourse has emerged.

The interpretation of Kant's political writings offered here has sought to resituate Kant's support for republics in a broader moral and political context. This highlights, among other things, Kant's view that the powerful members of the international system have wider obligations than those acknowledged in the 'separate peace' literature. Such obligations arise from the quintessentially (although not exclusively) liberal emphasis upon justice, at the domestic, international and cosmopolitan levels, as an essential requirement for lasting peace. Where, though, are the liberal voices engaged in the development of this insight? There is a contemporary literature engaged in developing the principles and practices upon which a just world order can develop, although it is to be found outside of the literature upon the 'separate peace'.

Probably the most wide-ranging work is the Keynesian (and to some extent Kantian) report of The Commission on Global Governance, *Our Global Neighbourhood.*[54] Woven throughout the report is a firm belief in the importance of meaningful democracy, which goes beyond the parliamentary realm to embrace the need for an active civil society with accountable practices and institutions. Richard Falk gives a stimulating review of the report in this volume (Chapter 4). He notes a number of positive features of the Report, but argues that it ultimately 'lacks political bite' and that it is prescriptively submissive to the powers that be.

Whilst I would support Falk's celebration of civil society in general, I would also want to defend the approach, and to some extent the substance, of the Report against his criticisms. *Our Global Neighbourhood* is helping to develop public consciousness of international relations away from neorealist and neoliberal concerns with system management, towards a terrain in which the moral consequences of dominant structures and practices must be faced. To this author, the articulation of alternative visions *of the big picture* in a way that links power to moral vision, is one of the Report's strengths. These are important features which are likely to facilitate rather than preclude a climate favourable to more radical positions. In addition, some of the reforms proposed by the Commission present specific proposals behind which it would be possible to muster considerable global support: such as a levy on foreign exchange transactions.[55]

Further reconsideration of what meaningful democracy might entail in contemporary conditions has been undertaken by Daniele Archibugi, David Held and the 'cosmopolitan democracy' project.[56] The concern of both groups with the question of greater accountability over the economic realm of activity is especially significant. Other writers have focused upon such questions as the notion of self-determination and minority rights, and the importance of 'constitutionalism' as a principle of global order.[57] Of course this is not to say that these various writers explicitly employ Kantian political philosophy to justify their projects. However, they do develop arguments which are in accord with the interpretation of Kant offered above.

Between the two literatures, there has been very little in the way of dialogue, although there are many latent linkages. The challenge for liberals is to reclaim the discourse upon liberal states and peace, and to develop this in terms of their own heritage: the crucial relationship between peace and justice.

Acknowledgement

The author would like to thank Christopher Brewin, Richard Devetak, Kimberley Hutchings, Andrew Linklater, Hidemi Suganami, Peter Wilson and the anonymous *Millennium* referees for comments on earlier drafts of this chapter.

Notes

1. Michael Doyle, 'Kant, Liberal Legacies, and Foreign Affairs, Part 1', *Philosophy and Public Affairs*, Vol. 12, No. 3 (1983), pp. 205–35; 'Kant, Liberal Legacies, and Foreign Affairs, Part 2', *Philosophy and Public Affairs*, Vol. 12, No. 4 (1983), pp. 323–53; 'Liberalism and World Politics', *American Political Science Review*, Vol. 80, No. 4 (1986), pp. 1151–69; 'Liberalism and International Relations', in Ronald Beiner and William J. Booth, *Kant and Political Philosophy: The Contemporary Legacy* (London: Yale University Press, 1993), pp. 173–203.

2. A notable exception is Cecelia Lynch, 'Kant, the Republican Peace, and Moral Guidance in International Law', *Ethics and International Affairs*, Vol. 8 (1994), pp. 39–58.

3. David Forsythe, *Human Rights and Peace: International and National Dimensions* (London: University of Nebraska Press, 1993), pp. 50, 156; Jack Levy, 'Domestic Politics and War', *Journal of Interdisciplinary History*, Vol. 18, No. 4 (1988), pp. 653–73; Georg Sørensen, 'Kant and Processes of Democratization: Consequences for Neorealist Thought', *Journal of Peace Research*, Vol. 29, No. 4 (1992), pp. 397–414. Although Fukuyama's thesis is rooted in his interpretation of Hegel's philosophy, significant here is his explicit reference to Doyle in the text, and the immediate context which draws upon liberal writers including Kant. See Francis Fukuyama, 'The End of History?', *The National Interest*, Vol. 16 (Summer 1989), p. 18. Bruce Russett does not explicitly acknowledge Doyle's reading of Kant, although there do not seem to be any significant differences between their respective interpretations. See Bruce Russett, *Grasping the Democratic Peace: Principles for a Post-Cold War Order* (Princeton, NJ: Princeton University Press, 1993).

4. Christopher Layne, 'Kant or Cant: The Myth of Democratic Peace', *International Security*, Vol. 19, No. 2 (1994), pp. 5–49, and Denny Roy, 'Neorealism and Kant: No Pacific Union', *Journal of Peace Research*, Vol. 30, No. 4 (1993), pp. 451–4.

5. Benjamin Netanyahu, *A Place among the Nations: Israel and the World* (London and New York: Bantam Press, 1993).

6. Doyle, 'Kant, Liberal Legacies, and Foreign Affairs, Part 1', pp. 229–32; Doyle, 'Liberalism and World Politics', pp. 1160–2; and Doyle, 'Liberalism and International Relations', pp. 189–92.
7. Doyle, 'Kant, Liberal Legacies, and Foreign Affairs, Part 1', p. 206; 'Liberalism and World Politics', p. 1151; and 'Liberalism and International Relations', p. 173. Doyle does not use quotation marks for the term, and it is stressed as a particular approach only by myself. See John MacMillan, 'Democracies Don't Fight: A Case of the Wrong Research Agenda?', *Review of International Studies*, Vol. 22, No. 4 (1996).
8. Doyle, 'Liberalism and World Politics', p. 1161; 'Liberalism and International Relations', p. 191, and Russett, *Grasping the Democratic Peace*, p. 32.
9. Read 'liberal state' in terms of the current usage. See, for example, Hidemi Suganami who notes that 'the key terms – "liberal", "libertarian", "democratic", "republican", "free", and "elective", and so on – are sufficiently similar in meaning to warrant the use of "liberal" to represent them all', Hidemi Suganami, *On the Causes of War* (Oxford: Clarendon Press, 1996), p. 101. Kant himself was referring, among other things, to the separation of power between the legislative and executive branches of government. While it is true that Kant was wary of rule by the *demos*, his reasoning behind the claim that republics would be pacific indicates that he would be comfortable with a liberal democracy. Chris Brown, however, questions whether Doyle's 'liberal states' correspond with Kant's notion of republicanism. Chris Brown, *International Relations Theory: New Normative Approaches* (London and New York: Harvester Wheatsheaf, 1992), p. 41. Throughout the piece, I refer to liberal states according to this current usage.
10. Russett, *Grasping the Democratic Peace*, p. 136.
11. Doyle, 'Kant, Liberal Legacies and Foreign Affairs, Part 2', p. 344, and Russett, *Grasping the Democratic Peace*, 3, p. 4.
12. These concerns are in the spirit of nineteenth-century Anglo-Saxon liberals and radicals and their twentieth-century heirs. See, for example, Alan J. P. Taylor, *The Troublemakers* (London: Hamish Hamilton, 1957), and Michael Howard, *War and the Liberal Conscience* (Oxford: Oxford University Press, 1981).
13. Russett, *Grasping the Democratic Peace*, p. 32.
14. Netanyahu, *A Place among the Nations*, p. 248, emphasis in original.
15. Fukuyama, *The End of History and the Last Man* (Harmondsworth: Penguin, 1992), pp. 282–3.
16. Netanyahu, *A Place among the Nations*, p. 244.
17. This is discussed further in MacMillan, 'Democracies Don't Fight'.
18. Doyle, 'Kant, Liberal Legacies, and Foreign Affairs, Part 1', p. 230; and the neglected but stimulating discussion of the proper course for a liberal foreign policy in 'Kant, Liberal Legacies, and Foreign Affairs, Part 2', pp. 343–9. In a short discussion entitled 'Democracy and Peace', in Bruce Russett, Harvey Starr and Richard J. Stoll (eds.), *Choices in World Politics: Sovereignty and Interdependence* (New York: W. H. Freeman, 1989), pp. 245–60, Russett foregrounds the linkage between peace and justice, though in his main (and later) work on the subject, *Grasping the Democratic Peace*, this theme was not prominent.

19. Lynch, 'Kant, the Republican Peace ...', p. 42.
20. Immanuel Kant, 'Metaphysics of Morals', p. 171, and 'Idea for a Universal History with a Cosmopolitan Purpose', pp. 47–8, both in Hans Reiss (ed.), *Kant's Political Writings*, trans. H. Nisbet, second edition (Cambridge: Cambridge University Press, 1991), pp. 131–75 and 41–53 respectively. Although Kant was sceptical, he insisted upon a duty to strive towards 'perpetual peace' in the absence of proof that the objective was impossible. For Kant's scheme of perpetual peace, see 'Perpetual Peace: A Philosophical Sketch', also in Reiss (ed.), *Kant's Political Writings*, pp. 93–130.
21. Kant, 'Metaphysics of Morals', p. 174.
22. Brown, pp. 34–5. For the six preliminary articles, see Kant, 'Perpetual Peace', pp. 93–7.
23. Kant, 'Metaphysics of Morals', p. 174.
24. Kant, 'Perpetual Peace', p. 104. Kant actually means a confederation.
25. On this topic see Christopher Brewin, 'The Duties of Liberal States', in Cornelia Navari (ed.), *The Condition of States* (Milton Keynes: Open University Press, 1991), pp. 197–215.
26. For an interesting (and pertinent) argument on the rights of states to restrict their involvement in the world economy, see Immanuel Kant, 'On the Common Saying: "This may be True in Theory, but it does not Apply in Practice"', in Reiss (ed.), *Kant's Political Writings*, p. 80n.
27. Kant, 'Metaphysics of Morals', pp. 164–75.
28. Kant, 'Perpetual Peace', pp. 98–108.
29. Kant, 'Perpetual Peace', p. 112.
30. It is unfair to regard this as the only reason why Kant thought republics would be more pacific than non-republics, since the principles of right upon which republics are founded are probably the more important restraining influence upon the use of force. However, there is no guarantee that republics will necessarily act according to these principles – as they frequently demonstrate.
31. Kant, 'Perpetual Peace', p. 100.
32. The liberal response to this claim is likely to be a demand for *more* democratization, see Howard, *War and the Liberal Conscience*, 11, p. 76. For the argument that political practices can be made more responsible and humane if decision makers directly face the consequences of their actions (and hence local, regional and global participatory democracy is to be developed), see Robyn Eckersley, *Environmentalism and Political Theory: Towards an Ecocentric Approach* (London: UCL Press, 1992), pp. 170–6.
33. Kant, 'Perpetual Peace', p. 102, emphasis added.
34. Doyle, 'Kant, Liberal Legacies, and Foreign Affairs, Part 1', p. 226.
35. Kant, 'Perpetual Peace', p. 104.
36. *Ibid.*, p. 99.
37. *Ibid.*, p. 99n, emphasis in original.
38. *Ibid.*, p. 104.
39. Kant, 'Metaphysics of Morals', p. 171, emphasis added.
40. Kant, 'Idea for a Universal History', p. 47, emphasis in original. See also Kant, 'Theory and Practice', in Reiss (ed.), *Kant's Political Writings*, p. 92.
41. Kant, 'Perpetual Peace', p. 101, emphasis in original.

42. Andrew Hurrell, 'Kant and the Kantian Paradigm in International Relations', *Review of International Studies*, Vol. 16, No. 3 (1990), p. 195.
43. Kant, 'Perpetual Peace', p. 101.
44. Kant, 'Metaphysics of Morals', p. 175.
45. Barry Buzan, *People, States and Fear: The National Security Problem in International Relations* (Brighton: Harvester Press, 1983), pp. 157, 173–213.
46. 'No state shall forcibly interfere in the constitution and government of another state.' Kant, 'Perpetual Peace', p. 96. The legitimacy of humanitarian intervention is not, to my knowledge, an issue that Kant addressed directly and is beyond the reach of this discussion.
47. Kant, 'Metaphysics of Morals', p. 170.
48. *Ibid.*
49. Kant, 'Perpetual Peace', p. 101.
50. *Ibid.*, p. 118.
51. For a brief discussion of this aspect of Kant's attitude towards the current system of international law, see Hurrell, 'Kant and the Kantian Paradigm', pp. 187–9.
52. Kant, 'Perpetual Peace', p. 118n. In the same footnote, Kant also writes that the creation of a lawful constitution based on the principles of freedom is the only one which will last.
53. This point is particularly pronounced throughout the 'Metaphysics of Morals'.
54. The Commission on Global Governance, *Our Global Neighbourhood* (Oxford: Oxford University Press, 1995).
55. *Ibid.*, pp. 217–21.
56. See David Held, 'Democracy: From City-States to a Cosmopolitan Order?', in Held (ed.), *Prospects for Democracy* (Cambridge: Polity Press, 1993), pp. 13–52, and Daniele Archibugi and David Held (eds.), *Cosmopolitan Democracy: An Agenda for a New World Order* (Cambridge: Polity Press, 1995).
57. See Will Kymlicka, *Liberalism, Community and Culture* (Oxford: Clarendon Press, 1989), and Andrew Linklater, 'Liberal Democracy, Constitutionalism and the New World Order', in Richard Leaver and James L. Richardson, *Charting the Post-Cold War Order* (Boulder, CO: Westview Press, 1993), pp. 29–38.

Part II

Globalization and Liberalism in Contemporary International Relations

4
Liberalism at the Global Level: Solidarity *vs.* Cooperation

Richard Falk

Liberalism at the international level has always been vague and ambiguous. It seems to have been initially associated with Woodrow Wilson's championship of political democracy, the related idea of self-determination and the possibility of a more peaceful and morally acceptable world in which security is managed by collective procedures within international institutions. This Wilsonian orientation, which is generally identifiable by support for a stronger United Nations, persists to a substantial extent, and has often been called 'liberal internationalism'. It tends to be combined with a projection onto the global stage of such domestic features of a liberal democratic state as elections, separation of powers, due process, human rights, and the Rule of Law.[1] The liberal orientation extended to international relations often advocates gradual increases in international cooperation by way of institutional arrangements. This international reliance on liberalism in its domestic setting is rarely coupled with a long-range comprehensive plan that culminates in the establishment of a liberal global state.[2]

A second, less understood, yet complementary approach to liberal internationalism has been persuasively traced back recently to Immanuel Kant, especially his contention that liberal states, loosely organized into a cooperative league, are unlikely to wage war against one another, and thus create a zone of peace that could, in theory, be enlarged until encompassing the planet. Kant also insisted upon a universal duty of 'hospitality' to strangers and foreigners as a means of inhibiting hostile relations among states and as an encouragement to the growth of global commerce.[3]

Yet, the new geopolitics of world order tends to be economistic in the sense of being restructured in accordance with global market forces. These dynamics have generated a setting for political life that is increasingly associated with 'globalization'. There are varied and often contradictory human consequences associated with globalization, a reshuffling to some extent of 'winners' and 'losers', but overall with polarizing effects that are widening disparities both within and among states. One generalized pattern, reinforced by several other trends, including the prominence of financial markets and the repudiation of Keynesian approaches to macro-economic policy, is to weaken the role of the state with respect to the active promotion of human betterment by way of public goods expenditures. Whether this pattern is *structural* (the pressures of competitiveness in a world where capital is mobile) or *ideological* (a push toward private sector hegemony in relation to the social agenda) need not be resolved.[4] The relevant point is that, to the extent that the state is converted into an agency role on behalf of world capital, it loses its liberalizing capacity. Hence, the widespread endorsement of democracy and human rights as the foundation for political legitimacy is no assurance that the state will seek to ameliorate the hardships endured by the poor and vulnerable.

In this regard, it seems appropriate to examine the report of the Commission on Global Governance, *Our Global Neighbourhood*, both as liberal text and as confirmation of the reality in an illiberal world.[5] This examination discloses a tension within the text, as well as a marginalized audience. Note that part of the contention is that the liberal political sentiment is antithetical to radical solutions, believing in the triumph of the good by way of incremental reform.

Without being philosophically, or even ideologically, explicit about it, *Our Global Neighbourhood* embodies both traditions of liberal internationalist thought. Apparently reflecting prevailing ideological attitudes, there is a renewed stress on the sanctity of private ownership of property and a generalized reliance upon the market to produce a brighter human future for humanity. The publication of this report in 1995 provided a provisional test as to whether the liberal internationalist orientation retained its earlier attractiveness as a practical, yet non-threatening type of idealism, which appealed to those elements in society that recognized, with varying degrees of clarity, the need and possibility of a better world order, yet believed that its achievement would depend on evolutionary and procedural, not revolutionary and substantive, means. Such an approach rested upon the capacity of receptive political leaders to pursue policies based on the long-term rational self-interest of their governments and citizenry, as well as the larger human community. It also presented itself as an alternative to Marxism-Leninism and socialism as a means to reconcile morality with modernization. The 'romantic' or sentimental component of liberalism involves the resolution of tensions between national and human interests, as well as between classes, races and genders, by the application of reason to achieve long-term well-being. Both conservative and left radical thought, in contrast, believe that hierarchy and conflict are endemic to the human condition as it has so far unfolded, and that any change for the better depends on struggle, that stability requires coercive control, and that a belief in eventual harmony rests on the transformation of the human condition in fundamental respects.

Our Global Neighbourhood is self-consciously based on the geopolitical opportunities to create a more cooperative world order in the aftermath of the Cold War and the practical necessity of doing so to handle the complexities and interdependencies that are increasingly characteristic of international life. Such a rationalist faith underpins a wide-ranging coherent set of implementing proposals that generally move in the direction of institutionalizing and democratizing international life, including extensions of the Rule of Law in a variety of reformist directions and the acknowledgement of transnational social and market forces as generating important global actors other than the governments of sovereign states. So long as many leading governments were led by liberals and social democrats in a generally supportive climate of opinion, these sorts of reformist ideas related to decency, fairness and sustainability would be likely to exert some influence, and were generally dominant in the West. Yet, they nevertheless remained deferential to realist thinking in the domain of security and subordinate to strategic goals in the old geopolitical atmosphere of conflict among leading states that dominated the global scene during the decades between the end of the Second World War and the fall of the Berlin Wall.[6]

But what about in the closing years of the twentieth century? On one side, liberal internationalism is severely challenged by 'the neoliberal consensus' that virtually disavows governmental responsibility for social goals, and entrusts the future to the dynamics of the market, including priorities set by the flow of capital.[7] As such, liberal wise 'men' (including women) of the sort that make up the Commission on Global Governance would seem to have little to say in a political climate that is increasingly distrustful of the role of governments in improving the quality of national or international life, and no longer needful of a morally attractive alternative to socialist claims. This perception of irrelevance is reinforced by several additional influential considerations: the discrediting of utopianism and all forms of social engineering in reaction to the collapse of the Soviet Union and the profound postmodern distrust of meta-narratives, including universalizing programmes of reform.[8] Further, after a brief opportunistic embrace of the United Nations during the Gulf Crisis and War (1990–91), the undisputed global leader, the United States, reversed course and pushed the Organization back to the outer margins of geopolitics, even threatening its financial viability.

Also relevant is an epochal shift from industrialism to electronics as the defining mode of technological innovation for both society and the economy. Such a shift undercuts earlier modalities of political participation and generates the basis for inventive adaptation of various kinds. The idea of constitutional democracy was based on the centrality of electoral consent to the dynamics of governance within clearly defined territorial boundaries. Within an emergent cyberworld, however, these boundaries virtually disappear, non-territoriality seems paramount, and time and distance are conflated. Such an altered consciousness has difficulty responding seriously to a political sensibility that seems still constrained by the orientations of the industrial/statist era which, while not over, is being superseded.

Against such an array of considerations it is fair to ask why one should take *Our Global Neighbourhood* seriously at all. Why not just toss it in the nearest waste basket? Is not well-meant liberalism a siren call that was never seriously heeded even when the times were right? In a sense, it is plausible to answer all these questions in the affirmative, and yet proceed. We cannot know the durability of moods. The concern with global governance is an unavoidable preoccupation in an increasingly integrated world. However, there is at present a mood of disillusionment associated with any effort to augment global governance in relation to global security and well-being, a general disaffection accentuated by the rightward drift of foreign policy in the United States, and even affecting such relatively functional concerns as the environment. This overall atmosphere makes the core emphasis of *Our Global Neighbourhood* on strengthening the United Nations seem seriously out of sync with the manner in which, for better or worse, the world is currently drifting.

The combination of complexity and fragility of contemporary international life is likely to generate a series of politically relevant demands for a variety of institutional steps that amount to the creation of global governance even if the language used in this particular effort is ill-suited for such wider implications.[9] *Our Global Neighbourhood* offers us the most informed and persuasive arguments for more comprehensive regulation of international economic and political activity than is now available. As such, it provides many transnational social actors with a possibly helpful, even mobilizing, basis for engaging in political conversations about the future, even if its specific assessments and recommendations provide only starting-points on the road to equitable and attainable global governance. In this respect, the relevance of *Our Global Neighbourhood* is arguable despite the likely obsolescence of its liberal lineage and the related problematic character of the international Commission format.[10] It may indeed be questionable whether liberalism is tied to the formation of Commissions seeking to identify and promote some conception of the global public interest that is being neglected elsewhere.[11]

My assessment will first seek to locate the Commission on Global Governance within the framework of liberal internationalism, and then move on to an inquiry into the substance of its recommendations for coping with the main challenges in international life. A third section will briefly discuss the imagery of the world as 'neighbourhood', questioning the ethical and functional viability of such a metaphor at this time.

Against such an ambivalent background, it may be most useful to conceive of the Commission on Global Governance as an exemplar of a particular approach to global policy rooted in a given global setting. Let it be noted that successful individuals of considerable prominence devoted time and energy to the process of preparing such a report: that is, within élite circles the liberal mind-set still retains some purchase. Beyond this, funds were raised. When *Our Global Neighbourhood* appeared it received a modest amount of media attention and was used rather widely in adult education, civic action and academic circles, at least for a couple of years.

To elicit its wider significance, I propose first to locate the Commission on Global Governance more firmly within the framework of liberal internationalism, expressive, that is, of a consensus of relatively likeminded Commission members. On this basis, the next section will examine the substance of several recommendations for policy or institutional initiatives as responses to the major current challenges of international life. A further section will focus on the cohering metaphor of 'global neighbourhood' as a means to recast our understanding of a world order no longer constituted merely by sovereign territorial units, and question its adequacy. Finally, a short section will return to the double-linked question: the end of liberalism? the end of liberal-minded Commissions?

The idiom of the independent Global Commission

A distinctive, if minor, feature of recent decades has been the formation of independent Commissions of eminent persons drawn from a range of élite backgrounds, gathered together for a series of meetings that eventuates in a report on some sector of international public policy. The process was initially associated with the former West German Chancellor Willy Brandt, whose Commission was established in 1980 to provide an improved approach to international development policy, particularly a better way of addressing North/South issues. The impulse to form these Commissions is quintessentially liberal in its spirit: that is, wise and respected leaders incrementally promoting the capacity of the state system to meet more successfully such primary challenges as the management of North/South relations on development, security and the environment.[12] The fact that their likely period of existence is the short interval between 1980 and the present suggests a particular moment in the history of international relations, a period during which leading governments were seen to be insufficiently responsive to the world order challenges of the day and when the viewpoints of distinguished liberal statesmen expressed as a consensus were thought capable of exerting a galvanizing and somewhat cosmopolitan influence on both leaders and their publics, thereby expanding the slightly narrower nationalist, short-term outlooks of most governments.

The most prominent attempts after the Brandt Commission were the Independent Commission on Disarmament and Security (the Palme Commission), the World Commission on Environment and Development (the Brundtland Commission) and the South Commission (chaired by Julius Nyerere).[13] These Commissions have certain generic traits: their report is associated by informal name with a past, present or future head of state, their recommendations and findings are supported by research and consultancies with known experts ('the usual suspects') supervised by a small professional secretariat, and their prose style is such as to limit their real readership to a tiny band of devoted followers. Their influence, to the extent that it achieves results, has derived from a combination of eminence, which helps gain some media attention, and governmental status, which is capable of penetrating sympathetic sectors of national and international bureaucracies. By and large, aside from their usefulness to academic specialists and graduate students, the success story of these reports has to do with conceptual clarification and an impact on policy discourse, rather than with specific substantive reforms.

In this regard, the Palme Commission did briefly influence security discourse in the latter stages of the Cold War by introducing the idea of 'common security' as a corrective to 'national security'. Common security was introduced by the Palme Commission to call attention to the degree to which the prevailing statist view of security was becoming dysfunctional, that is, generating insecurity ('the security dilemma') as each side's military build-up was leading the other side to feel acute anxiety, and react feverishly and wastefully, in a manner designed to match or get ahead, inducing a spiral of actions and reactions that resulted in a destabilizing arms race.[14] Calling for common security was intended to encourage confidence-building between the superpowers as mutually beneficial, a recognition that traditional ideas of military superiority were outmoded in the nuclear age, but that a conceptual rigidity about security was partly responsible for producing self-destructive adjustments. In this respect, the role of the Palme Commission was to challenge outmoded thinking that did not attack the underlying premise of conflict at the core of the Cold War, but argued that it could be handled in a less dangerous and costly fashion if it could be acknowledged and integrated into policy that the greatest danger to both sides was not their adversary, but the possibility that the process itself was generating destructive results and risks. This critique of traditional statist approaches to security never reshaped policy planning in elite circles, especially in the West. Arguably, it was a precursor to the related notion of 'comprehensive security' put forward by the Soviet Foreign Ministry as a key aspect of 'new thinking' during the early period of Gorbachev's leadership.

The Brundtland Commission is undoubtedly the most successful of Commissions ever. The report, *Our Common Future*, effectively promoted the idea of 'sustainable development', which ingeniously and effectively joined environmental concerns centred in the North with developmental and social concerns centred in the South. This labelling of poverty as a form of pollution greatly facilitated an important rhetorical reconciliation of North and South viewpoints in the setting of global environmental politics, and became the main rallying cry at the Rio Earth Summit of 1992 and thereafter. The extent of this Commission's influence also reflected Gro Harlem Brundtland's effectiveness as chair, and the extent to which the formation of the

Commission and the report were formally associated with the UN system. Excellent timing that brought the report into being at a convenient moment for it to serve as the bible for the Rio preparatory process also helped it receive global attention by the media and NGOs. This prominence ensured that the report would be widely distributed, but again its main impact is upon consolidating a rhetorical consensus that helped reorient the environmental discourse. But again, whether that discourse altered behaviour in identifiable ways is dubious. It is true that following Rio a UN Commission on Sustainable Development was established, and does provide a forum for various voices to be heard on issues of environment and development. However, the Brundtland viewpoint never attempted to reconcile its perspectives with the powerful, somewhat contradictory, forces unleashed by economic globalization. As mentioned earlier, the burden of influence exerted by globalization is a downward pressure on both concerns about 'sustainability' and development to the extent responsive to the priorities of the poor rather than following the logic of capital, aligning development to the extent possible with profitability. In this regard, Brundtland never faced the difficulty, even intellectually, of actualizing sustainable development. In one respect, to reshape the discourse, but not the policy, has a regressive effect, inviting postures of hypocrisy and cynicism, and finally of despair.

It is against this general background that the Commission on Global Governance was formed in 1992, its report being published in 1995 under the deliberately enticing title of *Our Global Neighbourhood*, presumably an effort to appeal to a wider literate, yet non-technical, audience. Ingvar Carlson, the Swedish Prime Minister, was co-chair, along with Shridath Ramphal, a long eminent Third World statesman from Guyana who had served as Secretary-General of the Commonwealth in the period 1975–90. Each Commission has its own particular background, and this one on global governance originated in a meeting convened by Willy Brandt in 1990, at Königswinter, Germany, bringing together members from the earlier Commissions to assess the world situation, reaching a principal conclusion that although the ending of the Cold War was a positive development, future prospects for world order depended on strengthening multilateral capacities for coordinated action at the global level.

The initial mechanism encouraged by the Brandt initiative was a more modest gathering of eminent persons at the invitation of Carlson, Ramphal, and the then Minister of Development and Co-operation in the Netherlands, Jan Pronk. The result was a pamphlet endorsed by its participants, distributed as the 'Stockholm Initiative on Global Security and Governance'. The report was released in April 1991.[15] The Stockholm Initiative highlighted its recommendation to establish a Commission to build the case for a more effective system of security and governance in the aftermath of the Cold War. The Stockholm Initiative was heavily centred on strengthening the United Nations, an emphasis that reflected the mistaken idea that emerged in the early 1990s that the UN could at last properly discharge its collective security role now that the East/West deadlock had been broken. The experience of the Gulf War in 1991 was widely interpreted as confirming this understanding, revealing the potency of the United Nations as a political actor when its undertakings were fully backed by a geopolitical consensus, but also, somewhat incidentally, disclosing the dangers to the sovereign rights of lesser states that could result if the mandate of the UN was not restricted by respect for its own constitutional framework.[16]

The Commission on Global Governance obviously timed and conceived of its work as related to the fiftieth anniversary of the United Nations, quite possibly sensing an opportunity to do for the next half-century what the framers of the UN Charter had done at San Francisco in 1945. The authors of *Our Global Neighbourhood* fortunately widened the focus to encompass the whole governance process in international society, and although the UN system remained the institutional focus of its proposals, the underlying analysis and policy perspective was far broader and richer, responding especially both to the challenges of economic globalization and to the emergence of a rudimentary global civil society in the form of an array of transnational social forces agitating for democratizing change on matters ranging from the rights of women and indigenous peoples to the protection of the environment and the empowerment of the poor. Intellectually and politically this broader conception of global governance helps keep the report relevant to the concerns of the late 1990s, and avoids the utter embarrassment of glorifying the security functions of the United Nations at a time when its stature, through little fault of its own, is at an historic low. In this respect, the contrast in global mood between April 1991 immediately following the successful UN response to Iraqi aggression against Kuwait when the Stockholm Initiative was issued, and the release of the report in early 1995 when the UN demonstrated its inability to protect several 'safe havens' in Bosnia against vicious Serb attacks is quite stark. A steady rise in scepticism about all forms of internationalism during the 1990s has undoubtedly further muted the media impact of the report, making it seem like a forlorn cry from the wilderness. To appreciate this trend it is necessary to consider several factors, but especially the downward pressures on global public goods exerted by market forces and the downsizing direction of leadership provided by the US government.

The Commission on Global Governance had 28 members, including its two co-chairs, 15 of whom came from the geographical South, five of whom were women. Their membership included such influential figures in past and present UN activities as Barber Conable (head of the World Bank), Sadako Ogata (High Commissioner of Refugees), Maurice Strong (Secretary-General of the 1992 Rio Conference on Environment and Development, as well as the earlier 1972 Stockholm Conference on the Human Environment) and Brian Urquhart (UN Under Secretary-General for Special Political Affairs from 1972 to 1986). Jacques Delors, Eurocrat *par excellence*, was also a member, as was Europe's leading advocate of development assistance to the South, Jan Pronk. The Commission also had several members who either currently or recently held prominent government positions, including Ali Atalas (Indonesia), Oscar Arias (Costa Rica), Manual Camacho Solis (Mexico), Bernard Chidzero (Zimbabwe), Hongkoo Lee (South Korea) and Olara Otunnu (Uganda). There were also several moral authority figures on the Commission with credentials as respected activists, including Allan Boesak (South Africa), Wangari Maathai (Kenya) and Marie-Angelique Savane (Senegal). The inclusion of activists on the Commission was a departure from past practice, including the Stockholm Initiative, undoubtedly an acknowledegment that leaders in civil society could now be considered 'eminent', with their inclusion lending legitimacy and credibility to a report issued by the Commission, and possibly most likely to be read and acted or by mainstream transnational social forces. Such a partial listing of the Commission membership, fails to mention the remaining members whose prominence is more difficult to categorize, yet the entire membership fits easily in with a group operating from the assumptions of liberal internationalism in the 1990s.[17]

Note especially that representatives of business, finance and labour are not directly included among the membership, and that the ideological outlook of the Commission, as suggested by both Willy Brandt's patriarchal inspiration and the lineage of the co-chairs, is social democratic. In global terms the orientation is definitely pro-development and pro-reform, but decidedly also anti-radical and anti-reactionary. There is a statist bias (or credibility) arising from the credentials and close government connections of the great majority of members, and a geopolitical sensitivity expressed by choosing at least one Commissioner from each of the five permanent members of the Security Council, as well as one each from the two financial super-powers Germany and Japan, and from India, Brazil and Indonesia, countries each powerful in its particular region.

What this Commission profile depicts is in all probability the last stand of a global liberal establishment intending to shape a humanistic perspective that would influence world public opinion, as well as polit-ical leaders. This humanistic voice seeks to articulate the case for pru-dence and decency, a collective consciousness, without questioning the resistant structural assumptions of the established (statist) and emergent (globalized) world order. Is this kind of voice a politically irrelevant and financially wasteful indulgence, or does such a Commission allow transnational social forces, the vehicles of hope and struggle, to gain influence and legitimacy? The elite and media-visible identity of the Commission, and its statist character, would suggest a path of influence that is centred upon governments, and their crea-tures, international institutions, but it is in these arenas, at least at present, that recommendations of such a Commission seem to have virtually no purchase on political reality.

In my judgement, this Commission on Global Governance is likely to be the last such effort to address broad general concerns of interna-tional life for the foreseeable future.[18] The report seems likely to exert disproportionately little impact relative to the energy and resources devoted to its preparation and dissemination, and unlike its distin-guished predecessors, especially Palme and Brundtland, it has had no impact on public discourse, although it seems to have strengthened the academic tendency to consider more seriously a focus on 'global governance' as an element of mainstream international relations. The formation of a journal named *Global Governance* shortly after the issuance of the Carlson Report exhibits this influence. Beyond this, liberal sentiments seem no longer reflective of the prevailing mood in the main societies of the world, with even those leaders associated with liberal and social democratic outlooks converting at a rapid rate to some variant of market-oriented constitutionalism, and those with more radical viewpoints linking up with green politics or transnational movements. Given these considerations, *Our Global Neighbourhood* comes across as an outmoded homily on global reform rather than a creative contribution to policy discourse.

Assuredly, this does not mean that the substantive goals of liberal internationalism are outmoded, any more than socialist values can be pronounced extinct as a result of the Soviet failure, but what is likely is that neither liberalism nor socialism will be the explicit political means by which these ends are pursued in the future. A new political language with its own distinctive orientation towards history and action will be required. In many respects the surge of green politics in the 1980s was such a move, but it has so far proved unable to mobilize support along a broad enough spectrum to challenge neoliberalism to any appreciable extent beyond strictly environmental concerns, which were incorporated into the programmes of mainstream political parties, blunting the focused appeals of environmentally concerned parties.

Liberal internationalism for the mid-1990s

Our Global Neighbourhood can be read in several different ways. Its manifest intention is to exert substantive influence in official policy circles relating to governments and international institutions, especially by providing concrete proposals for reform; these proposals are well considered, do not challenge existing geopolitical or geoeconomic structures and offer sensible ways to reach goals that have been previously widely endorsed by influential sectors of public opinion, including the leaders of major governments. On this level, the proposals descended upon the world as a lead balloon. It is an unpleasant reality that liberal reformism cannot find receptive audiences these days either in relation to global institutional structure or with respect to the functioning of the world economy. Neither elites nor publics are receptive, and what visionary voices exist (for instance, Nelson Mandela, Auug San Suu Kyi, Vaclav Havel) are domestically, or at best regionally, preoccupied, although interestingly both Mandela and Havel have promotional statements that appear on the cover of *Our Global Neighbourhood*, perhaps reflecting personal ties between the Commission and the most morally sensitive world leaders.

Our Global Neighbourhood could also be usefully read as an informed and comprehensive portrayal of world order concerns in the mid-1990s. If this educative purpose is stressed, the results become more impressive. The report presents information accurately and elegantly, often relying on simple tables to summarize data on key trends. Because the report advocates reforms based on ethical principles it offers a gentle critique of the ways in which international political life is organized. As a critique, *Our Global Neighbourhood* is not penetrating enough to be illuminating, as it avoids any real questioning either of structural features of world order or of the ideological consensus that prevails among Western elites. As might be expected, the report rejects extremism in all forms, while assuming against the evidence that it will be possible to reconcile globalization with humanist values without a sustained political struggle.

Three further positive contributions of the report can be mentioned. First of all, the report overcomes the liberal, pragmatic tendency to avoid an overall assessment. The point of departure for the report is so articulated: 'The world needs a new vision that can galvanize people everywhere to achieve higher levels of cooperation in areas of common concern and shared destiny.'[19] As well, it explicitly acknowledges that 'ethnic cleansing in the Balkans, brutal violence in Somalia, and geno-cide in Rwanda' have undermined the confidence that existed three years earlier when the Stockholm Initiative was endorsed.[20] The unify-ing call for 'global governance' is put forward, then, in the report despite a 'deepening disquiet' about the receptivity of governments and the United Nations. This notion of global governance is broadly identified with 'the sum of the many ways individuals and institutions, public and private, manage their common affairs. ... It includes formal institutions and regimes empowered to enforce compliance, as well as informal arrangements that people and institutions either have agreed to or perceive to be in their interest.' That is, governance involves arrangements at all levels of social interaction from grassroots/local to those embodied in the UN system, and may help shape a post-Westphalian discourse in international relations.

Second, the report, unlike others in this genre that rest their policy claims on appeals to reason, acknowledges openly an adherence to certain values, as well as stressing the importance of an ethical frame-work of universal scope to guide policy-makers: 'We believe that all humanity could uphold core values of respect for life, liberty, justice and equity, mutual respect, caring, and integrity. These provide a foun-dation for transforming a global neighbourhood based on economic exchange and improved communications into a universal moral com-munity in which people are bound together by more than proximity, interest, or identity.'[21] These values are derived from reliance on the normative metaphor of 'neighbourhood' which is treated both as descriptive of an integrated global reality and as prescriptive of how the peoples of the world should be connected for purposes of mutual well-being.[22] It appears to be a deepening of Marshall McLuhan's prophetic anticipation of 'a global village'.

The third normative contribution of the report is to acknowledge the emergence and significance of global civil society understood as 'a multitude of institutions, voluntary associations, and networks – women's groups, trade unions, chambers of commerce, farming or housing cooperatives, neighbourhood watch associations, religion-based organizations, and so on'.[23] The report strongly recommends extending the notion of democracy to include global civil society, thus indirectly challenging the exclusivist statist make-up of almost every international institution and also recognizing the need to validate new modes of political participation in light of the widespread popular 'disenchantment with the performance of government';[24] this disenchantment seems to be most pronounced in the most successful constitutional democracies at the present time.

The body of the report sets forth various ideas for realizing these three points of normative commitment without challenging too frontally the neoliberal consensus. The most revealing, and in certain respects disappointing, proposals relate to the challenge of economic globalization. After usefully summarizing the phenomenon of globalization the report recommends the establishment of an Economic Security Council, intended to be a more representative body addressing global economic policy than either the G-7 or the Bretton Woods institutions and more legitimate and effective than such UN bodies as ECOSOC or UNCTAD (both of which the report recommends eliminating).[25] The primary role of the new body would be to coordinate economic activity and to promote 'consensus' and 'dialogue' on the 'evolution of the international system'. The Economic Security Council 'would work closely with the Bretton Woods institutions, not in opposition to them'.[26] According to the proposal, the membership would be drawn from the five largest economies, together with an allocation of seats based on principles of regional representation.

It seems extremely unlikely that an Economic Security Council will be established in this period, especially if its mandate was seriously meant to protect vulnerable societies and peoples from various economic security threats. The language of the report makes it clear that it is not questioning the basic premises of neoliberalism, whether privatization or market-guided approaches to social and environmental policy, but adapting them to a world of increasing complexity and interdependence. At the same time, the ethical concerns of the global neighbourhood are somehow also to be taken seriously, yet to realize these valued ends would appear to place a premium on regulating the activities of corporations, banks and financial markets at least partly on the basis of social criteria, which would be at variance with the freedoms for the private sector so strongly endorsed by neoliberal precepts. The report stops short of proposing the regulation of global market forces, and even fails to link the sorts of societal disruption being caused by corporate wrong-doing (as in Bhopal), currency manipulations and banking operations that routinely launder and hide money stolen by organized crime and by corrupt leaders from their own peoples with market activity. In this respect the liberal orientation of the report is disappointing, but predictably so: formulating an attractive ethical framework, yet at the same time legitimating the very social and economic forces that obstruct the values at stake and proposing machinery that will not respond to the essence of the human challenge posed by globalization, which is to impose on governments a discipline of global capital that gives priority to market-driven concerns at the expense of human-oriented concerns and works against public sector initiatives.

The same tantalizing combination of forward-looking proposal and ideological capitulation to the status quo is associated with the other main policy ideas advocated. On weapons of mass destruction the report impressively calls for the elimination of nuclear weapons, as being '[w]eapons of mass destruction' that 'are not legitimate instruments of national defence',[27] to be carried out through a process of 10–15 years.[28] At the same time the report does not specifically challenge the reliance on this weaponry by the nuclear weapons states who show no signs of allowing proposals for elimination of nuclear weaponry to get even a foothold in the global agenda. For instance, no mention is made in the report of the World Court Project, an historic effort of civil society in collaboration with several governments to test the legality of threat or use of nuclear weaponry by a General Assembly request to the World Court. Indeed, subsequent to the report, the World Court did issue an historic Advisory Opinion on nuclear weapons that casts serious doubt on their legality.[29] The avoidance of such concreteness gives the report a tone of blandness associated with UN documents and is the clearest indication that its eminent endorsers do not intend to offend the powers that be. In this crucial respect, *Our Global Neighbourhood* takes a position that is the opposite of what one would expect from the most representative transnational forces that make up global civil society, namely, a clear indictment, identification of culprits, regulatory adjustments, resource allocations needed to reach goals and, most especially, endorsement of civil initiatives that challenge statist imperatives. In this respect, global civil society to the extent that it is a participatory presence tends to be more confrontational, whether it be Greenpeace organizing a campaign in mid-1995 to resist the resumption of French nuclear testing in the Pacific or the efforts of the 30,000 women drawn from NGO ranks, in Beijing, to oppose the Chinese official effort to keep the UN conference on Women and Development as anodyne and statist as possible. Arguably, these strands of effort are complementary, the élite Commissions making the prevailing discourse more receptive to the policy demands of social activists.

The same ambivalence pervades virtually all aspects of the report. A call is made for strengthening the Rule of Law in international life, but nothing is said about the failure by large constitutional states to constrain their own uses of force by reference to independent judicial assessments of the relevance of international law.[30] The familiar, yet still welcome, suggestions are made in some detail to extend the role of the World Court and to support the establishment of an International Criminal Court. There is also a rare specific criticism of the United States government and of France for their failure to respect the authority of the Court in the Nicaragua and Nuclear Testing Cases, respectively.[31] Again, these proposals directed at governments are unlikely to be acted upon in the foreseeable future, and give the report a tone of irrelevance. It would have been more engaging if there were an appreciation of the extent to which transnational civil initiatives are seeking to appropriate and extend the Rule of Law without awaiting the approval or action of governments. In this regard the Permanent Peoples Tribunal operating out of Rome for almost two decades is exemplary, as are efforts at law enforcement by way of citizen boycotts. Such genuine efforts to extend global governance by non-violent democratic means are not even mentioned as indicative of civil initiatives and innovations.[32]

The substantive material organized around reform proposals in the report is highly professional in its careful formulation and presentation. What it lacks is political bite. Although there is much that is constructively reformist and useful in the report, the overall impression is of the familiar kind of liberal internationalist agenda set forth at a time when the policy pendulum is swinging in a particularly illiberal direction in most countries and in international society generally. Although *Our Global Neighbourhood* is to be commended for its recognition and affirmation of the relevance of global civil society, it fails to address this relevance in politically significant ways, ignoring their radical tactics and, thereby, consigning these civil forces to talkshop roles that even if acted upon would tend to produce a coopted reality rather than bring about genuine extensions of the theory and practice of democracy.

The most honest interpretation of such criticisms is the question, 'But what could you expect?' Given the composition of the Commission, the problems of funding such an operation, and the dominant experience of its membership that the most essential dialogue on policy matters is with the representatives of the established order.[33]

The search for a mobilizing metaphor

The report will definitely be associated in policy and academic circles with the metaphor of global neighbourhood. Like such predecessor metaphors as 'spaceship earth' and 'a global village', the idea of global neighbourhood is intended to stress the implications of interdependence, but to do so in a manner that is less technocratic and more communitarian. In the words of the Commission: 'The changes of the last half-century have brought the global neighbourhood nearer to reality, a world in which citizens are increasingly dependent on one another and need to cooperate. Matters calling for a global neighbourhood action keep multiplying. What happens far away matters much more now.'[34] In an important sense, the global neighbourhood as metaphor creatively emphasizes the centrality of people at a time when markets and capital seem decisive, affirming, as well, the solidarity of humanity and the ethical need to promote fairness and caring. This frame of reference has no specific political implications and does not imply a liberal programme of reform. The report also lauds the beneficial effects of democracy, commerce and human rights, and thus embodies a kind of Kantian view that a peaceful and benevolent world can be constructed over time on the basis of these sorts of ideas.

However, the particular policy focus is less on fundamentals than on the practical benefits of cooperation for mutual benefit, an orientation that seeks small steps forward in contexts in which basic structures of wealth and power are treated as stable and acceptable. To be sure, the outbreak of ethnic conflict and political fragmentation is acknowledged, but in a manner that requires only small adjustments in what the report calls the 'old norms', namely those of 'sovereignty' and 'self-determination'.[35] The strict territorial postulates of sovereignty are to be somewhat relaxed in favour of protecting the fundamental rights of peoples and nations, but operational hard cases involving acute oppression are not discussed; a similar situation obtains with respect to self-determination. Vague support is given to moderate approaches to self-determination that do not involve shattering existing states or subjecting minorities to threatening state formations, but what to do about contradictory nationalisms struggling for primacy within the same territorial space is not addressed, or how to handle a captive nation entrapped within an imperial state (for example, Tibet).

The implication of the word neighbourhood as used in the report is friendliness, a shared concern for the well-being of neighbours and a willingness to help out in times of need. However, the modern world transmits other far more sinister conceptions of neighbourhood gang struggles for exclusive control, inter-ethnic hostility, class differentiation. Some of the worst instances of genocidal violence have occurred between those intimately linked by situation and tradition, including even ethnic identity.

Perhaps, more devastatingly, the premises of economic globalization involve indifference to those sectors of societies, regions and the world that are perceived by markets as not being currently productive for capital. Africa has been neglected in recent years. During the Cold War, geopolitical rivalry led both superpowers to compete for influence in sub-Saharan Africa by bestowals of economic assistance, as well as by devastating covert and overt intervention.[36] This tension between the ethical imperatives of the global neighbourhood and the dynamics of economic globalization are evaded, an evasion that has been characteristic of all Wilsonian variants of liberal internationalism. This evasion is more damaging in the contemporary setting because globalization-from-above has been so successful in subordinating the state to its goals.[37] To put the point starkly, the polarizing effects of unregulated global market forces are destroying existing levels of community, making the positive associations of neighbourhood more and more of a pipe dream, while the negative aspects of divisiveness and conflict become more and more of an actuality. In effect, the Commission never seriously asked the question 'What sort of neighbourhood?' By not posing the question, given the impact of globalization, the metaphor has a sentimental quality that invites disregard.

This evasion is particularly damaging to the report's attempt to acknowledge the relevance of transnational social forces, the globalization-from-below that constitutes the operational reality of global civil society. The ethical stress of neighbourliness suggests a people-oriented globalism, yet the report's strong endorsement of Bretton Woods institutions and approaches, as well as the dynamics of economic globalization, implies a market-oriented globalism. The same incoherence undermines the democratizing reforms proposed for the United Nations, calling for a Forum of Civil Society to meet prior to the General Assembly in the same facilities used by governmental representatives, and a Right of Petition for aggrieved individuals and groups that will be reviewed by an independent Council of Petitions, recommending a referral, if appropriate, to the Security Council, General Assembly and Secretary-General. These initiatives are not likely to be accepted, but even if they were, there is not much prospect that the statism of the United Nations could be challenged by these means, except at its edges. At most, such innovations would provide civil society with entry-points and mobilizing occasions, not for neighbourly discussion, but to posit demands and convey to wider audiences the depth and intensity of cleavages and perceived grievances, as well as to offer sites of struggle.

In the end, *Our Global Neighbourhood* falls somewhat clumsily between two stools, while endeavouring to straddle both. Its proposals and orientation are too reformist, humanist and populist to be acceptable to either leading states or the new élites of globalization. Yet these proposals and, even more so, the underlying analysis is insufficiently radical to satisfy typical orientations in global civil society: in particular, the embrace of economic globalization by the report invites suspicion given the general critical view that such a market-driven world accentuates the suffering of the poorest and most vulnerable sectors of international society. Perhaps, in the end, liberal internationalism is always better off avoiding the big picture, saving its energy for well-constructed, specific proposals that are a meeting-ground for enlightened sectors of the established order and the more moderate, gradualist elements in civil society. It is the case that the best thinking in the report happens to be focused on specific reform possibilities that are compatible with economic globalization.

It is probably a bad sign that eminent persons of liberal persuasion are currently out of fashion and that our future is being primarily shaped by numerous interactions among the many varieties of technocratic globalist, social reactionary and mean-spirited traditionalists, a strange interplay between advanced sectors of electronic capital (for example, Bill Gates' Microsoft) and various backlash phenomena associated with a variety of nationalist, ethnic and religious extremisms. We can comprehend this latest failure of liberal internationalism mainly through its inability to come sufficiently to terms with the advent of this era of globalization, and to cast its lot with transnational social forces rather than to remain content with the established order. In the context of global governance, liberalism has managed to promote the idea of international organization, but only as an *instrument* of statecraft and geopolitics, not as an *alternative* based on a real shift from unilateralism and militarism to world community procedures. When the liberal becomes more radical, as in proposals for world government, the outlook seems even more sterile, confusing a coherent alternative to statism as a blueprint with a viable political engagement with transforming social forces. To overcome the tendency to be either too compliant in relation to geopolitics or too oblivious to its foundational relationship with the exercise of power in international life is the major challenge facing world order thinking.

Neither Commissions of eminent persons nor academic approaches are likely to advance the cause of global governance very far under existing conditions. The best hope on both fronts is to be bold in critique and receptive in approach to the potential role of transformative elements in global civil society. This may be an impossibility given the nature of the Commission format, and highly difficult within academic circles given the realist orthodoxy that prevails, especially in the centres of geopolitical influence.

Thus, the prospects for constructive approaches to global governance, despite the urgencies associated with the social and ecological harm being done and threatened by unregulated market forces, are not very encouraging. There are some hopeful lines, however, that deserve attention beyond what can be expected from global Commissions: new coalitions between sectors of global civil society and disadvantaged states in the South; compromises struck at the regional level between economistic projects of elites and the more social goals of citizens, as in Europe; new surges of normative energy arising from ecological and political breakdowns of order that threaten core interests of global market forces; more focused initiatives, as on the oceans, that raise awareness in ways that do enable limited forms of global governance to emerge.[38]

Notes

1. Ann-Marie Slaughter, 'International Law in a World of Liberal States', *European Journal of International Law*, Vol. 6, No. 4 (1995), especially p. 6; and idem, 'The Real New World Order', *Foreign Affairs*, Vol. 76, No. 5 (1997), pp. 183–97. See also Andrew Moravcsik, 'Liberalism

and International Relations Theory' (Center for International Affairs, Harvard University, Working Paper, No. 92–6, 1992). The aptness of the analogy between domestic political structures and world order thinking has been a matter of continuous controversy. The main various positions are usefully analysed in Hidemi Suganami, *The Domestic Analogy and World Order Proposals* (Cambridge: Cambridge University Press, 1989).

2. The liberal perspective tends to be incrementalist, accepting the statist framework as the foundation of world order; advocacy of world government is associated with a paradigm jump that has the main idea of overcoming statism. See David Ray Griffin, 'The Need for (Democratic) Global Government' (undated paper), and Grenville Clark and Louis B. Sohn, *World Peace Through World Law*, third revised edition (Cambridge, MA: Harvard University Press, 1966).

3. These Kantian ideas have been influentially presented and assessed for their contemporary relevance by Michael W. Doyle, 'Liberalism and World Politics', *American Political Science Review*, Vol. 80, No. 4 (1986), especially pp. 1155–62.

4. See Paul Hirst and Grahame Thompson, *Globalization in Question: The International Economy and the Possibilities of Governance* (Cambridge: Polity Press, 1996).

5. *Our Global Neighbourhood: The Report of the Commission on Global Governance* (Oxford: Oxford University Press, 1995).

6. It is important to appreciate that liberal internationalism was generally subordinated to a realist view of the state and its modes of perceiving and deciding, and should be conceived as mainly a normative commentary of marginal relevance to the conduct of statecraft. That is, in the security domain of war/peace relations realism always provided the underpinning for liberal internationalism. Also, as Henry Kissinger is fond of pointing out, the United States was alone among major states to being susceptible to liberal internationalist posturing, often, he argues, at the expense of a clearheaded pursuit of national interests. See, for example, Henry Kissinger, *Diplomacy* (New York: Simon and Schuster, 1994), especially pp. 804–35. For a bold 1990s attempt to reassert the old geopolitics see Zbigniew Brzezinski, *The Grand Chessboard: American Primacy and Geostrategic Imperatives* (New York: Basic Books, 1997).

7. The terminology of neoliberalism invites confusion, as if implying that neoliberalism was a continuation and adaptation of liberal internationalism; the history of liberalism is complex and contradictory, and includes an early eighteenth-century emphasis, most obviously in the writing of John Locke, on property rights and minimalist government; however, liberal internationalism has all along emphasized the realization of liberal values and procedures through the agency of governmental initiative, whereas neoliberalism de-emphasizes the social dimensions of liberalism while seeking to minimize governmental activism, especially in relation to economic policy, including any assumption of public sector responsibility for the basic needs of vulnerable individuals and groups.

8. Of course, it is misleading to associate liberalism with utopianism; it is more properly understood as an anti-utopian manifestation of a pragmatic,

problem-solving orientation, as in the work of John Dewey. Nevertheless, the prevailing outlook in this period has been to lump all reformist thinking together, especially so condemning policies dedicated to social well-being that rely upon governmental activism; in this respect, the anti-utopianism formerly directed against the Marxist-Leninist traditions of thought is easily, if inappropriately, redirected to liberalism and social democracy. Having slain the largest ideological dragon impeding a full-scale embrace of market logic, it becomes opportune to hunt down various lesser dragons, among which the idea of compassionate governance is the most formidable.

9. For example, the ambitious moves towards, regional and global institutionalization in Maastricht arrangements for Europe and through the creation of the World Trade Organization as a sequel to GATT definitely move towards economic governance but such labels are avoided: also the normative implications of such governance schemes may tilt the distribution of benefits even further in a polarizing direction to the benefit of the rich and privileged. It is important to appreciate that global governance can be either beneficial for or detrimental to the achievement of human well-being, and in this crucial respect, resembles the appraisal of the strong territorial sovereign state as harmful or hurtful in relation to world order values.

10. This irrelevance is explained later.

11. Since the original version of this chapter appeared in *Millennium: Journal of International Studies* in 1995, I have myself served as an active member of the Independent World Commission on the Oceans, chaired by Mario Soares, former President of Portugal. By focusing on the oceans, a subject-matter that is not part of the traditional liberal agenda, and a natural foundation for the life process of the planet, two difficulties that constrained the Commission on Global Governance are removed: (1) ideological consensus is far less necessary, although relevant to the extent that a more equitable approach to access, use and enjoyment of the oceans is at stake; (2) awareness is itself a valuable goal, giving greater value to information, inspirational approaches, and a coherent perspective. Whether such differences will indeed save the Oceans Commission from the fate of the liberal Commissions cannot be assessed until after its report has appeared and been discussed, which is expected to occur in late 1998.

12. These Commissions should be distinguished from global conferences under UN auspices on similar issues that provide arenas and sites of struggle for governments and for transnational social forces; also distinct, yet related, was the Trilateral Commission that brought together in a continuing format private sector elites in Japan, Europe and North America, exerting a significant influence on political elites in the North during the 1970s, but relinquishing their role by the mid-1980s as their neoliberal orientation had become operative policy.

13. For concise background information on these Commission activities, see 'Common Responsibility in the 1990s', The Stockholm Initiative on Global Security and Governance, 22 April 1991 (hereinafter referred to as 'The Stockholm Initiative'), pp. 6–9, and *Our Global Neighbourhood*, pp. xiv–xvi and 359.

14. In the 1980s there arose a fairly widespread view that the instabilities of the arms race were more dangerous to world peace than the foreign policy goals of either superpower, that the danger of catastrophic war came from an obsolete system rather than from the expansionism of either side in the Cold War.

15. *Our Global Neighbourhood*, pp. 361–86 for a description of formation, working plan, and make-up of the Commission.

16. For a critical assessment of the UN overreach in the Gulf Crisis, see Richard Falk, 'Reflections on the Gulf Experience: Force and War in the UN System', in Tareq Y. Ismael and Jacqueline S. Ismael (eds.), *The Gulf War and the New World Order* (Gainesville, FL: University of Florida, 1994), pp. 25–39.

17. For a full listing of members, with mini-biographies of each, see *Our Global Neighbourhood*, pp. 361–86.

18. By last such effort, I mean mainly the ideologically homogeneous liberal orientation rather than the global Commission format; it is more likely that if Commissions are formed in the future their composition will be more ideologically representative of contending positions, or possibly, homogeneously expressive of neoliberalism. Also possible, if funding can be acquired, would be a Commission dominated by activist and civil society perspectives. In other words, what is unlikely is the recurrence of Commissions dominated by liberal internationalist perspectives, especially if devoted to very general reformist goals.

19. *Our Global Neighbourhood*, p. 1.

20. *Ibid.*, p. 2.

21. *Ibid.*, p. 49.

22. The final section will consider whether 'neighbourhood' is a helpful metaphor at this time when the encounters of modernism, traditionalism and postmodernism are so intense.

23. *Our Global Neighbourhood*, p. 32.

24. *Ibid.*, p. 33.

25. *Ibid.*, p. 155.

26. Both quotations are from *ibid,*, p. 156.

27. *Ibid.*, p. 338.

28. *Ibid.*, pp. 340–1.

29. See ICJ AO.

30. See Richard Falk, 'The Extension of Law to Foreign Policy: The Next Constitutional Challenge', in Alan S. Rosenbaum (ed.), *Constitutionalism: The Philosophical Dimension* (Westport, CT: Greenwood, 1988), pp. 205–21. On why this cannot happen with the jurisprudential confines of international law, see Anthony Carty, *The Decay of International Law* (Manchester: Manchester University Press, 1986).

31. *Our Global Neighbourhood*, p. 312.

32. Antonio Cassese and Edmond Jouve (eds.), *Pour un droit des peuples* (Paris: Berger-Levrault, 1978).

33. In fact, as earlier argued, the most receptive audience is likely to be interested segments of global civil society despite the failure of the report to represent their views and tactics with accuracy. Is the need for respectability so great that this mismatch between the content and tone of the report and its greatest potential audience cannot be rectified? At issue here is partly differ-

ing styles of presentation and uses of language. The elite make-up of
Commissions encourages a bureaucratic reluctance to speak plainly, to rely
on finger-pointing illustrations, whereas activist groups insist upon mobilizing rhetoric and as vivid as possible reliance on 'cases' that show the need
for action.
34. *Our Global Neighbourhood*, p. 336. Is this last assertion generally true? Why
did Somalia seem to mean more during the Cold War than since 1989?
Why was so little done in response to genocidal outbursts in Rwanda?
35. *Ibid.*, pp. 67–75.
36. For one graphic account of the negative impact of Cold War priorities on
the internal struggles in southern Africa, see Victoria Brittain, *Hidden Lives,
Hidden Deaths* (London: Faber, 1988).
37. See Jeremy Brecher and Tim Costello, *Global Village or Global Pillage:
Economic Reconstruction from the Bottom Up* (Boston, MA: South End Press,
1994), and Smitu Kothari, 'Where Are the People? The United Nations,
Global Economic Institutions and Governance', paper given at UN Fiftieth
Anniversary Conference, The United Nations: Between Sovereignty and
Global Governance? (Melbourne, Australia, 2–6 July 1995).
38. The efforts of the Independent World Commission on the Oceans are
illustrative of both opportunities and obstacles.

5

At Home Abroad, Abroad at Home: International Liberalization and Domestic Stability in the New World Economy*

John Gerard Ruggie

The two most enduring contemporaneous accounts of the inter-war period are E. H. Carr's *The Twenty Years' Crisis* and Karl Polanyi's *The Great Transformation*.[1] The perspectives from which the two authors wrote could barely have differed more. Carr is best remembered today for pulverizing the idealist foundations of liberal internationalism, and thereby preparing the ground for the postwar ascendancy of realist discourse in the academic study of international relations. Polanyi's intellectual pedigree and legacy are more complex. He delivered a searing indictment of the social destructiveness of unregulated market forces and the moral mutilation he attributed to market rationality. For these views, Polanyi was later adopted by the New Left. However, he anchored his critique in an organic conception of society that was, in point of fact, deeply conservative in the traditionalist sense of that term.

Despite their differences, Carr and Polanyi reached similar conclusions about the future of the world economy. Both believed they had witnessed, in Polanyi's words, 'the passing of capitalist internationalism'; or, as Carr depicted it, the 'abnormal, *laissez-faire* interlude of the nineteenth century'.[2] Further, both felt that the drive to reimpose social and political imperatives on the self-regulating market, which had swept the industrialized countries in the 1930s, would be extended into the international arena after the war. 'Internationally,' Carr felt, 'the consequences of absolute *laissez-faire* are as fantastic and as unacceptable as are the consequences of *laissez-faire* within the state.'[3] Polanyi concurred that '[o]ut of the ruins of the Old World, the cornerstones of the New can be seen to emerge: economic collaboration of governments *and* the liberty to organize national life at will'.[4]

For nearly half a century, the economic collaboration of governments that Carr and Polanyi foresaw has been pursued within a form of multilateralism consistent with the maintenance of domestic stability, what I have elsewhere called the embedded liberalism compromise.[5] Societies were asked to embrace the change and dislocation attending international liberalization. In turn, liberalization and its effects were cushioned by the newly acquired domestic economic and social policy roles of governments. At the same time, the measures adopted to effect domestic cushioning were expected to be limited in duration, commensurate with the extent of external disruption and compatible with the long-term expansion of international economic transactions.

Due in part to the success of this postwar arrangement, capital has become globally more mobile, as well as more transnationalized in organization and integrated in scope, than Carr or Polanyi could ever have imagined. We are, therefore, entering an entirely new era in the evolution of the world economy. In this chapter, I develop a provisional schematic formulation of this new world economy's key institutional features and consequences. I focus on three sets of issues in particular: the growing role of domestic domains as issues of contention in international economic policy; the denationalization of control over significant decisions regarding production, exchange and employment; and the growing difficulty experienced by governments in living up to their part of the domestic social compact on which postwar liberalization has hinged.

Some observers may find the new world economy 'fantastic', in the positive sense of the word, because of its presumed global efficiency and welfare effects. However, it could end up being 'fantastic' as Carr meant: fanciful, due to doubts about its domestic political viability. In some respects, then, the world in 1995 finds itself faced with a challenge that is not unlike the one it faced in 1945: devising compatible forms of international liberalization and domestic stability. However, there are two critical differences. First, the ability and willingness of the United States to act in support of the overall international economic order is considerably less today than in 1945. Second, the lack of consensus on core conceptual issues regarding the international and domestic policy realms alike suggests that the intellectual context today is also less conducive to a successful resolution. The combination of these factors implies that considerable turmoil may lie ahead.

Contested domestic domains

It was no secret to economists in the 1930s that imperfect competition, and patterns of domestic industrial organization more generally, produced significant effects on international trade.[6] Articles 46–54 of the Charter of the International Trade Organization (ITO) reflected these concerns, as they sought to curtail a variety of restrictive business practices that might affect trade flows. By virtue of Article 46, for instance, members of the ITO would have pledged 'to prevent ... business practices affecting international trade which restrain competition, limit access to markets, or foster monopolistic control, whenever such practices have harmful effects on the expansion of production or trade ...'[7] In the immediate postwar years, these concerns were removed from the international trade agenda through a two-step process. The first was the defeat of the ITO in the US Senate, which left conventional point-of-entry barriers as the sole portfolio of the quickly assembled General Agreement on Tariffs and Trade (GATT). Second, GATT then avoided the related conceptual problems posed by state-trading nations, such as the Soviet Union, by calling for state-trading enterprises in their external purchases and sales simply to behave like private economic units: 'solely in accordance with commercial considerations', in the words of Article XVII of the GATT, that is, in response to factors such as price, quality, transportation costs and similar terms of purchase or sale.[8] Thus, the external significance of divergent domestic institutional factors was assumed away.

Now that point-of-entry barriers have become progressively lowered or eliminated, the impact of domestic economic policies and institutional arrangements on international economic transactions has soared in salience. Over a decade ago, Richard Blackhurst, a well-known GATT staff economist, foresaw 'the twilight of domestic economic policies'.[9] Blackhurst noted that, in distinguishing between 'international' and 'domestic' economic policy, a shift was taking place from a definition of international as border measures, to *any* policy which had an 'important' impact on international transaction flows, no matter what the instrument was or where it was applied. Moreover, Blackhurst predicted that,

> barring either a major retreat into protectionism such as occurred in the 1930s or a massive reduction in the level of government intervention in the economy, the reclassification will continue into the foreseeable future, aiming towards an end point where few eco-

nomic policies of any consequence will be considered primarily domestic.[10]

To some extent, this trend affects monetary relations as well as trade. However, it is more advanced in trade, and also more intense because domestic trade relief measures make compensatory and retaliatory moves more readily accessible. The GATT, and now the World Trade Organization (WTO), was designed, in the words of one legal scholar, 'to maintain a balance of [external] concessions and obligations, not to restructure nations'.[11] Yet, 'restructuring nations', at least certain aspects of nations, is what trade disputes increasingly have come to be about. Below, I describe briefly some of the issues in contention.

Domestic structures

One of these issues concerns domestic economic structures: defined broadly to include both government policies and policy networks, as well as patterns of private sector industrial organization. Sylvia Ostry, a former official of the Organization for Economic Cooperation and Development (OECD), differentiates three stylized forms among the leading capitalist countries: the pluralist market economy characteristic of the United States, the social market economy of continental Europe and Japan's corporatist market economy.[12] For the moment, Ostry would accept behaviour, tastes and institutions that have 'cultural and historical roots' as 'given', because the 'appropriate domain for international policy co-operation is government policy'.[13] To reconcile the most serious trade effects of economic policy differences among these three forms of market economies, Ostry suggests, requires convergence in the following areas: competition policy, including merger law; research and development policies, especially subsidies; the asymmetry of access in the investment area, which largely targets Japan; and financial regulation as it affects corporate governance, such as, for example, bank ownership of firms.[14] Even if we accept Ostry's concession to culture and history, achieving policy convergence in the remaining areas on her list is a daunting task.

The deepest difference on each of these policy dimensions lies between Japan and the other two. The Japan case makes clear that a narrow focus on specific policies alone, as Ostry recommends, is simply not practical. Among the factors that have been identified as shaping Japan's trade and investment posture are its labour market, capital markets and systems of ownership, production and distribution; the economic role of the state; and, indeed, the nature of its electoral system.[15] Scholars disagree on whether differences in domestic economic structures are declining, as liberal economists tend to believe, or are more enduring features of Japanese society.[16] Alas, policy-makers elsewhere lack the luxury of waiting to find out who is right.

As difficult as it is, however, the highly charged case of Japan masks a more generic problem that would be with us in any event. Now that border barriers have been reduced to insignificant levels, domestic economic structures *ipso facto* are taking centre stage in international trade disputes. If they diverge systematically and have 'important' effects on international transaction flows, then an international political problem potentially exists.

The domestic economic structures of one's trading partners typically enter the trade policy agenda via 'unfairness' claims. Potentially, this has at least four deleterious consequences. First, what constitutes 'fairness' tends to be determined unilaterally by the aggrieved party. As Robert E. Hudec points out, 'there are relatively few international agreements regulating the substance of such claims, and there is no recognised tribunal to adjudicate them in common law fashion'.[17] GATT had nothing to say on the subject, and progress within the WTO is likely to remain modest, focused largely on such traditional issues as anti-dumping and countervailing duties.

Second, by their nature, fairness claims call for unilateral concessions on the part of the accused party: '[t]o say that certain conduct is unfair is to say that the guilty party must correct it for that reason alone'.[18] As Ryutaro Komiya and Motoshige Itoh characterize US demands regarding those Japanese trade practices which it deems to be unfair: '[u]sually trade negotiations between two countries take the form of give-and-take, but in these negotiations, which have been going on almost continuously since 1976, the subject matter has been simply how much and how soon Japan would make concessions, with the United States offering little if anything in exchange'.[19] In contrast, GATT processes, and presumably corresponding processes in the WTO, rest on mutual concessions as the basis for agreement, unless specific legal obligations can be shown to have been violated. When it comes to fairness claims, therefore, the GATT and WTO are in the impossible position of having to cope with structural asymmetries by means of symmetrical accommodation.

Third, if policy harmonization were to become the preferred vehicle for dealing with the international effects of domestic policies and arrangements, questions such as these would arise immediately: Harmonization to whose standard? Who decides whose standard will become the norm, and how? In addition, the slippery slope of policy harmonization is steep, as indicated by the 240 items raised by the United States in the US–Japan Structural Impediments Initiative talks.[20] Fourth, and finally, unilateral measures can become the instrument of choice to achieve, for instance, market access abroad, as has often been the case for the United States in relation to Japan. When these measures are generalized across multiple issues and numerous countries the likelihood of retaliation and cycles of escalation can only grow.

In addition to the 'fairness' of domestic policies and institutional arrangements, the differential impact of domestic standards is becoming a critical trade policy issue. Labour and environmental standards are the most intrusive. Former Vice-President Al Gore announced to officials from 109 countries assembled to sign GATT's Uruguay Round accord in Marrakech, Morocco, in April 1994, that Washington would seek to give pride of place to environmental and labour standards in future WTO negotiations.[21]

In short, the premise that differences in domestic economic structures and practices could be ignored in organizing the international trade regime no longer holds. Intrinsically, the issue has little to do with protectionism, although, of course, it is susceptible to capture by protectionist forces. It has everything to do with the growing irrelevance of the traditional distinction between 'internal' and 'external' policy domains, or the contestation of where, precisely, the one ends and the other begins. There are no simple solutions to the policy problems posed by this transformation. Blackhurst recommends that governments adopt new multilateral rules to defend themselves from pressures originating at home no less than abroad:

> general international rules are at least as useful in protecting a government from domestic interest groups as they are in protecting it from abuses by other governments. It is no paradox that the observance of general rules *increases* a government's freedom and ability to pursue genuine national interests.[22]

However, the process will be more difficult than Blackhurst supposed. As Peter Cowhey and Jonathan Aronson have suggested, even narrowly construed commercial policy requires a subtle but significant shift, away from trade *per se*, towards both formal and informal conditions governing market access.[23] Moreover, because non-border policy measures are in the hands of a variety of domestic agencies other than trade ministries, the international trade policy process will increasingly involve international agencies in addition to WTO. Finally, the inclusion of environmental and labour standards entangles trade relations in very intimate domains of domestic social policy.

Intangibles

The blurring of boundaries between domestic and international realms is both hastened and deepened by the growing significance of traded services. Services used to be 'invisible' appendages to merchandise trade: shipping, insurance and tourism. Today, the list is longer and the magnitude higher. It now includes information services; various financial, professional and business-related services; construction; cultural services; and many more. Their volume has reached somewhere between one fifth and one quarter of total world trade, although, because of definitional and statistical anomalies, the balance of world services imports and exports is routinely off by $100 billion or so per annum, and that still understates hard-to-measure services that are embodied in traded products, such as design, engineering or data processing.[24] The expansion of traded services is due to transnationalized goods production; technological developments, especially the informatics revolution; and domestic deregulation, particularly of capital markets and telecommunications.

The institutional challenge posed by traded services is not quantitative, however, but qualitative. The GATT was designed for merchandise trade: ballbearings and bananas cross frontiers, passing through customs houses on the way. Invisibles were left uncovered by GATT. Indeed, according to an etymological survey by William J. Drake and Kalypso Nicolaidis, services had not been regarded as being 'traded' before 1972, when they were first so construed in an OECD experts' report: 'the group took a huge leap by suggesting tentatively that the transactions in services could be considered trade, that the principles and norms for trade in goods might apply, and that the challenge in the emerging transition was to avoid "protectionism".[25] As the world's largest producer and 'exporter' of services, the United States quickly embraced these notions. The United States pushed for GATT rules to govern traded services as early as the Tokyo Round of the 1970s, but with little success. The United States also had great difficulty getting services onto the agenda of the Uruguay Round, and when it did succeed the victory initially appeared largely symbolic.[26] Even so, in the end, the Round did produce a General Agreement on Trade in Services (GATS).

Essentially, the GATS consists of a set of general principles, a number of special conditions or exceptions and initial liberalization commitments.[27] Traded services generally are to be governed by the classical GATT principles of non-discrimination and transparency of domestic rules and regulations, but countries have the right to exclude specific services from the principles of national treatment and the right of market access. Safeguards provisions are included and mechanisms for dispute settlement provided for. In short, trade in services will be brought under the GATT/WTO umbrella, with an ultimate balance of obligations between domestic and international objectives which is more qualified than for merchandise trade and also more individualized.

It is important to realize, however, that the GATS only marks the conclusion of one chapter in a continuing story of very difficult economic diplomacy. It brings within the conventional trade framework that portion of traded services which countries are willing to include. A number of highly contentious issues remain beyond the reach of this framework. Intrinsically, this fact has little to do with what one normally regards as trade barriers or protectionism, but stems largely from the unique attributes of services that differentiate them from goods.

First, because the concept of services has no well-established place in economic theory, its definition tends to be *ad hoc* and arbitrary: intangible activities not included in agriculture, mining and manufacturing. Attempts to define services more theoretically have focused on their being non-storable, therefore requiring simultaneity in provision and use.[28] However, this insight has generated endless lists that can be endlessly argued about, rather than a finite and universally agreed set. With tongue only half in cheek, the *Economist* once proposed defining services as '[t]hings which can be bought and sold but which you cannot drop on your foot';[29] but in fact architectural plans, computer disks and magnetic tapes, not to mention Big Macs in Moscow or Budapest, can be dropped on one's foot. In short, unlike the case of merchandise trade, in traded services the very definition of the phenomenon remains subject to strategic behaviour by governments. There is no reason to expect that contested definitions will yield to consensus simply because a GATS has been reached.

Second, governments typically regulate domestic service industries more rigorously than other economic activities. Entry into many services, such as medicine, law or accounting, is strictly licensed.

Governments often still reserve the right to approve utilities prices, which in many places still include transportation and telecommunications. Financial institutions, such as banks, insurance firms and securities traders, are subject to prudential supervision. Finally, in many countries, the state still owns outright certain service industries. Most of these regulatory objectives and instruments were not designed with trade in mind. Where they apply, the principles of non-discrimination, transparency and national treatment should moderate somewhat the impact of differences in national regulatory environments, but they will not eliminate the problem.

Furthermore, despite what Drake and Nicolaidis characterize as the 'revolution in social ontology' that reconceived services,[30] the fact remains that relatively few services are 'traded' in any recognizable sense of the term. In merchandise trade, the factors of production and the consumers stand still while the finished product moves. In traded services, the factors of production do the moving while the product is fixed in location. Thus, trade in services amounts to provider-mobility across borders. However, why, for example, should provider-mobility encompass US banks offering financial services in Seoul, but not South Korean construction workers providing their services in Seattle? This issue exercised developing countries during the GATS negotiations and will remain contentious in the future. Indeed, because of the difficulty of accommodating such trade-offs in the domestic policies of the OECD countries, it would not be entirely surprising if a second 'ontological revolution' were to occur somewhere down the road: this time, tying services more closely to the realm of investment policy rather than trade.

Finally, one suspects that services-related conflicts will be higher in the Asia-Pacific region, particularly vis-à-vis Japan, than elsewhere among the industrialized countries. Regulatory environments are more opaque, inviting the imputation of worst-case motivations, and if past experience from the difficulties encountered in the areas of direct foreign investment and patent protection is any guide, then in Japan, at any rate, the efficacy of institutional solutions (like the right of establishment) may prove elusive and generate as many bilateral disputes as they resolve.[31]

In conclusion, the postwar trade regime was intended to achieve and maintain a sustainable balance between the internal and external policy objectives of governments, in keeping with the embedded liberalism compromise. It was not designed to restructure domestic institutional arrangements. Yet, domestic restructuring is what the trade policy agenda increasingly has come to be about. Highly politicized trade policy disputes and potential instability in trade relations appear to be the virtually inevitable consequence of successful liberalization.

Globalization

Much has been written about globalization and nearly as much has been dismissed as 'globaloney'. Milton Friedman has put the negative case most categorically, as is his wont: '[t]he world is less internationalised in any immediate, relevant, pertinent sense today than it was in 1913 or in 1929'.[32] Friedman contends that the divergence between the price of the same good in different countries, which became distinctly pronounced after the Great Depression, has remained in place despite steadily decreasing transportation costs, thus 'demonstrating vividly how powerful and effective government intervention has been in rendering the law of one price far less applicable after 1931 than it was before'.[33]

Friedman's observation that the world economy is far from being a single economy governed by the law of one price is largely correct, but also irrelevant to the point at issue. Globalization today is assuming various microeconomic forms of increasingly extensive, diverse and integrated institutional webs forged within markets and among firms across the globe. Illustrating the poverty of conventional concepts, this phenomenon is typically described as 'off-shore' markets and 'off-shore' production, as if they existed in some ethereal space waiting to be reconceived by the economic equivalent of relativity theory.

Most international economists have devoted little attention to these organizational forms because institutional economics is not much in vogue among them. The conventional notions of international politics do not go far to describe or explain them either, whether the liberal proclivity to discover that sovereignty is everywhere at bay, or the realist security blanket under which nothing ever fundamentally changes. At the moment, little can be established conclusively about this transformation because no official definitions exist of the relevant categories of analysis, and so no uniform data are collected. Nevertheless the simplest of typologies, the distinction between markets, hierarchies and networks will help us intuitively to grasp the issues at stake.[34] It derives from the work of the otherwise unlikely pairing of business school economists and their economist counterparts on the left, together with organizational political scientists and sociologists. A stylized discussion of these forms and their implications follows.

Markets

One of the core premises of the postwar economic regimes was that international economic transactions are conducted at arm's length between distinct and disjoint national economies. Several private sector institutional transformations have called this premise into question, as well as the policy measures based on it. The first concerns the mediating mechanism of the market itself.

The most significant institutional changes exhibited by international financial markets are their growth, diversification and integration across national economies, beyond even the wildest expectations of policy-makers when they first decided to unleash them. Once an adjunct of trade, financial transactions now tower over annual trade flows. In addition to old-fashioned investment capital, there are international markets in currencies and equities, as well as derivatives of all of these, including options, futures and swaps. Although they are physically separated, these markets are global in that they 'function as if they were all in the same place',[35] in real time and around the clock.

This evolution, perhaps revolution is the more appropriate term, has serious consequences for economic policy-making. Virtually by definition, taken for granted cause–effect relations and trade-offs between exchange rates and trade balances, say, or between interest rates and exchange rates, are confounded by the complexities of this new financial world. Richard N. Cooper summarizes the general point thus: '[w]hen markets evolve to the point of becoming international in scope the effectiveness of traditional instruments of economic policy is often greatly reduced or even nullified'.[36]

Similarly, the international markets for goods and services have expanded and diversified. Their most significant institutional change, however, is the fact that they have become overshadowed altogether by new organizational forms which internalize both production and exchange within global corporate structures. I briefly describe two characteristic forms and their implications for policy.

Hierarchies

The rate of increase in international production, that is, production by multinational enterprises outside their home countries, began to exceed the rate of increase in world trade in the 1960s. Sometime in the 1980s, the actual volume of international production began to exceed trade flows. Today, the worldwide sales of multinational firms, at $5.5 trillion, are only slightly less than the entire US Gross Domestic Product (GDP). Multinationals based in the United States play a major role in international production: their revenues from manufacturing abroad are now twice their export earnings.[37]

A recent US Department of Commerce study sought to measure what the US position in world markets would look like if the standard balance-of-trade measure were combined with the net effects of sales by US-owned companies abroad, and by foreign-owned companies in the United States. It found that, on this more inclusive indicator of global sales and purchases of goods and services, the United States has consistently been earning a surplus, rising from $8 billion in 1981 to $24 billion in 1991, even as its trade deficit deteriorated during the same period from $16 billion to $28 billion.[38] The strategies of US-owned multinationals, as well as the assessment of these firms by stock markets, reflect this broader US net position in world markets. US labour, in contrast, lives in the world of the standard balance-of-trade figures. The growing gap between the two expresses a fundamental source of dislocation in the American political economy.[39]

The fact that US firms now produce more abroad than they export is in itself important. However, an even more profound institutional shift follows from it: the dominant mode of organizing goods production and exchange in the world economy is increasingly 'through administrative hierarchies rather than external markets'.[40] The process began simply enough. For a variety of reasons, firms set up subsidiaries abroad to service local markets. Over the course of 30 years or so, this process gradually was transformed into systems of sourcing, production and distribution that have been described as 'the global factory'.[41]

As a result of this transformation, the template, the mental picture of the economic world, on the basis of which postwar economic policy-making and the international economic regimes were conceived, has been rendered obsolete. In that picture, production was national, and countries were linked into an international division of labour by arm's length trade, portfolio investment and direct investment in raw materials sectors or to secure local market access. Today, in significant measure the international division of labour is becoming *internalized* at the level of firms. Integrated administrative structures that span the globe increasingly manage the design, production and exchange of parts, components and finished products; the allocation of strategic resources, including funds and skills; and the synoptic plans that rationalize these processes, including their location, for success in a competitive environment that is itself increasingly global. In short, for virtually every major industry, whether manufactures or services, the primary mode for the international organization of economic transactions has shifted away from reliance on international markets towards global administrative hierarchies.[42] Thus, even as borders everywhere have become more open, in this specifically institutional sense, global production and exchange may be said to have become more 'closed'. Even though states are actively involved in bargaining with firms about conditions of access, for example, nowhere is economic policy-making remotely equipped to deal with the systemic policy consequences of this shift.

One direct consequence is the growth of intra-firm trade: trade among subsidiaries or otherwise related parties. At the moment, few official and uniform intra-firm trade statistics are collected. Episodic studies show that it is growing at a rate considerably more rapid than conventional trade and they indicate that intra-firm trade is far less sensitive than conventional trade to such policy instruments as exchange rates.[43] Other policy-related concerns include transfer pricing for the purposes of cross-subsidization and to minimize tax obligations.

Furthermore, this institutional transformation has begun to turn the conduct of trade policy into a metaphysical exercise, poignantly captured by Robert Reich's question: '*Who* is US?'[44] The US International Trade Commission (ITC), for example, not long ago confronted a case of anti-dumping brought by a Japanese firm producing typewriters in the United States, against a US firm importing typewriters into the United States from off-shore facilities in Singapore and Indonesia.[45] In making its decisions, what weights should government assign to the nationality of ownership, the locale of production and contributions to the economy, when these are no longer covariant? The growing tendency by US firms to internationalize research and development in costly high-technology sectors has raised related concerns.[46]

Finally, this institutional transformation challenges what was perhaps the central relationship in the entire postwar American political economy. As Cowhey and Aronson depict its prevailing model of industrial organization, the federal government assumed that its primary role was to manage levels of consumer spending, provide R&D funding and otherwise help socialize the costs of technological innovation via military procurement and civilian science programmes. The major US companies would take it from there.[47] Today, it is getting harder to determine not only whether something is a US product, as

Reich observes, but more importantly, whether the legal designation, 'an American corporation', describes the same economic entity, with the same consequences for domestic employment and economic growth, that it did in the 1950s and 1960s.[48] The NAFTA debate about how many US jobs would be lost or gained made it clear how little is known about the links between transnationalized production and trade policy, on the one hand, and domestic employment and economic growth, on the other. It also demonstrated that previous premises about the nature of economic entities and relationships no longer fully capture essential features of the US political economy.

This form of, in essence, denationalization may be welcomed by trade theorists and academic specialists in trade law, in the belief that it will enhance global economic efficiency and welfare while decreasing government intervention, and thereby will reduce trade disputes. However, it may have just the opposite effect. If governments find that their array of policy tools, including the relatively benign option of the 'new protectionism', no longer suffices to achieve their objectives, there is no telling what measures they might turn to in exasperation. The most constructive posture of 'cosmopolitan' policy analysts, therefore, is not to applaud the failure of 'parochial' governments, but to help them devise new means to do their jobs.

Networks

Even as analysts and policy-makers are trying to assimilate the consequences of globally integrated structures of production and exchange, the corporate world has already pushed ahead with the next generation of institutional innovations. Generically, these have been described as network forms of organization. In large-scale, high-technology sectors they are more commonly known as 'strategic alliances':[49]

Networks ... are especially useful for the exchange of commodities whose value is not easily measured. Such qualitative matters as know-how, technological capability, a particular approach or style of production, a spirit of innovation or experimentation, or a philosophy of zero defects are very hard to place a price tag on. They are not easily traded in markets nor communicated through a corporate hierarchy.[50]

In addition, the sheer size of investments and magnitudes of risks in many rapidly changing areas of high technology are increasingly beyond the capacity of even the largest firms, driving them to establish alliances.[51]

Paraphrasing Walter Powell's typology, networks are a collaborative form of organization, based on complementary strengths, characterized by relational modes of interaction, exhibiting interdependent preferences, stressing mutual benefits and bonded by reputational considerations. The field of strategic alliances is dominated by technology-intensive industries, such as semiconductors, telecommunications, commercial aircraft and automobiles. The major home bases of firms entering into alliances are the United States, European Union (especially Germany), Japan and Korea. Finally, Powell suggests that, as the globally integrated firm is discovering strategic alliances at the high end of R&D and in some instances production, it is also rediscovering the market at the low end of standardized components.[52]

Numerous questions attend the future of strategic alliances, especially concerning their viability and permanence. As the *Economist* warns: 'Managing such vaguely defined relationships is difficult enough at the best of times; distance, language and culture bring added complications. Add to this the fact that many networks are in the business of closing plants and refashioning markets, and you have a recipe for trouble.'[53] However, if networks were to become a central and permanent feature of international economic organization, then the focus of collective economic policy-making inevitably would shift towards questions of global industrial policy. At a minimum, it would entail negotiating market access, as Cowhey and Aronson suggest, but negotiating market shares might not be far behind.[54]

In sum, the reconfiguration of global structures of production and exchange, via markets, hierarchies and networks, increasingly has rendered problematical core assumptions on the basis of which governments throughout the capitalist world had pursued the domestic objectives of economic growth, full employment, and social stability. No new consensus is at yet at hand on how, or even whether, these objectives can be successfully combined in the new world economy.

Welfare capitalism

In the autumn of 1993, the editors of the *Economist* thought they had detected, and vigorously applauded, a new grand economic strategy on the part of the Clinton administration. This purported to offer Americans what the journal described as a 'new deal': '[i]ts outlines are simple: you accept change (such as the North American Free Trade Agreement) and we'll help to give you [occupational, health care, and personal] security'.[55] The *Financial Times* later that year, even while editorially basking in 'the most capitalist Christmas in history', reflected on the pressing need for a new deal for the entire capitalist world:

> [t]he world is changing rapidly; the Atlantic nations in general and Europe in particular face competition from the younger, harsher, more robust capitalism of south Asia. ... Even the middle classes, who have benefited most from economic growth, fear that they may lose what they have, while those outside note that however rich the super-rich may get, large-scale unemployment persists. Lower down the income scale the picture is far worse. ... If welfare capitalism is to be sustained, its managers must find new means of controlling its cost, and minimising the cost to employers. Radical policies, centred around the notion of giving the poor a hand-up rather than a hand-out must be pursued.[56]

These two British publications are among the most irrepressible and articulate advocates anywhere of free markets and free trade. What, then, possessed them to worry about the economic security of workers and sustaining welfare capitalism and, even more curiously, to suggest that governments have a role to play in achieving those objectives? The answer is surprisingly simple. Both realize that the extraordinary success of postwar international liberalization has hinged on a domestic social compact between state and society. Both see that this social compact is everywhere fraying; and both fear that if it unravels altogether, so too will international liberalization.

Social expenditures began to rise rapidly in the OECD countries in the 1960s, and now average roughly one third of GDP. However, contrary to widespread misconceptions in the United States, these expenditures levelled off some time ago. In the United States they nearly doubled, from roughly 10 per cent of GDP in 1960 to just under 19 per cent in 1975. They peaked there, and by 1985 had drifted lower than a decade before. Indeed, in 1985, only Spain and Japan devoted a smaller share of GDP to social expenditures than the United States.[57] On the other hand, the US economy has generated far more jobs than any other in the OECD for the past two decades, though the uniformity of their quality is in dispute and long-term unemployment has increased.[58]

In Western Europe, the social safety net has held up more firmly than in the United States, but at the cost of eroding competitiveness and an anaemic rate of job creation. Production costs are among the highest in the world, thanks to generous benefits and high payroll taxes, and the workforce is immobile and inflexible. As a result, unemployment is at a postwar high, averaging 11 per cent. The situation is far worse in Eastern Europe. It remains masked in Japan by the employment practices of firms, but is a latent threat.[59] Surveying these trends, Paul McCracken, who chaired President Nixon's Council of Economic Advisers, reached a sombre conclusion in a *Wall Street Journal* article: '[t]hose entering the work forces in Western Europe and even in the US confront labour market conditions more nearly resembling those of the late 1930s than those prevailing during the four decades or so following World War II.'[60]

Budget deficits and tax-averse publics make it impossible for governments to expand the web of social policies that has characterized welfare capitalism since the Second World War. Even for the most social democratic and neo-corporatist welfare states, the costs have become unsustainable. Moreover, there is a growing sense that some of these policies have become part of the problem, not the solution. This is not only because of their financial burden, but also because many are perceived not to work well any longer and are even thought to create perverse disincentives. US Labor Secretary, Robert Reich, reflected a growing consensus, when he proposed that several job-related social programmes be terminated: '[i]nvesting scarce resources in programs that don't deliver cheats workers who require results and taxpayers who finance failure.'[61]

Efforts radically to overhaul the capitalist welfare state cannot focus only on retrenchment, however, if the project of international liberalization is to remain domestically viable. To succeed, these efforts must 'review and redesign', not merely 'slash and trash', in the words of Lloyd Axworthy, Canada's Liberal Minister of Human Resources.[62] Kenneth Clarke, Britain's former Conservative Chancellor of the Exchequer, echoed the sentiment: 'I intend,' he said at the outset of a speech, 'to extol the virtues of both a flexible labour market and a strong welfare state. ... I believe that, properly directed, the two complement one another.'[63] Further, in January 1994, President Clinton warned the allies at the NATO summit that, unless the United States, Europe and Japan create greater economic and social opportunities at home, 'it will be difficult for the people of ... all our nations to continue to support [a] policy of involvement with the rest of the world.'[64]

So, the compromise of embedded liberalism has come around full circle. Once again, governments are groping to find a mutually compatible set of policies for international and domestic stabilization. However, they are doing so in an institutional context wherein little remains the same except an implicit normative commitment to sustain both, and in an international political environment in which their common enemy is not a clear and present geopolitical threat, but more diffuse fears of the consequences of policy failure.

Conclusion

The new world economy that has emerged over the past few decades poses significant challenges to governments because it is disembedded in several key dimensions. The first is in its policy templates: the mental maps of spaces and structures with which policy-makers visualize the basic contours of their world. These have been severely strained and even left behind by the breakdown in the distinction between domestic and international policy realms, the growing role of the ontologically ambiguous transactions called traded services and the shift from markets to hierarchies and networks as core forms in the global organization of production and exchange. The second, related source of disembeddedness is the world of policy-making itself. International as well as domestic economic policy targets are increasingly elusive because instrumentalities are no longer as effective. This loss of efficacy, in turn, reflects the fact that the theoretical, conceptual and statistical bases of policy too often still reflect previous policy templates and the cause–effect relations that pertained in that earlier world. Last, the new world economy is increasingly disembedded from the domestic social compact between state and society on which the political viability of the postwar international economic order has hinged. Policy attitudes towards the new world economy have shifted in the direction of neoliberalism to an extent that is beginning to be of concern even to staunch guardians of market orthodoxies in the leading financial journals of Britain and the United States.

Constructing a contemporary analogue to the embedded liberalism compromise will be a Herculean task. Last time around, the most decisive negotiations took place, in essence, between two countries: the United States and Britain. This time, partly because of the diffusion of economic power but also due to the nature of the issues themselves, the relevant parties must include all leading capitalist nations, in many instances the newly industrializing countries, and in some cases members of the poorer developing world. What is more, last time around there was widespread consensus about what needed to be done and how to do it in the professional circles on which policy-makers drew in the relevant 'epistemic communities', as I have called them elsewhere.[65] Today, it is more appropriate to speak of epistemic disarray in the community of scholars and policy analysts. Finally, the overall international geostrategic situation is very different today, requiring more precise and balanced quids-pro-quos in international economic relations.

It is exceedingly unlikely that any new grand bargain can be forged, except in the most general of terms. At best, we are likely to see a series of normative framework agreements and their specific operationalization in specific sectors, based on varying levels of commitments, made by shifting groups of countries. Making sure that these minilateral and plurilateral schemes recognize the organic link between domestic social and economic security on the one hand, and the durability of international systems of production and exchange on the other, is the toughest challenge of all.

Notes

* An earlier version of this chapter was presented as the 1994 Jean Monnet Lecture at the European University Institute in Florence.

1. E. H. Carr, *The Twenty Years' Crisis, 1919–1939: An Introduction to the Study of International Relations*, second edition (New York: Harper & Row, 1964, first edition 1939), and Karl Polanyi, *The Great Transformation: The Political and Economic Origins of Our Time* (Boston, MA: Beacon Books, 1944, reprinted 1957).

2. Polanyi, *ibid.*, p. 248 and Carr, *ibid.*, p. 116.

3. Carr, p. 121.

4. Polanyi, pp. 253–4, emphasis in original.

5. John Gerard Ruggie, 'International Regimes, Transactions, and Change: Embedded Liberalism in the Postwar Economic Order', *International Organization*, Vol. 36, No. 2 (1982), pp. 379–415. See also Ruggie, 'Embedded Liberalism Revisited: Institutions and Progress in International Economic Relations', in Emanuel Adler and Beverly Crawford (eds.), *Progress in Postwar International Relations* (New York: Columbia University Press, 1991), pp. 201–34.

6. Two works that readily come to mind are Edward Chamberlin, *The Theory of Monopolistic Competition* (Cambridge, MA: Harvard University Press, 1929), and Joan Robinson, *The Economics of Imperfect Competition* (London: Macmillan, 1931).

7. Articles 47 through 52, as well as Article 54, further defined the salient terms and specified the remedies available under the ITO. Article 53 made special provisions for handling restrictive practices in traded services. The

118   *John Gerard Ruggie*

full text is reprinted in Clair Wilcox, *A Charter for World Trade* (New York: Macmillan, 1949), pp. 281–7.

8. These words were taken almost verbatim from the ITO Charter, which the Soviets had a hand in drafting. See Jacob Viner, 'Conflicts of Principle in Drafting a Trade Charter', *Foreign Affairs*, Vol. 25, No. 4 (1947), pp. 612–28, and Herbert Feis, 'The Conflict Over Trade Ideologies', *Foreign Affairs*, Vol. 25, No. 2 (1947), pp. 217–28.

9. Richard Blackhurst, 'The Twilight of Domestic Economic Policies', *The World Economy*, Vol. 4, No. 4 (1981), pp. 357–74.

10. *Ibid.*, p. 363.

11. Patricia Kalla, 'The GATT Dispute Settlement Procedure in the 1980s: Where Do We Go from Here?', *Dickinson Journal of International Law*, Vol. 5, No. 1 (1986), p. 95.

12. Sylvia Ostry, 'Beyond the Border: The New International Policy Arena', in *Strategic Industries in a Global Economy* (Paris: Organization for Economic Cooperation and Development, 1991), pp. 83–4.

13. *Ibid.*, p. 84.

14. *Ibid.*, pp. 87–9.

15. This expansive view is held not only by the so-called 'revisionists', but also by Japanese analysts and relatively dispassionate US observers. See Chalmers Johnson, 'The Japanese Political Economy: A Crisis in Theory', *Ethics & International Affairs*, Vol. 2 (1988), pp. 79–97; Shigeto Tsuru, *Japan's Capitalism: Creative Defeat and Beyond* (Cambridge: Cambridge University Press, 1993); Daniel I. Okimoto, *Between MITI and the Market: Japanese Industrial Policy for High Technology* (Stanford, CA: Stanford University Press, 1989); and Dennis J. Encarnation, *Rivals beyond Trade: America Versus Japan in Global Competition* (Ithaca, NY: Cornell University Press, 1992). On the nature of the electoral system as it affects Japan's multilateral commitments, see Peter F. Cowhey, 'Elect Locally – Order Globally: Domestic Politics and Multilateral Cooperation', in John Gerard Ruggie (ed.), *Multilateralism Matters: The Theory and Praxis of an Institutional Form* (New York: Columbia University Press, 1993), pp. 157–200.

16. The two positions are illustrated, respectively, by Jagdish N. Bhagwati, *The World Trading System at Risk* (Princeton, NJ: Princeton University Press, 1991), pp. 24–44; and Kozo Yamamura, 'Will Japan's Economic Structure Change? Confessions of a Former Optimist', in Yamamura (ed.), *Japan's Economic Structure: Should It Change* (Seattle, WA: Society for Japanese Studies, University of Washington, 1990), pp. 13–64.

17. Robert E. Hudec, '"Mirror, Mirror, on the Wall": The Concept of Fairness in United States Trade Policy', paper presented at the 'Roundtable on Fair Trade, Harmonization, Level Playing Fields and the World Trading System: Economic, Political and International Legal Questions for the 1990s', Columbia University, 10 January 1992, p. 1.

18. *Ibid.*

19. Ryutaro Komiya and Motoshige Itoh, 'Japan's International Trade and Trade Policy, 1955–1984', in Takashi Inoguchi and Daniel I. Okimoto (eds.), *The Political Economy of Japan, Volume 2, The Changing International Context* (Stanford, CA: Stanford University Press, 1988), p. 203.

20. Timothy J. McNulty, 'Deal Opens Japan Market to US Satellites', *Chicago Tribune*, 4 April 1990, p. C-3.
21. See Editorial, 'Exporting Labor Standards', *Washington Post*, 10 April 1994, p. C-6; Alan Riding, 'Gore Insists Environment is a Trade Issue', *New York Times*, 15 April 1994, p. D-1; and William Drozdiak, 'Historic Trade Pact Signed, But Global Tensions Persist', *Washington Post*, 16 April 1994, p. A-12.
22. Blackhurst, 'The Twilight of Domestic Economic Policies', p. 369, emphasis in original.
23. Peter F. Cowhey and Jonathan D. Aronson, *Managing the World Economy: The Consequences of Corporate Alliances* (New York: Council on Foreign Relations, 1993), Chapter 8.
24. William J. Drake and Kalypso Nicolaidis, 'Ideas, Interests, and Institutionalization: "Trade in Services" and the Uruguay Round', *International Organization*, Vol. 46, No. 1 (1992), p. 37 and n. 1.
25. *Ibid.*, p. 45.
26. For a brief summary, see 'Nothing to Lose but its Chains: A Survey of World Trade', *The Economist*, 22 September 1990.
27. See Drake and Nikolaidis, 'Ideas, Interests and Institutionalization'; and John M. Curtis and Robert Wolfe, 'Nothing is Agreed until Everything is Agreed: First Thoughts on the Implications of the Uruguay Round', in Maureen Appel Molot and Harald von Riekhoff (eds.), *A Part of the Peace: Canada Among Nations 1994* (Ottawa: Carleton University Press, 1994), 101–28.
28. See Jagdish N. Bhagwati, 'Trade in Services and the Multinational Trade Negotiations', *World Bank Economic Review*, Vol. 1, No. 4 (1987), pp. 549–69.
29. 'A Gatt for Services', *The Economist*, 12 October 1985, p. 20.
30. Drake and Nicolaidis, 'Ideas, Interests and Institutionalization', p. 38.
31. See Encarnation, *Rivals beyond Trade, passim.*
32. Milton Friedman, 'Internationalization of the U.S. Economy', *Fraser Forum* (February 1989), p. 10.
33. *Ibid.* Kenneth Waltz made a similar case in a controversial paper a quarter of a century ago, using as his measures of internationalization: (1) the size of the external sector of the major economic powers relative to their domestic economies, and (2) the degree of intersectoral specialization in their trade. See Kenneth N. Waltz, 'The Myth of National Interdependence', in Charles P. Kindleberger (ed.), *The International Corporation* (Cambridge, MA: MIT Press, 1970), pp. 205–23. With intra-sectoral trade flows dominating among the major economies, the second part of Waltz's definition is a truism. The first is less the case today than it was in 1970, but more importantly it is also less relevant, for reasons I will discuss presently.
34. The standard conceptual works are Oliver E. Williamson, *Markets and Hierarchies* (New York: Free Press, 1975), and Walter W. Powell, 'Neither Market nor Hierarchy: Network Forms of Organization', *Research in Organizational Behavior*, Vol. 12 (1990), pp. 295–336. For a suggestive application of these concepts to the evolution of international corporate strategies and structures, see Stephen J. Kobrin, 'Beyond Geography: Inter-Firm Networks and the Structural Integration of the Global Economy'

(Philadelphia, PA: William H. Wurster Center for International Management Studies, Wharton School, University of Pennsylvania, Working Paper 93-10, November 1993).

35. John M. Stopford and Susan Strange, *Rival States, Rival Firms: Competition for World Market Shares* (Cambridge: Cambridge University Press, 1991), p. 40.

36. Richard N. Cooper, *Economic Policy in an Interdependent World* (Cambridge, MA: MIT Press, 1986), p. 96. A senior executive of Gillette, a major multinational consumer products firm, gives concrete expression to this generalization: '[i]n the long run currency fluctuations, up and down, don't mean a whit in the decision where to manufacture'. Cited in Louis Uchitelle, 'U.S. Corporations Expanding Abroad at a Quicker Pace', *New York Times*, 25 July 1994, p. D-2.

37. 'The Discreet Charm of the Multicultural Multinational', *The Economist*, 30 July 1994, pp. 65–6.

38. J. Steven Landefeld, Obie G. Whichard and Jeffrey H. Lowe, 'Alternative Frameworks for U.S. International Transactions', *Survey of Current Business*, Vol. 73, No. 12 (1993), pp. 50–61.

39. Japanese multinationals exhibit a more pronounced tendency to import from home country suppliers rather than purchasing locally, thereby adding fuel to US–Japan trade disputes. See Encarnation, *Rivals beyond Trade;* Mordechai E. Kreinin, 'How Closed is Japan's Market? Additional Evidence', *The World Economy*, Vol. 11, No. 4 (1988), pp. 529–42; and United Nations Centre on Transnational Corporations, *World Investment Report, 1991: The Triad in Foreign Direct Investment* (New York: United Nations, 1991).

40. Stephen J. Kobrin, 'An Empirical Analysis of the Determinants of Global Integration', *Strategic Management Journal*, Vol. 12 (1991), p. 20.

41. Joseph Grunwald and Kenneth Flamm, *The Global Factory: Foreign Assembly in International Trade* (Washington, DC: The Brookings Institution, 1985).

42. Kobrin's work is particularly helpful in conceptualizing this transformation. See Kobrin, 'Beyond Geography' and 'Empirical Analysis'. For a critical account of its consequences, in the industrialized countries as well as the Third World, see Richard J. Barnet and John Cavanagh, *Global Dreams: Imperial Corporations and the New World Order* (New York: Simon & Schuster, 1994).

43. See Jane Sneddon Little, 'Intra-Firm Trade: An Update', *New England Economic Review* (May/June 1987), pp. 46–51; Mark Cassons, *Multinationals and World Trade* (London: Allen & Unwin, 1986); and the earlier but still useful study by Gerald C. Helleiner, *Intra-Firm Trade and the Developing Countries* (London: Macmillan, 1981).

44. Robert Reich, *The Work of Nations* (New York: Knopf, 1991), Chapter 25.

45. The case involved Brothers Industries Ltd, a Japanese concern assembling typewriters in Bartlett, Tennessee; and Smith Corona, a US concern doing the same off-shore. Adding another element of complexity, Hanson PLC, a British group, owned 48 per cent of Smith Corona. See Robert B. Reich, 'Dumpsters', *The New Republic* (10 June 1991), p. 9; and David E. Sanger, 'A Twist in Fair Trade Case: Japanese Charge a U.S. Rival', *New York Times* (12 August 1991), p. D-1. Sanger's story also recounts that Chrysler almost inadvertently filed an ITC claim against *itself* when it charged Japanese

firms with dumping minivans in the US market – one of the vehicles covered by the definition was made for Chrysler by Mitsubishi. The Brothers request was subsequently denied, the ITC concluding that the firm was not enough of a domestic producer to claim injury.

46. Andrew Pollack, 'Technology without Borders Raises Big Questions for US', *New York Times* (1 January 1992), p. 1.
47. Cowhey and Aronson, *Managing the World Economy*, pp. 16–17.
48. Reich points out that of the $20,000 an American consumer paid in 1991 for a Pontiac Le Mans, about $6,000 went to South Korea for parts and operations, $3,500 to Japan, $1,500 to Germany, and an additional $1,400 to various suppliers of products and services in these and other countries. Less than $8,000 of the total was paid for goods and services that were produced in the United States. See Reich, *The Work of Nations*, p. 113.
49. See Powell, 'Neither Market nor Hierarchy', and Kobrin, 'Beyond Geography'. The most extensive discussion to date of the policy implications of strategic alliances is Cowhey and Aronson, *Managing the World Economy*.
50. Powell, 'Neither Market nor Hierarchy', p. 304.
51. Kobrin, 'Beyond Geography', stresses this particular causal factor.
52. Powell, 'Neither Market nor Hierarchy'.
53. 'The Discreet Charm', p. 66, and 'Does it Matter Where You Are?', *The Economist*, 30 July 1994, p. 13.
54. Cowhey and Aronson, *Managing the World Economy*, Chapters 8–10.
55. 'In Search of Security', *The Economist*, 16 October 1993, p. 25.
56. 'Capitalism at Christmas', *Financial Times* (24 December 1993), p. 6.
57. OECD, *The Future of Social Protection* (Paris: Organisation for Economic Cooperation and Development, 1988), Table 1, p. 10.
58. As the senior economist of the National Association of Manufacturers – which is not usually closely allied with labour – recently stated: '[t]here are large numbers of temporary, part-time and contract workers out there who are counted as employed but are in reality competing for permanent jobs'. Cited in Louis Uchitelle, 'A Matter of Timing – Debate on the Fed's Latest Rate Increase Focuses on Capacity and Wage Demands', *New York Times*, 18 August 1994, p. D-16.
59. See Ferdinand Protzman, 'Rewriting the Contract for Germany's Vaunted Workers', *New York Times* (13 February 1994), p. E-5; 'Europe and the Underclass', *The Economist* (30 July 1994), pp. 21–3; Steve Coll, 'Economic Change, Social Upheaval', *Washington Post* (7 August 1994), p. A-1; and Drozdiak, 'New Global Markets'.
60. Paul McCracken, 'Costlier Labor, Fewer Jobs, Unemployment – The Crisis Continues', *Wall Street Journal* (7 January 1994), p. A-10.
61. Cited in Frank Swoboda, 'Reich Targets Several Job Programs', *Washington Post* (28 January 1994), p. A-1.
62. Cited in Geoffrey York, 'Grits Vow Radical Social Reform', *Globe and Mail* (Toronto) (1 February 1994), p. A-7.
63. Cited in 'Mr. Clarke's Manifesto', Editorial, *Financial Times* (5 May 1994), p. 17.
64. Cited in E. J. Dionne, Jr., 'Europe's Preoccupation', *Washington Post* (11 January 1994), p. A-11.

65. John Gerard Ruggie, 'International Responses to Technology: Concepts and Trends', *International Organization*, Vol. 29, No. 3 (Summer 1975), pp. 569–70. For an application to the postwar economic negotiations, see G. John Ikenberry, 'A World Economy Restored: Expert Consensus and the Anglo-American Settlement', *International Organization*, Vol. 46, No. 1 (Winter 1992), pp. 289–321.

6
Globalization, Market Civilization and Disciplinary Neoliberalism

Stephen Gill

The present world order involves a more 'liberalized' and commodified set of historical structures, driven by the restructuring of capital and a political shift to the right. This process involves the spatial expansion and social deepening of economic liberal definitions of social purpose and possessively individualist patterns of action and politics.[1] Current transformations can be related to Braudel's concept of the *'longue durée'*, in so far as the structure and language of social relations is now more conditioned by the long-term commodity logic of capital. Capitalist norms and practices pervade the *gestes répétés* of everyday life in a more systematic way than in the era of welfare-nationalism and state capitalism (from the 1930s to the 1960s), so that it may be apposite to speak of the emergence of what I call a 'market civilization'.

By market civilization, I mean a contradictory movement or set of transformative practices. The concept entails, on the one hand, cultural, ideological and mythic forms understood broadly as an ideology or myth of capitalist progress. These representations are associated with the cumulative aspects of market integration and the increasingly expansive structures of accumulation, legitimation, consumption and work. They are largely configured by the power of transnational capital. On the other hand, market civilization involves patterns of social disintegration and exclusionary and hierarchical patterns of social relations. Indeed, whilst the concept of the *longue durée* suggests the lineage and depth of market practices, it can be argued that a disturbing feature of market civilization is that it tends to generate a perspective on the world that is ahistorical, economistic, materialistic, me-oriented, short-termist and ecologically myopic. Although the governance of this market civilization is framed by the discourse of globalizing neoliberalism and expressed through the interaction of free enterprise and the state, its coordination is achieved through a combination of market discipline and the direct application of political power. In this sense, there has been a 'globalization of liberalism', involving the emergence of market civilization: neoliberal globalization is the latest phase in a process that originated before the dawning of the Enlightenment in Europe, and accelerated in the nineteenth century with the onset of industrial capitalism and the consolidation of the integral nation-state.[2]

The purpose of this chapter is to probe aspects of this situation which, following Antonio Gramsci, we call one of 'organic crisis'. This crisis involves a restructuring of prevailing ideas, institutions and material capacities that constitute historical structures of world order. As Gramsci put it: '[i]n every country the process is different, although the content is the same. And the content is the crisis of the ruling class's hegemony. ... A "crisis of authority" is spoken of ... this is precisely ... a general crisis of the state.'[3] When we introduce the issues of power and justice into our examination of neoliberal forms of globalization, what is emerging is a politics of supremacy, rather than a politics of justice or hegemony. For example, a situation of bourgeois hegemony implies the construction of an historical bloc that transcends social classes and fuses their direction into an active and largely legitimate system of rule. This implies a fusion of economic, political and cultural elements of society (state and civil society) into a political alliance or coalition that combines coercion and consent. That is, the creation of such a bloc presupposes opposition and a means for incorporating or defeating it in a process of struggle. Whilst there is no compromise by the leading class fraction on the fundamentals of the mode of production, there is nevertheless an inclusion, politically, of a significant range of interests. Subordinate classes thus carry weight within the formulation of state policy. By a situation of supremacy, I mean rule by a nonhegemonic bloc of forces that exercises dominance for a period over apparently fragmented populations, until a coherent form of opposition emerges.

In the present era, this supremacist bloc can be conceptualized as commensurate with the emergence of a market-based transnational free enterprise system, which is dependent for its conditions of existence on a range of state–civil society complexes. It is both 'outside' and 'inside' the state: it forms part of the 'local' political structures as well as serving to constitute a 'global' political and civil society. Thus, in my sketch of the power structures of contemporary global politics, with significant local variations, a transnational historical bloc is formed,

with its nucleus largely comprising elements of the G-7 state appara-
tuses and transnational capital (in manufacturing, finance and services), and associated privileged workers and smaller firms (for
example, small and middle-sized businesses linked as contractors or
suppliers, import–export businesses and service companies, such as
stockbrokers, accountants, consultancies, lobbyists, educational entrepreneurs, architects and designers).[4]

One vehicle for the emergence of this situation has been policies
that tend to subject the majority to market forces whilst preserving
social protection for the strong (for example, highly skilled workers,
corporate capital or those with inherited wealth). These policies are
cast within a neoliberal discourse of governance that stresses the
efficiency, welfare and freedom of the market, and self-actualization
through the process of consumption. However, the effects of these
policies are hierarchical and contradictory, so that it is also possible to
say that the neoliberal turn can itself be interpreted as partly a manifestation of a crisis of governmental authority and credibility, indeed
of governability, within and across a range of societies. It represents
what Gramsci called 'a rift between popular masses and ruling
ideologies' expressed in widespread 'scepticism with regard to all
theories and general formulae ... and to a form of politics which is not
simply realistic in fact ... but which is cynical in its immediate
manifestation'.[5]

Indeed, partly because aspects of this political-civilizational pattern
provoke resistance and political counter-movements, many associated
political forms are 'illiberal', authoritarian and anti-democratic in
nature. Here, prevailing class forces of transnational capital seek to
stabilize their dominance in a global situation that approximates
'passive revolution'. Passive revolution refers politically to a situation
characterized by 'dominance without leadership' or 'dictatorship
without hegemony'.[6] Where necessary, this may entail limited formal
democratization in a strategy that involves either *transformism* (the
'formation of an ever-more extensive ruling class' through incorporation and absorption of rival elites, often leading to their 'annihilation
or decapitation', for example, Salinas' Mexico), or *Caesarism* (for
example, 'where the forces in conflict balance each other in a
catastrophic manner' a dictatorial tendency prevails, perhaps as in
Yeltsin's Russia).[7]

Thus, the statement that we are in a situation of organic crisis
suggests that, whilst there has been a growth in the structural power of
capital, its contradictory consequences mean that neoliberalism has

failed to gain more than temporary dominance over our societies. To investigate this proposition further, the chapter begins with a brief methodological statement, and then examines the precise form of the politics of supremacy embodied in contemporary globalization and disciplinary neoliberalism.

Analysing power and knowledge in the global political economy

The dominant forces of contemporary globalization are constituted by a neoliberal historical bloc that practises a politics of supremacy within and across nations. The idea of an historical bloc, a concept which is one of the most fundamental innovations of Gramsci's political theory, is consistent in some ways with what Foucault called a 'discursive formation': a set of ideas and practices with particular conditions of existence, which are more or less institutionalized, but which may be only partially understood by those that they encompass.[8] Both concepts allow us to make sense of the way that practices and understandings come to pervade many areas of social and political life, in complex, perhaps unpredictable and contested, ways.

Karl Marx's concept of 'commodity fetishism'[9] (the ways in which the exchange of commodities in the money form masks the conditions and struggles associated with the production of commodities) can also be related to the content of the prevailing cultural discourse, in so far as it enables us to identify the basic social form that it presupposes: the way in which capitalist commercialization shapes outlooks, identities, time-horizons and conceptions of social space. The increasingly widespread commodification of social relations is partly reflected in the growing cultural preoccupation with surface textures and symbols rather than historical depth, and with architectural collage and immediacy, that characterizes some forms of postmodernism.[10] David Harvey notes (perhaps forgetting the potential impact of new technologies) that, for Foucault, the only irreducible element is the human body, which is the particular 'site' at which discursive repression is ultimately experienced and localized.[11] For Foucault, nevertheless, this very individualized and localized 'moment' is also where 'resistance' to repressive discourse can occur.[12]

Foucault's approach is useful in the way that it highlights the constitution and constraints of particular discursive forms, and for its emphasis on the way in which certain forms of power and knowledge serve to constitute particular aspects of civilization. However, despite its preoccupation with localized, capillary forms of power/knowledge, the Foucauldian view often lacks a convincing way of linking these forms of power to macro-structures. Foucault identifies a 'great transformation' at the start of the nineteenth century that produced a new 'historical, comparative grammar'. This was an 'archaeological rupture' in modes of thought so general that it came to bear on 'the general rules of one or several discursive formations', including, as he notes, both Ricardian and Marxian political economy.[13] Yet, how does Foucault explain this transformation? He speaks elusively of multiple determinations, but strangely missing from his explanation of this epistemological revolution is any sustained analysis of the rise of capital as a social relation, or indeed any attempt to speak of capital's power, either specifically or in general. A discussion of historical struggle over the modalities of power and knowledge is also missing.

Thus, despite the Foucauldian preoccupation with the problematic of power/knowledge as localized and institutionalized by discourse, with localized resistance through interventions in the systems of power/knowledge (in a political economy where knowledge is viewed as the principal form of production and power resource), there is little by way of an emancipatory dimension to this perspective and no adequate link between macro- and micro-structures of power in the approach. Even in a world where we might accept the postulate of multiple identities and a radical sense of discontinuity in forms of representation and human consciousness, unless our social perspective is one of the ostrich, it seems difficult to ignore the overwhelming evidence of a tremendous growth of inequality over the past two decades: income has been radically redistributed between labour and capital in an era of stagnating growth in most of the OECD nations. Indeed, the concentration of capital has proceeded very much along the lines anticipated by Marx, and thus must be central to any explanation of the present global transformation; just as the incipient forms of capitalist industrialization were central to the epistemological changes in the nineteenth century, and to the new representations of political economy, that were revealed by Foucault's archaeological excavations.

My approach, then, uses certain Foucauldian ideas, but repositions them within an historical materialist framework to sketch a model of power that is able to account for those who are included and those who are excluded or marginalized in the global political economy. Whereas Foucault tends to depict power relations in an all-encompassing way, perhaps the usefulness of his concepts of discursive formation and panopticism is more specific. They apply to some members of what John Kenneth Galbraith calls the 'culture of contentment': people who are exemplars of the commodified and normalized society *par excellence*.[14] These people are Foucault's willing victims, who hold credit cards and provide or call for the wider provision of personal information that can be manipulated in data bases.

By contrast, the marginalized are both within the societies of the culture of consumption and elsewhere in the world. They may have forms of knowledge that are not amenable to rationalization and discipline in the sense implied by Foucault, and they may not necessarily cooperate with normalizing practices. They may actively seek to develop counter-hegemonic forms of power/knowledge. South Africa, the archetypal 'panoptic' society, is an example of the exercise of this kind of power. Here, state violence and surveillance could not prevent change. Thus, Foucault represents a cry of outrage at the taming of the individual, and he inaugurates a purely defensive strategy of localized resistance. However, historical materialism goes much further in an attempt to theorize and to promote collective action to create an alternative form of society: even from within a prison, as Gramsci's notebooks show so clearly. This is why it is necessary to theorize the problem of change in local and global dimensions, and to look beyond the currently fragmented forms of opposition to neoliberal supremacy.

The meaning of 'globalization'

In this section I ask what is meant by the concept of 'globalization' as used in conventional political discourse in the OECD countries. We need to ask: 'globalization of what, where, and for whom?'

In their post-1945 phase, contemporary processes of globalization are unparalleled, at least in terms of their scale and extension: there have been massive increases in productive power and compressions of time and space. This has occurred in the context of tremendous and unprecedented population growth which began to rise significantly from the late eighteenth century onwards.[15] Indeed, according to Eric Hobsbawm, globalization is one counterpart to an unprecedented social and cultural revolution, at least in the OECD nations. Here, the peasantry as a class has been effectively eliminated; thus bringing to an end the seven or eight millennia of human history of the peasantry in a major portion of the world, as well as consolidating the trend towards a more urbanized, rationalized and marketized form of world economy. For the first time in history there is 'a single, increasingly integrated and universal world economy largely operating across state frontiers ("transnationally") and therefore increasingly across the frontiers of state ideology'.[16]

Thus, globalization is part of a broad process of restructuring of the state and civil society, and of the political economy and culture. It is also an ideology largely consistent with the world-view and political priorities of large-scale, internationally mobile forms of capital. Politically, it is consistent with the outlook of affluent minorities in the OECD and in the urban elites and new middle classes in the Third World. The current phase of economic globalization has come to be characterized increasingly not by free competition as idealized in neo-classical theory, but by *oligopolistic neoliberalism*: oligopoly and protection for the strong and a socialization of their risks, market discipline for the weak.

Of course, 'globalization' as a process is not amenable to reductionist forms of explanation, because it is many-faceted and multidimensional and involves ideas, images, symbols, music, fashions and a variety of tastes and representations of identity and community. Nevertheless, in its present mythic and ideological representations, the concept serves to reify a global economic system dominated by large institutional investors and transnational firms which control the bulk of the world's productive assets and are the principal influences in world trade and financial markets. For example, in 1992, the 300 largest transnational firms controlled about 25 per cent of the world's $20 trillion stock of productive assets; the top 600 corporations with annual sales over $1 billion accounted for over 20 per cent of the world's total value-added in manufacturing and agriculture.[17] There were about 37,000 transnational corporations by 1992, with 170,000 affiliates (up from 7,000 in the early 1970s). These firms had cumulative foreign direct investment of about $2 trillion, one third of which was controlled by the 100 largest corporations. The top 100 had global sales of $5.5 trillion, a sum roughly equal to the GNP of the United States. The 1992 value of world exports of goods and non-factor services was around $4 trillion, of which a third was intra-firm trade between parents and affiliates of transnationals.[18] Transnationals are large capital and knowledge-intensive firms that altogether employ about 72 million people, of whom 15 million are in developing countries. Most workers in transnational corporations are well paid, and tend to enjoy better working conditions than those in local firms. Directly and indirectly, transnationals account for around 5 per cent of the global workforce, although they control over 33 per cent of global assets.[19] In the financial markets, by 1994 the daily flow of foreign exchange trans-actions world-wide may have exceeded $1 trillion or 'roughly the foreign exchange holdings of all the central banks of the major indus-trialized nations'.[20] This is despite the fact that perhaps no more than 10 per cent of all financial transactions are related to real economic activity (that is, to finance trade flows or capital movements). Much of the rest is related to speculative activity, money laundering and tax evasion, as well as the offsetting of risk.

In this context, partly as a consequence of the global decline of the left and the rising power of transnational capital, political life in many parts of the world has come to be configured, to a degree, by 'neolib-eral' economic and political principles over the past two decades. This process has been hastened by the collapse of communist rule and has been articulated in different ways mainly by conservative political leaders like Margaret Thatcher, Ronald Reagan, Brian Mulroney and, more recently, by Newt Gingrich and the new cohort of Republicans in the US Congress.[21] What seems to be emerging in present-day global-ization is an intensification of the *longue durée* of commodification (the shaping of social relations by making labour and nature into exchange-able commodities) not only among the New Right and neoliberal ideo-logues, but also among the élites and emerging middle classes in the Third World.

With respect to the dominant discursive formation of our time, the neoliberal concept of 'globalization' suggests that the privatization and transnationalization of capital are either inevitable or desirable from a broad social viewpoint. In this sense, the concept of globalization exhibits positive and negative forms of ideology. A positive aspect is the equation of free competition and free exchange (global capital mobility) with economic efficiency, welfare and democracy, and a myth of virtually unlimited social progress, as represented in television advertising and other media, and in World Bank and IMF reports. A negative aspect is how neoliberal market forces are often said to have marginalized non-market alternatives, especially from the political left. Thus, some equate globalization with the unfolding of a business Hegelian myth of the capitalist market ('the global information stan-dard') as the Absolute Idea: global financial markets are said to be 'civilizing', although implacable and gigantic, forces for good govern-ment.[22] Some equate neoliberal globalization with the 'end of history', although, as implied in his invocation of Nietzsche's dispirited and pathetic 'Last Man', for Francis Fukuyama the victory of liberalism is a hollow one, since the post-communist Last Man, for whom liberalism

is the only global alternative, is doomed to boredom: a morbid repeti-
tiveness simulates death; a condition that may be palliated by satellite
television showing World Cup soccer.[23]

None the less, as Galbraith has shown, the privileges of the politically
powerful and economically strong have been reinforced in the OECD
nations since the late 1960s, often to the detriment of the vast majority
of the population.[24] The neoliberal shift in government policies has
tended to subject the majority of the population to the power of market
forces whilst preserving social protection for the strong. In the Third
World, the counterpart to Galbraith's 'culture of contentment' are urban
elites and ruling and emerging middle classes who benefit from the
consumption patterns and incorporation into financial and production
circuits of transnational capital.[25] Recent growth in enclave residential
development, private provision of security and private insurance and
health care suggests that access to what were often considered to be
public goods under socialized provision is now increasingly privatized,
individualized and hierarchical in nature. More broadly, there has been a
transformation of the socialization of risk towards a privatization and
individualization of risk assessment and insurance provision. Nevertheless, this process is hierarchical: for example, burdens of risk are
redistributed, marketized and individualized (for example, associated with
illness, old age or pensions) as opposed to being fully socialized through
collective and public provision.[26]

Despite enormous increases in global output and population since
the Second World War, a significant polarization of income and of life
chances has been central to the restructuring process of the last 20
years. For the 800 million or so affluent consumers in the OECD, there
is a counterpart number starving in the Third World, with one billion
more that have no clean drinking water or sufficient food to provide
basic nutrition.[27] More than half of Africa's population lives in
absolute poverty. In the 1980s, the income of two-thirds of African
workers fell below the poverty line. A disproportionate burden of
adjustment to harsher circumstances has fallen on women and children and weaker members of society, such as the old and the dis-
abled.[28] Many of these people also live in war-torn societies, where
huge quantities of cheap mass-produced conventional weapons have
accumulated, including over 100 million landmines: 'weapons that
never miss'. One million landmines exploded under Third World
victims in the last 15 years.[29]

A re-emergence of serious global public health problems may be indicated by the growth in contagious diseases once thought to have been

conquered in the march of medical progress (for example, cholera or anthrax), as well as in diseases associated with environmental degradation and pollution (for example, asthma, allergies, and new viruses such as HIV). During the decades since the Second World War life expectancy increased steadily throughout the world. This process has now apparently gone into reverse in a number of countries (notably in the former communist-ruled nations of Eastern Europe):

> [t]he resurgence of epidemics is a crucial indicator of the state of our world, not only in terms of human suffering, but also in terms of development more generally. It implies the breakdown of the social controls that usually prevent such diseases, hygiene, nutrition, resistance to infection, immunization programmes, housing.[30]

The price of many medical products marketed by transnational pharmaceutical firms has risen and the relaxation of trade barriers, and other market forms of restriction and regulation, has made it simpler to dump expired or unsafe medicines in parts of the Third World.[31] Globally, public health and educational provisions have been reduced, partly because of neoliberal structural adjustment pressures on most governments to exercise monetary restraint, cut budgets, repay debts, balance their international trade, devalue their currencies, remove subsidies and trade and investment barriers and, in so doing, restore international creditworthiness and thereby extend the market civilization globally. Such pressures emanate from agents in the global financial markets and from international organizations like the World Bank and IMF, as well as from within these societies. In many parts of the Third World and in the former Soviet Union, economic liberalization has been welcomed as a means of reforming the old, unaccountable political order.

From a socio-historical perspective, then, a remarkable feature of contemporary world society is how more and more aspects of everyday life in OECD nations have come to be premised upon or pervaded by market values, representations and symbols, as time and distance are apparently shrunk by scientific-technological innovation, the hyper-mobility of financial capital and some types of information flows. Commercialization has configured more aspects of family life, religious practice, leisure pursuits and aspects of nature. Indeed, processes of commodification have progressively encompassed aspects of life that had been viewed as inalienable.[32] Increasingly, patent rights over human genes and tissue, plants, seeds and animal hybrids are obtained routinely by pharmaceutical and agricultural corporations, including the DNA of 'endangered peoples' (that is, aboriginal or native peoples). These private 'intellectual' property rights are being internationalized and extended into the legal regimes of the world through the new World Trade Organization. Such developments are taking place when, in much of the OECD, there has been little political debate over the repercussions of biotechnology and genetic innovation, to say nothing of the privatization of life-forms.[33] At the same time, large numbers of people are almost totally marginalized from enjoyment of the fruits of global production.

In this sense, the 'social question' is posed anew today, and, as in the nineteenth century, it is posed both locally and globally. Indeed, this tendency is inherent in the expansion of capital which serves to disintegrate and to transform the existing social order. Capital tends to supplant the old with an order that is radically new and historically unprecedented. Thus, social taboos are overcome and capital exerts growing influence over the most sensitive rituals of different civilizations (provided that they offer opportunities for profit):

[t]he American way of death has cast its pall over Europe. Service Corporation International, the US's largest burial business, spent £306m on buying 15 per cent of the UK market last year and is now paying FFr2.05bn to take a 30 per cent share of French funerals. But there is sound business strategy behind this apparent megalomania. Funeral parlours offer vast potential economies of scale. Centrally locating hearses, embalmers and attendants ... and there are added benefits from bulk buying. ... Tax and accounting differentials mean the deal will enhance earnings even before operating improvements. ... Competition and monopolies issues have restricted further US acquisitions while a flat death rate has constrained organic growth. A fragmented European market provides a vast new customer base. There is the risk that xenophobia might provide the kiss of death for such deals. But its Australian operations have demonstrated few barriers to international undertaking.[34]

In this quintessential representation of the ideology of transnational neoliberalism, even the rites of death and burial are associated with profit. Megalomania is conflated with sound business strategy and equated with the maximization of efficiency through the exploitation of economies of scale. These have been inhibited in the United States because of the government's anti-monopoly legislation; and, not least, because people are not dying in sufficient numbers. At least in the former Soviet bloc, death rates have risen dramatically since the collapse of communist rule. Nevertheless, this author worries at the risk to the venture posed by the cultural particularities of other countries, which are viewed as xenophobic barriers to the expansion of capital.

To recapitulate: the current phase of globalization is part of a social and cultural transformation in which links between work, effort, savings and life-chances (and death) more generally are reified through ideological representations commensurate with a growth in the power of capital. Social interaction, work patterns and leisure become increasingly monetized, marketized and abstracted; not necessarily in ways that ordinary people cannot understand. At the most obvious transactional level, for example, most citizens in Latin America and Asia can calculate complex financial transactions, such as the interplay between commodity prices, inflation rates, exchange rates and the nominal rate of interest. In principle, such calculations are no more complex than those made in financial dealing rooms in London, Singapore, Tokyo and New York. However, the calculations of the former are more likely to be matters of immediate survival, indeed of life or death, for the individuals concerned, and are not linked to extravagant bonuses. In this way, the health/sickness/death of the 'market' is globally incorporated, at the micro-level of the individual, as it were, into popular consciousness and action; that is, into 'the structures of everyday life'.[35]

By implication, this situation involves methods by which patterns of privilege can be defended from encroachment and possible expropriation by those who have been subordinated and marginalized. In the terminology of Fred Hirsch, privileged consumption and production patterns of a small section of the world's population are, in effect, the 'positional goods' of the global political economy, which the contemporary systems of policing and military power are increasingly designed to protect.[36]

The following two sections elaborate other dimensions of power associated with the globalization of neoliberal politico-economic forms.

'Disciplinary' neoliberalism

In social theory, the term 'discipline' is used in a number of slightly different ways. Max Weber defined the concept of discipline as follows:

'[t]hose who obey are not necessarily obedient or an especially large mass, nor are they necessarily united in a specific locality. What is decisive for discipline is that obedience of a plurality of men is rationally uniform.'[37] 'Rational uniformity' can be observed in classes, status groups and political parties, which are all phenomena of the distribution of power in society: 'discipline' is, therefore, a form of the exercise of power within social organizations. For Emile Durkheim, (self-) discipline, or the restraint of one's inclinations, is a means to develop reasoned behaviour and thus foster the moral growth of the healthy personality: unregulated emotions can produce *anomie*.[38] For Michel Foucault, 'discipline' is sometimes used in ways that approximate Weber and Durkheim, but generally the term is used to indicate both a modernist framework of understanding that underpins a terrain of knowledge, and a system of social and individual control: '[t]he Enlightenment, which discovered the liberties, also invented the disciplines.'[39]

The concept of discipline advanced here combines macro- and micro-dimensions of power: the structural power of capital; the ability to promote uniformity and obedience within parties, cadres, organizations and especially in class formations associated with transnational capital (perhaps involving self-discipline in the Durkheimian sense); and particular instances of disciplinary power in a Foucauldian sense. Thus, 'disciplinary neoliberalism' is a concrete form of structural and behavioural power; it combines the structural power of capital with 'capillary power' and 'panopticism'.[40] In other words, neoliberal forms of discipline are not necessarily universal nor consistent, but they are bureaucratized and institutionalized, and they operate with different degrees of intensity across a range of 'public' and 'private' spheres. In this sense, discipline is both a transnational and a local dimension of power, and these dimensions of discipline are one dimension of the supremacist transnational historical bloc that I have sketched in the previous section of this chapter.

New constitutionalism and global governance

Disciplinary neoliberalism is institutionalized at the macro-level of power in the quasi-legal restructuring of state and international political forms: the 'new constitutionalism'. This discourse of global economic governance is reflected in the conditionality policies of the Bretton Woods organizations, quasi-constitutional regional arrangements such as NAFTA or Maastricht, and the multilateral regulatory framework of the new World Trade Organization. It is reflected in the global trend towards independent central banks, with macroeconomic policy prioritizing the 'fight against inflation'.[41]

New constitutionalism is a macro-political dimension of the process whereby the nature and purpose of the public sphere in the OECD has been redefined in a more privatized and commodified way, with its economic criteria defined in a more globalized and abstract frame of reference. The accountability of governments to 'markets' is mainly to material forces and the sentiments of investment managers in the bond markets and to the conditionality of the Bretton Woods organizations. It has grown in a period of fiscal crisis and in accordance with the growing salience of 'new constitutionalist' discourses of global governance. The new constitutionalism can be defined as the political project of attempting to make transnational liberalism, and if possible liberal democratic capitalism, the sole model for future development. It is therefore intimately related to the rise of market civilization.

New constitutionalist proposals are often implicit rather than explicit. Nevertheless, they emphasize market efficiency, discipline and confidence; economic policy credibility and consistency; and limitations on democratic decision-making processes. Proposals imply or mandate the insulation of key aspects of the economy from the influence of politicians or the mass of citizens by imposing, internally and externally, 'binding constraints' on the conduct of fiscal, monetary, trade and investment policies.[42] Ideology and market power are not enough to ensure the adequacy of neoliberal restructuring. It is worth noting that the United States is the least likely of any country to submit to such constraints, although its leaders insist that they be applied systematically to other states. None the less, even the autonomy of the United States, Japan and the European Union is constrained in matters of macroeconomic policy by the globalization of finance and production. Smaller and less self-sufficient states tend to be correspondingly more sensitive and vulnerable to global financial pressures.

In effect, new constitutionalism confers privileged rights of citizenship and representation on corporate capital, whilst constraining the democratization process that has involved struggles for representation for hundreds of years. Central, therefore, to new constitutionalism is the imposition of discipline on public institutions, partly to prevent national interference with the property rights and entry and exit options of holders of mobile capital with regard to particular political jurisdictions. These initiatives are also linked to efforts to define appropriate policy, partly by strengthening surveillance mechanisms of international organizations and private agencies, such as the bond raters. Governments in need of external financing are forced to provide data. One reason for this is to make domestic economic and political agents and trends more transparent to global supervisors in the IMF or Bank for International Settlements (BIS), as well as to the increasingly influential private bond-rating agencies such as Moody's and Standards and Poor. Indeed, initiatives based on new constitutionalist surveillance assumptions were launched at the G-7 Summit in Halifax, Nova Scotia, in June 1995.[43] The G-7 leaders opted to strengthen surveillance mechanisms under the aegis of the IMF, World Bank and BIS, after the failure of existing methods of surveillance was revealed by the Mexican financial crisis of 1994–95.

By contrast, traditional notions of constitutionalism are associated with political rights, obligations and freedoms, and procedures that give institutional form to the state. Constitutions define, describe and outline the rights and obligations of citizens; common policy-making institutions with authority over the entire polity; the limits to the scope of action of these institutions; and, of course, enforcement mechanisms and ratification and amendment procedures.[44]

Turning to recent examples of neoliberal forms of regionalization, there is a difference in kind between North America and Western Europe. Here, I represent both examples more as projects than as exemplars of the final crystallization of neoliberal dominance. For example, questions of European unification have been made more complex not only by German unification, but also by the accession of new Nordic members and the prospect of further enlargement to encompass former communist-ruled nations. NAFTA is also undergoing considerable turbulence and contestation, not only within each member nation, but also more broadly in Latin America.

The European Union has citizenship for individuals from member countries and has partly accountable mechanisms for negotiation, ratification, amendment and enforcement, and for incorporating and weighting the interests of the smaller European nations. However, although social and welfare policy and regulation have been institutionalized in the EU since the Treaty of Rome, for example with respect to migrant workers (Article 51), equal treatment of men and women (Article 119), protection of workers (Article 118) and the health and safety of workers (Article 118 and 118a of the Single European Act), implementation has been patchy despite the influence of trades unions, some political parties and, in some cases, the European Court for Human Rights. In large part, this inconsistency has been the result of employer opposition. A further reason is the development of unaccountable intergovernmental agencies.[45] Nevertheless, the political centre of gravity of European political economy has recently tilted towards definitions which reflect a financial and free trade conception: that is, a neoliberal view of Europe, as opposed to the more social democratic idea of 'social Europe'.[46] This is reflected in many of the Maastricht provisions, especially the proposals for a largely unaccountable European central banking system, and fiscal/public debt provisions intended to be binding on all future governments in the EU.

North American arrangements are more hierarchical and asymmetrical, understood both in inter-state terms and in terms of the class structures of each nation. NAFTA is premised upon a low level of political institutionalization and a hub-and-spoke configuration of power, with the United States at the centre of a continentalized political economy. This is even more the case with the Caribbean Basin Initiative, which can unilaterally be terminated by the United States.[47] The United States has negotiated the implicit right to monitor and control large areas of Canadian political life in the US–Canada Free Trade Agreement. The US–Canada Agreement specifies that each side has to notify the other 'party' by advanced warning, of *intended* federal or provincial government policy that *might* affect the other side's interests, as defined by the agreement.[48] Because of its huge economic integration with the United States, this is a situation which necessarily affects the vast majority of Canadian economic activity, but not vice versa. Thus, Canadian governments no longer can contemplate an independent or interventionist economic strategy. In both NAFTA and the US–Canada Agreement there are no transnational citizenship rights other than those accorded to capital, and these are defined to favour US-registered companies. Finally, NAFTA can be amended only by agreement of all signatories. Whilst these arrangements place binding constraints on the policies of Canada and Mexico, to a certain degree, the United States retains constitutional autonomy and important prerogatives: its trade law is allowed to override treaty provisions, notwithstanding the rights of redress that are available to participants through the dispute settlement mechanisms.[49]

In other words, the US government is using access to its vast market as a lever of power, linked to a reshaping of the international business climate, by subjecting other nations to the disciplines of the new constitutionalism, whilst largely refusing to submit to them itself, partly for strategic reasons. Indeed, one of the arguments expressed by former

European Union President Jacques Delors in favour of comprehensive West European economic and monetary union was strategic: to offset economic unilateralism from the United States, in matters of money and trade.

Thus, an American-centred global neoliberalism mandates a separation of politics and economics in ways that may narrow political representation and constrain democratic social choice in many parts of the world. New constitutionalism, which ratifies this separation, may have become the *de facto* discourse of governance for most of the global political economy. This discourse involves a hierarchy of pressures and constraints on government autonomy that vary according to the size, economic strength, form of state and civil society, and prevailing national and regional institutional capabilities, as well as the degree of integration into global capital and money markets.

Panopticism and the coercive face of the neoliberal state

The panopticon is a word for 'sees all', which was coined from the Greek by Jeremy Bentham and popularized by Foucault.[50] We can define panopticism as 'a dystopia latent in modernity: the possibility of developing a system of control which reduces the individual to a manipulable and relatively inert commodity'.[51] If it were ever to be achieved, a condition of panopticism would ensure 'a surveillance which would be both global and individualising whilst at the same time keeping the individuals under observation [through the illumination of space]'.[52] Foucault's use of the term suggests that it is possible to render the human condition obedient and acquiescent to the various forms of observation, enquiry and experimentation that are demanded by scientific progress and social order in what he calls the 'disciplinary society': something which, according to Blanchot, Foucault denounced and ultimately identified with Nazism.[53]

Use of panoptic practices antedates modern bureaucratic systems and technical innovations and goes back at least as far as the administrative, military and labour control systems of ancient imperial China, or, more recently, the Ottoman empire. Clearly, there can be no all-seeing eye of power. There can only be mechanisms of surveillance that are intended to maximize discipline in the Weberian sense noted above. Indeed, these mechanisms of surveillance may be more intensive and important for the reproduction of the neoliberal transnational historic bloc amongst its ruling classes and élites, than among subordinate elements in society. Some suggest that there is evidence of a recent tendency towards increasing use of technologically sophisticated surveillance capabilities by private firms and the state, whilst not denying that many new technologies are socially empowering, liberating and decentralizing in nature.[54] However, it is crucial to stress that a technological 'revolution' does not necessarily entail or indeed imply a basic change in social relations, for example in the relations of exploitation and alienation in capitalism.

Contemporary surveillance practices by corporate and governmental bureaucracies are nevertheless important. Populations are constructed statistically as manipulable entities in databases: that is, they are monitored and objectified for purposes of social control or profit, for example in the huge private data corporations that specialize in commercially useful information about individuals and households.[55] Some OECD social security ministries have shifted to more rigorous monitoring of clients, with some introducing 'workfare' programmes (analogous to Bentham's management schemes for paupers and prisoners[56]) and ensuring the 'transparency' and 'inspectability' of claims and activities. More recently, because of restructuring of production, increased migration and the growth of transnational criminal networks, policing changes have involved reorganized surveillance capacities. In this process, it is worth noting that the mobility of capital is not matched by a corresponding mobility or freedom of labour. Indeed, new OECD citizenship rights are increasingly regulated by a commodity logic and sold by governments to raise revenue and attract investment and, if possible, skills.[57] Collection of information about populations may also be used to discipline individuals via sanctions or inducements: such as the denial or provision of private credit, health and insurance, or genetic testing and biological monitoring of workers to identify and perhaps exclude those who are unfit or potentially costly to corporate health plans.

One possible explanation for these surveillance tendencies is that pressures are placed upon the state by the interaction between fiscal crises in local, regional and national governments (especially since the mid-1970s), and the globalization of financial markets and the mobility of transnational corporations. Driven to raise operating finance on the more globalized financial markets, governments are pressured into providing a business climate judged attractive by global standards in order to win and retain foreign direct investment.

Such developments have also accompanied major restructurings of tax systems in the OECD and elsewhere: these have reduced marginal tax rates on capital and high-income earners and have attempted to broaden the tax base, in order to create a more 'activist tax state' with increasingly regressive taxes. Traditional forms of state intervention in the economy to promote redistribution have declined, and socialization of risk for the majority of the population has been eroding. Indeed, on the basis of a comprehensive global survey, Sven Steinmo suggests that the Swedish case is most striking, since it signals a massive shift away from the redistributive welfare-nationalist form of state in a neoliberal direction.[58] As noted above, in the 1980s this has also gone with an emphasis on the restructuring of the state through the tactics of marketization and privatization. Governments have had to pay increased attention to collecting tax revenues and raising cash through privatization, in an age where the ideology (but not the reality) of the balanced budget has come to prevail in economic rhetoric. According to an OECD study, these developments have allowed companies to allocate debt and investment strategies according to varying state policies.[59]

In sum, governments in the OECD and elsewhere have invested heavily in new technologies to create and manipulate databases for tax collection, social security, immigration, social control and criminal enforcement.[60] Thus, disciplinary neoliberalism, under conditions of increasing fiscal crisis, may tend to make aspects of civil society and the state form more panoptic, and indeed coercive, in nature.

Indeed, neoliberal forms of discipline are hierarchical both in the sense of social classes and in terms of inter-state politics. At the heart of the global economy there is an internationalization of authority and governance that involves not only international organizations (such as the BIS, IMF and World Bank) and transnational firms, but also private consultancies and private bond-rating agencies which act, as it were, as arbiters of the supply of capital for public finance and corporate investment, partly acting as 'private makers of global public policy'.[61] I call this politico-economic structure and the internationalization of authority that it entails, the 'G-7 nexus'. It tends to be represented in everyday political discourse and the mass media as an abstract, hyper-rational and largely uncontested set of social forces and processes. A technocratic representation of IMF surveillance and conditionality reinforces this, epistemologically and ideologically.

Discussing the bond-raters and allocation mechanisms in the capital markets, Timothy J. Sinclair notes that 'more abstract investment standards will establish greater potential for ties between domestic and foreign interests ... [perhaps] reinforcing the impression that investment is a neutral technical activity, rather than a struggle for resources between competing societal interests'.[62] Indeed, in 1995, following the

Mexican financial crisis, a draconian economic adjustment, indeed a 'shock therapy' programme, was undertaken under United States, IMF and World Bank supervision. It provoked the worst Mexican recession since the 1930s and a massive rise in unemployment and social misery. The United States, the IMF and a less than unanimous G-7 tended to represent the package as the only way in which Mexico could repair its tattered credit rating and restore its credibility with foreign investors. This representation was also used later to justify the attempt by the G-7 nations to increase the surveillance and economic veto power of the IMF with respect to its indebted Third World membership.[63]

Neoliberal contradictions and the movement of history

Neoliberal forms of rationality are largely instrumental and are concerned with finding the best means to achieve calculated ends. For neoliberals, primary motivations are understood in a possessively individualistic framework. Motivation is provided by fear and greed, and is reflected in the drive to acquire more security and more goods. Yet, any significant attempt to widen this pattern of motivation would entail an intensification of existing accumulation and consumption patterns, tending to deplete or to destroy the eco-structures of the planet, making everyone less secure and perhaps more vulnerable to disease (even the powerful). Thus, if North American patterns of accumulation and consumption were to be significantly extended, for example to China, the despoliation of the global eco-structure would be virtually assured. Even so, the central ideological message and social myth of neoliberalism is that such a possibility is both desirable and attainable for all: in so far as limitations are recognized, this is at best through a redefinition of the concept of 'sustainable development' so as to make it consistent with the continuation of existing patterns of accumulation and consumption.[64]

Whilst existing patterns of consumption have a more or less exclusive quality, depending on the form and place of consumption, their very existence requires that public goods be provided locally and globally so as to underpin production, consumption and exchange processes. Governments throughout the world are required to regulate and compensate for the social, economic and ecological problems attendant upon existing patterns of consumption and production. This means that the state must find ways to sustain the tax base and to police and regulate the market society. This may prove difficult when prevailing economic ideology and the organization of the world economy validate, on the one hand, cuts in public expenditure and reducing the scope of state action, and, on the other, a burgeoning black or informal economy and a tendency for organized criminal syndicates to grow in strength.[65] Nevertheless, as new constitutionalist arrangements suggest, globally to extract surplus, capital depends on national and global public goods provision.

Therefore, the logic of neoliberalism is contradictory: it promotes global economic integration (and hence the need for global public goods), but also generates depletion of resources and the environment, as well as undermining the traditional tax base and the capacity to provide public goods. Indeed, neoclassical economic thinking, which lies at the heart of neoliberal discourse, tends to ignore, with impunity, ecological constraints such as the laws of thermodynamics.[66] Moreover, neoliberal macroeconomic policies, aligned to the ideology of the competition state, may generate a more conflictual inter-state dynamic that may prolong economic stagnation for the vast majority of the world's population, through, for example, competitive austerity and beggarthy-neighbour currency depreciation.[67]

According to Walter Benjamin, within myth the passage of time takes the form of predestination, such that human control is denied.[68] Thus, the operation of the neoliberal myth of progress in market civilization is intended implicitly to engender a fatalism that denies the construction of alternatives to the prevailing order, and thus, negates the idea that history is made by collective human action. Whilst it might be argued that the generation of such a myth is central to the hegemony of capital, we might recast it in Polanyian terms: neoliberalism holds out the reified prospect of a 'stark utopia'.[69] As Adam Smith intimated in *The Theory of Moral Sentiments*, and as Polanyi pointed out, a pure market system is a utopian abstraction and any attempt to construct it fully would require an immensely authoritarian application of political power through the state.[70] One reason for this is the recent tendency for exploitation to intensify, in part because of the apparent domination of production and the state by finance. This would raise doubts about the viability of a minimal or 'night-watchman' state, as portrayed in liberal ideology.[71] Indeed, it can be shown that many of the neoliberal forms of state have been authoritarian. In some cases, this has involved considerable coercive power to destroy opposition or eliminate the possibility of a third way: such as in Chile in 1973, or in post-communist Eastern Europe.

Restructuring along market-driven lines tends to generate a deepening of social inequality, a rise in the rate and intensity of the exploitation of labour, growth in social polarization, gender inequality, a widespread sense of social and economic insecurity and, not least, pervasive disenchantment with conventional political practice. Such a situation may also open the door to the appeals of extremist political movements, whilst more broadly giving rise to resistance and counter-mobilization. Indeed, in the context of the growing salience of biological discourses concerning social life, one might suggest that there may be a social Darwinist dimension to the neoliberal world order.[72] This proposition is supported by evidence of the renaissance of fascism and atavistic forms of nationalism.

Thus, whilst the restructuring of forms of state along neoliberal lines has apparently accelerated in recent years, there are indications that remaking state and society along these lines lacks moral credibility, authority and legitimacy. This is partly because the rule and the burdens of market forces are most frequently imposed hierarchically on the weaker states and social actors, whilst the more powerful receive tax write-offs, state subsidies and other prerogatives. However, one should be careful not to overstate the degree to which this represents the universalization of a new form of world order. In fact, the very existence of the neoliberal structural adjustment programmes of the World Bank and of IMF stabilization measures shows that economic liberalization has a very long way to go before it can be considered the new development paradigm for the majority of the world's population.

Indeed, such policies are contested even within the ranks of the G-7, and the conflicts between the different models of capitalist development this entails can be expected to continue. One reason for G-7 conflicts is that the socio-economic systems of Germany and Japan are less attuned to pure market forces. For example, in Japan, important political forces seem to have adopted the Hirschian view that the very operation of capitalist market forces depends upon their restraint, and on the maintenance of traditional systems of obligations and institutions that cause people to behave *as if* they respect the law, and accept not only the contractual but also the customary nature of market transactions.[73]

Thus, we should not conflate propaganda with history. History has not 'ended' and alternatives are created politically. In *The Great Transformation*, Polanyi argued that a 'double movement' of free economic and self-protecting social and political forces operated to configure global politics in the 1930s.[74] The New Deal, fascism, Nazism and populist movements of left and right reflected opposition to global *laissez-faire* and the power of financial capital. For Gramsci, the 1930s involved the death throes of the old order and the struggle of a new order to be born.[75] By analogy, one can suggest that today we may be in, or entering into, a period of a new 'double movement': one that certainly manifests many morbid symptoms. The coming years will probably involve a substantial intensification of political conflict. It seems likely that this will incorporate the contradictory political tendencies associated with, on the one hand, democratic and progressive forces, and, on the other, the growing forces of reaction, such as the resurgence of fascism and certain forms of fundamentalist politics or criminal elements in world politics. Indeed, a new double movement would be different in character from that of the 1930s, not least because its concerns would be more global and wide-ranging in nature, and might include nuclearism, the proliferation of conventional weapons, ecology, gender questions, the globalization of organized crime and the re-regulation of new global information and financial grids.

Put differently, there is a growing contradiction between the tendency towards the globality and universality of capital in the neoliberal form and the particularity of the legitimation and enforcement of its key exploitative relations by the state. Whereas capital tends towards universality, it cannot operate outside or beyond the political context, and involves planning, legitimation and the use of coercive capacities by the state. This forms the key substantive problem for a theory of international relations, at least as seen from an historical materialist perspective. In this context, one of the main tasks of political economy today is to understand and theorize the possibilities for the transformation of these dimensions of world order, in the context of consciousness, culture and material life.

This chapter has highlighted part of the terrain of struggle that will configure the politics of the emerging world order, which it has defined as a politics of *supremacy* rather than hegemony. It can also be read as part of a research agenda on the material and mental limits, contradictions and political opportunities for counter-supremacist forces. These seek to redefine questions of international relations by drawing on critical perspectives on epistemology, ontology, theory and practice, by highlighting the contestability of, and contradictions in, the practice of neoliberal discourse.[76] The chapter may contribute to a wider emancipatory project that seeks to use new forms and modes of knowledge to transcend the dominant economism and reductionism of our time, and to contribute to the possibility for new intersubjectivities and intellectual and material networks. The motivation for this is that a critical and historicist reading of present trends suggests that, in the absence of major changes in lifestyle, consumption patterns and public goods provisions, the current configuration of world order and neoliberal forms of global governance is unsustainable.

Finally, this chapter has posed the implicit question whether the phrase 'neoliberal market civilization' is an oxymoron, in so far as the concept of civilization implies not only a pattern of society, but also an active historical process that fosters a more humanized, literate and civil way of life, involving social well-being on a broad and inclusive basis. Looking beyond the confines of this chapter, which can only scratch the surface of a huge and complex set of questions and problems, the key world order problem for the future might be said to involve the creation of a peaceful and tolerant coexistence between differentiated civilizational forms, in ways that provide material and political conditions of high quality. This requires effort to redress the vast inequalities of the present age and a double democratization of forms of state and civil society in both global and local dimensions of political life.

Acknowledgement

I would like to thank Randy Persaud for valuable comments on a first draft of this chapter, and the Canadian SSHRC for research support.

Notes

1. Stephen Gill, 'Political Economy and Structural Change: Globalizing Elites in the Emerging World Order', in Yoshikazu Sakamoto (ed.), *Global Transformation: Challenges to the State System* (Tokyo: United Nations University Press, 1994), pp. 169–99.
2. Fernand Braudel, *The Structures of Everyday Life: The Limits of the Possible*, Volume I of *Civilisation and Capitalism, 15th–18th Centuries*, trans. S. Reynolds (New York: Harper and Row, 1981). Whether this process is associated with a condition of becoming or being civilized is for the reader to decide.
3. Antonio Gramsci, *Selections from the Prison Notebooks of Antonio Gramsci*, ed. and trans. Q. Hoare and G. Nowell Smith (New York: International Publishers, 1971), p. 210.
4. For an elaboration of this historical bloc, see Stephen Gill and David Law, 'Global Hegemony and the Structural Power of Capital', *International Studies Quarterly*, Vol. 36, No. 4 (1989), pp. 475–99.

5. Gramsci, *Prison Notebooks*, p. 276.
6. *Ibid.*, pp. 105–6, 120 and 114. A situation of passive revolution either involves stalemate between opposed blocs of forces, or is when bourgeois class forces have not sufficiently developed or advanced politically for their leadership to take a legitimate, consensual and hegemonic form. Thus, the power of the state and authoritarian politics prevail in the process of socioeconomic restructuring. For an interpretation of the USSR using these concepts, see Kees van der Pijl, 'Soviet Socialism and Passive Revolution', in Stephen Gill (ed.), *Gramsci, Historical Materialism and International Relations* (Cambridge: Cambridge University Press, 1993), pp. 237–58. For an application to India, see Partha Chatterjee, *Nationalist Thought and the Colonial World: A Derivative Discourse* (London: Zed Books, 1986).
7. Gramsci, *Prison Notebooks*, pp. 58 and 219. On transformism, see pp. 58ff. On progressive and reactionary forms of Caesarism, see pp. 219–23.
8. Michel Foucault, *The Archaeology of Knowledge*, trans. A. M. Sheridan Smith (London: Tavistock, 1972), pp. 31–40.
9. Karl Marx, *Capital, Volume I*, trans. Ben Fowkes (Harmondsworth: Penguin, 1976).
10. Examples of this tendency include the British 'heritage' industry and theme-parks, theme-park casinos and wax museums in the United States and elsewhere, and architectural forms that create collage fantasies that annihilate any meaningful sense of history. See Umberto Eco, *Travels in Hyperreality* (New York: Harcourt Brace, 1986), pp. 1–58.
11. David Harvey, *The Condition of Postmodernity* (Oxford: Blackwell, 1989), pp. 39–65.
12. 'It's true that during these extraordinary events [May 1968, at the Sorbonne] I often asked: but why isn't Foucault here? Thus granting him his power of attraction and underscoring the empty place he should have been occupying.' Maurice Blanchot, 'Michel Foucault as I Imagine Him', in Michel Foucault and Blanchot, *Foucault/Blanchot*, trans. J. Mehlman and B. Massumi (New York: Zone Books, 1990), p. 63.
13. Foucault, *Archaeology of Knowledge*, pp. 176–7.
14. John Kenneth Galbraith, *The Culture of Contentment* (New York: Houghton Mifflin, 1992).
15. Braudel, *The Structures of Everyday Life*, pp. 31–101.
16. Eric Hobsbawm, *The Age of Extremes* (Toronto: Penguin Books, 1994), pp. 287–343.
17. 'A Survey of Multinationals', *The Economist* (27 March 1993).
18. United Nations Conference on Trade and Development, *World Investment Report* (Geneva: UN, 1993).
19. United Nations Research Institute for Social Development, *States of Disarray: The Social Effects of Globalization* (Geneva: UNRISD, 1995), p. 154.
20. Morris Miller, 'Where is Global Interdependence Taking Us?, *Mimeo*, p. 12, citing BIS statistics. Subsequently published with same title in *Futures*, Vol. 27, No. 2 (1995), pp. 125–44.
21. Neoliberalism is also associated strongly with some neoclassical political economists, especially in traditions established during and after the Second World War at the LSE (by F. A. von Hayek) and later at the University of Chicago (by Harry Johnson and Milton Friedman), as well as by postwar

political scientists at the Virginia public choice school (inspired by James Buchanan and William Niskanen).

22. Walter Wriston, *The Twilight of Sovereignty: How the Information Revolution is Transforming Our World* (New York; Scribner's, 1992).

23. 'For most of post-historical Europe, the World Cup has replaced military competition as the chief outlet for nationalist striving to be number one. As Kojève once said, his goal was to re-establish the Roman Empire, but this time as a multinational soccer team': Francis Fukuyama, *The End of History and the Last Man* (New York: Avon Books, 1992), p. 319.

24. Galbraith, *The Culture of Contentment*.

25. On Latin America, see Celso Furtado, 'Transnationalisation and Monetarism', *International Journal of Political Economy*, Vol. 17, No. 1 (1987), pp. 15–44; on Africa, see Fantu Cheru, *The Silent Revolution: Debt, Development and Democracy* (London: Zed Books, 1989). On the somewhat different conditions in East Asia, see Frederic C. Deyo, *The Political Economy of the New Asian Industrialism* (Ithaca, NY: Cornell University Press, 1987).

26. The IMF and World Bank have recently pressed for the privatization of public pension provision, especially in the Third World, to create larger local capital markets. See, for example, Estelle James, 'Averting the Old-Age Crisis', *Finance and Development*, Vol. 32, No. 2 (1995), pp. 4–7, and the rest of the special issue of this World Bank/IMF journal.

27. Of course, there has been substantial improvement in basic living conditions. The UNDP showed that nearly 70 per cent of world population lived in 'abysmal' conditions in 1960; by 1992, only 32 per cent suffered such conditions. Global GNP rose seven-fold since 1945 from $3 trillion to $22 trillion. World population more than doubled from 2.5 billion to 5.5 billion; per capita income more than tripled. See United Nations Development Programme, *Human Development Report, 1994* (New York: Oxford University Press, 1994). However, in this report, UNDP adds, 'we still live in a world where a fifth of the developing world's population goes hungry every night ... and a third lives in abject poverty – at such a margin of human existence that words simply fail to describe it – the richest billion people command 60 times the income of the poorest billion. ... Poor nations and rich are afflicted by growing human distress ... food production must triple if people are to be adequately fed, but the resource base for sustainable agriculture is eroding' (pp. 1–2).

28. UNRISD, *States of Disarray*, pp. 110–26.

29. *Ibid.*, pp. 48 and 114.

30. *Ibid.*, p. 26.

31. *Ibid.*, pp. 26–7.

32. Herbert Gottweis, 'Genetic Engineering, Democracy, and the Politics of Identity', *Social Text*, Vol. 13 (1995), pp. 127–52.

33. John Vidal and John Carver, 'Like Lambs to the Gene Market', *Guardian Weekly* (1 January 1995), p. 17. On the commodification of the human body involving the sale of eggs, sperm, kidneys and the patenting of genes, see Andrew Kimbrell, 'The Body Enclosed: The Commodification of Human "Parts"', *The Ecologist*, Vol. 25, No. 4 (1995), pp. 134–40. I am grateful to David Law for this reference.

34. 'Fatal Attraction', Lex Column, *Financial Times* (11 July 1995).

35. Braudel, *The Structures of Everyday Life*.
36. Fred Hirsch, *The Social Limits to Growth* (Cambridge, MA: Harvard University Press, 1976), pp. 27–54.
37. Max Weber, 'The Meaning of Discipline', in *From Max Weber: Essays in Sociology*, ed. and trans. H. H. Gerth and C. Wright Mills (New York: Oxford University Press, 1946), p. 253.
38. Frank Pearce, *The Radical Durkheim* (London: Unwin Hyman, 1989), pp. 80, 139 and 205.
39. Michel Foucault, *Discipline and Punish*, trans. A. Sheridan (New York: Pantheon Books, 1977), p. 222.
40. Michel Foucault, *Power/Knowledge: Selected Interviews and Other Writings*, ed. and trans. C. Gordon *et al.* (New York: Pantheon Books, 1980), and Gill and Law, 'Global Hegemony'.
41. Stephen Gill, 'Economic Globalization and the Internationalization of Authority: Limits and Contradictions', *Geoforum*, Vol. 23, No. 3 (1992), pp. 269–84.
42. See Stephen Gill, 'The Emerging World Order and European Change', in Ralph Miliband and Leo Panitch (eds.), *New World Order? Socialist Register 1992* (London: Merlin Press, 1992), especially pp. 167–72.
43. 'G-7 Proposals to Strengthen Bretton Woods Institutions', *IMF Survey*, Vol. 24, No. 13 (1995), pp. 201–5.
44. Stephen Clarkson, 'Constitutionalizing the Canadian–American Relationship', in Duncan Cameron and Mel Watkins (eds.), *Canada under Free Trade* (Toronto: Lorimer, 1993), p. 4.
45. On the relevant legislation, see Laura Cram, 'Calling the Piper without Playing the Tune? Social Policy Regulation: The Role of the Commission in European Community Social Policy', *Policy and Politics*, Vol. 21, No. 2 (1993), pp. 85–95. The 1985 Schengen Convention's impact on immigration and the 1976 Trevi Group on terrorism, extremism and international violence are examples of unaccountable agencies: see Rosemary Sales, 'Race, Gender and European Integration', presented at the International Studies Association, Washington DC, March 1994.
46. On the balance between neoliberal and social Europe, see Martin Rhodes, 'The Social Dimension of the Single European Market: National versus Transnational Regulation', *European Journal of Political Research*, Vol. 19, Nos. 2–3 (1991), pp. 245–80; Martin Rhodes, 'The Future of the "Social Dimension": Labour Market Regulation in post-1992 Europe', *Journal of Common Market Studies*, Vol. 30, No. 1 (1992), pp. 23–51; Wolfgang Streek and Phillippe Schmitter, 'From National Corporatism to Transnational Pluralism: Organised Interests in the Single European Market', *Politics and Society*, Vol. 20, No. 4 (1992), pp. 507–12; Kevin Doogan, 'The Social Charter and the Europeanisation of Employment and Social Policy', *Policy and Politics*, Vol. 20, No. 3 (1992), pp. 167–76; and Allan Cochrane and Doogan, 'Welfare Policy: The Dynamics of European Integration', *Policy and Politics*, Vol. 21, No. 2 (1993), pp. 85–95.
47. Hillbourne A. Watson, 'NAFTA under Global Regionalization and Restructuring: Implications for North America and the Caribbean', discussion paper, Howard University, Washington DC (1994), pp. 24–7.
48. Clarkson, 'The Canadian–American Relationship', pp. 13–14.

49. Clarkson notes that the United States 'maintained intact the sovereignty of Congress to pass new trade measures that could supersede the trade agreement'. *Ibid.*, p. 12.
50. See the Preface to Volume 4 of Jeremy Bentham, *The Works of Jeremy Bentham* (Edinburgh: William Tait, 1859), published under the supervision of Bentham's executor, John Bowring. See also Foucault, *Discipline and Punish*, pp. 195–228, and 232.
51. Stephen Gill, 'The Global Panopticon?: The Neo-liberal State, Economic Life and Democratic Surveillance', *Alternatives*, Vol. 20, No. 1 (1995), p. 2.
52. Foucault, *Power/Knowledge*, p. 6.
53. Blanchot, 'Michel Foucault', p. 86.
54. Abbe Mowshowitz, 'The Emerging Network Marketplace', Strategic Research Workshop on 'New Technology, Surveillance and Social Control', Queen's University, Kingston, Ontario, Canada, 14–16 May 1993.
55. Oscar H. Gandy Jr., *The Panoptic Sort: A Political Economy of Personal Information* (Boulder, CO: Westview Press, 1993).
56. Bentham, *Works*, Volume 4, pp. 37–171, and especially pp. 55 and 69ff.
57. For example, Canadian citizenship can be obtained by those who bring $200,000 in investment funds into the country.
58. Sven Steinmo, 'The End of Redistribution? International Pressures and Domestic Tax Policy Choices', *Challenge: The Journal of Economic Affairs*, Vol. 37, No. 6 (1994), pp. 9–17.
59. Organization for Economic Cooperation and Development, *Economies in Transition* (Paris: OECD, no date given), cited in *ibid.*, p. 14.
60. On the privatization of crime control and incarceration, see Nils Christie, *Crime Control as Industry: Towards Gulag Western Style?* (London: Routledge, 1993).
61. Timothy J. Sinclair, 'Between State and Market: Hegemony and Institutions of Collective Action under Conditions of International Capital Mobility', *Policy Sciences*, Vol. 27, No. 4 (1994), pp. 447–66.
62. *Ibid.*, p. 461.
63. This representation was made throughout various articles in the *IMF Survey*, in 1995. For example, see Vol. 24, No. 11, p. 177, or Vol. 24, No. 17, p. 267.
64. See the World Commission on Environment and Development, *Our Common Future*, 'The Brundtland Report' (Oxford: Oxford University Press, 1987), especially p. 51, and the Commission on Global Governance, *Our Global Neighbourhood* (Oxford: Oxford University Press, 1995), pp. 208–16.
65. The tax-evading 'informal sector' might be redefined to include all agents who evade taxes, such as transnational firms through transfer pricing and those that place funds in offshore tax havens.
66. Elmar Altvater, *The Future of the Market: An Essay on the Regulation of Money and Nature after the Collapse of 'Actually Existing Socialism'*, trans. P. Camiler (New York: Verso, 1993), and Martin O' Connor (ed.), *Is Capitalism Sustainable? Political Economy and the Politics of Ecology* (New York: Guildford Press, 1994).
67. Gill, 'The Emerging World Order', and Gregory Albo, '"Competitive Austerity" and the Impasse of Capitalist Employment Policy', in Ralph Miliband and Leo Panitch (eds.), *Between Globalism and Nationalism* (London: Merlin Press, 1994), pp. 144–70.

68. S. Buck-Morss, *The Dialectics of Seeing: Walter Benjamin and the Arcades Project* (Cambridge, MA: MIT Press, 1989), pp. 78–82.
69. Karl Polanyi, *The Great Transformation: The Political and Economic Origins of Our Time* (Boston, MA: Beacon, 1957), p. 3.
70. On the view that Smith's economics is a form of utopianism, see A. Skinner, 'Introduction', in Adam Smith, *The Wealth of Nations* (Harmondsworth: Penguin, 1967), pp. 29–97. Polanyi noted that, for Smith, '[n]o hidden hand tries to impose the rites of cannibalism in the name of self-interest', *Great Transformation*, p. 112.
71. See, for example, Friedrich A. von Hayek, *The Road to Serfdom* (London: Routledge and Kegan Paul, 1944), and Milton Friedman, *Capitalism and Freedom* (Chicago, IL: University of Chicago Press, 1962).
72. Elaine Draper, *Risky Business: Genetic Testing and Exclusionary Practices in the Hazardous Workplace* (Cambridge: Cambridge University Press, 1991).
73. Hirsch, *The Social Limits to Growth*, pp. 117–58.
74. Polanyi, *The Great Transformation*, pp. 130–4.
75. Gramsci, *Prison Notebooks*, p. 276.
76. Other attempts to develop such a research agenda can be found in Stephen Gill and David Law, *The Global Political Economy* (Baltimore, MD: Johns Hopkins University Press, 1988), and Gill (ed.), *Gramsci*.

7
Global Civil Society: An Ethical Profile

Mervyn Frost

The moment of optimism which accompanied the collapse of communism and the end of the Cold War has come and gone. In the wake of the bipolar world a global civil society has emerged. The most manifest and the strongest component of this is the global market economy. Initial hopes that this globalization would usher in a liberal, democratic and just world order have faded. The optimistic reading of the 'End of History' thesis has come in for severe criticism from many quarters. Indeed, many of the chapters in this book may be understood as criticisms of naïve expectations about the imminent emergence of a freer and more democratic world order. Common themes, both in this book and elsewhere, refer to the ways in which the spread of global civil society (capitalism) has advanced inequality, undermined democracy, increased instability and brought forth contradictions which undermine the possibility of a more emancipated world order.

In order to make these criticisms, social scientists have focused on the power differentials that have emerged through the operation of what Justin Rosenberg calls the 'empire of civil society'.[1] They have, for the most part, been interested in laying bare the emerging structures of power in our capitalist world. Although these efforts have been broadly sociological, most of the literature is moved by a clear ethical concern to highlight how justice, democracy, equality and human freedom are being threatened by the global power of capitalism. Scholarly interest is guided by the thought that if we could but understand the current structures of power we might, in the long run, learn how to bring about reform (or revolution).

In this chapter, I wish to argue that social scientists' preoccupation with the structure of power in global civil society has led them to ignore another equally important feature of this society, which is its ethical structure. They have been inclined to treat the global capitalist economy (a major component of global civil society) as a structure of power without ethical content. I aim to rectify this. In civil society we constitute one another as rights holders. This is an ethical standing that we value highly and that can only be achieved within this kind of society. While I do not contest that it is important that we analyse the pattern of power that emerges from the operation of our global civil society over time, I wish to stress that it is equally important that we take note of the forms of ethical being which this particular practice makes possible. This is of particular importance when attempting to conceptualize the possible reform of our current institutions.

It is my contention that, in general, we misunderstand the ethical significance of global civil society. From an ethical point of view, this society has a number of features which are quite remarkable, but seldom remarked on. The aim of this chapter is to bring some of these features to light. This is a limited exercise focusing on but one of the hierarchy of social institutions within which we constitute one another as valued individuals. A full profile of the ethical practices within which we are constituted as such would require a consideration of the ethical dimensions of other important institutions, such as the family, the state and the system of sovereign democratic states.[2]

There are several preliminary points about what I am *not* attempting in this chapter which I wish to make clear, in order to prevent misunderstanding later on. First, although I focus on civil society defined in a way that includes market relations, I want to make it quite clear that I am not concerned to argue the libertarian case. I am not putting the argument that civil society, defined as a society of rights holders, is the pre-eminent social practice and that other institutions, such as the state, are impediments to the good ethical effects which would pertain if civil society – understood as the market – were allowed to operate freely. On my view, libertarians misunderstand the *ethical* significance of the state. For them it is but an *instrument* for the protection of pre-existing rights. I would argue that the democratic state is a necessary component for our constitution as free ethical beings. Second, in this chapter I do not attempt a discussion of the extremely important role of the democratic state in the ethical constitution of free individuals. For the purposes of this chapter, I will simply leave the whole task of an ethical evaluation of the democratic state to one side. Third, I declare at the outset that I am fully aware that a practice such as civil society, once it is in motion, produces over time a set of what we might call 'structurally determined outcomes'. It produces a set of power relations among the actors which we need to take account of when we contemplate the question: 'What, from an ethical point of view, ought we to do now?' Although important issues are at stake here, I shall not be considering them in this chapter. These features of civil society have often been commented upon, most notably by Marxist scholars.[3] The features on which I wish to comment are less often brought to light.

Let me make two more preliminary points before we get to the subject in hand. First, a guiding motif in what follows is that we constitute one another as valued beings in a number of practices. We may constitute one another as members of a university (my writing this chapter is an act undertaken as a constituted member of that practice). At the same time, the members of the university are engaged in different constituting practices, as members of families, churches, political parties, liberation movements, and so on. Each practice has its rules of conduct: the university expects of me conduct in accordance with research accreditation norms, with its norms pertaining to teaching, with its rules spelling out my relationship to my head of department, and so on. Underlying these are deeper values which the practice promotes. In this case, values such as the pursuit of knowledge, the transfer of skills of analysis, the inculcation of tolerance for diverse points of view, and so on. Since each of us participates in a number of practices it follows that the values embedded in them might conflict. For example, the values promoted by university life might conflict with those embedded in the fundamental religious practice in which you participate. It may then be that in some sense your life could be shown to be incoherent. What is required in one practice contradicts the requirements of another. I take it that a key task of ethical theory is to bring to light the values promoted by the practices within which we are participants, with a view to showing up such incoherencies across practices. In this chapter, I will attempt to highlight some of the main ethical features of global civil society. Second, and as a final preliminary point, in this chapter I am engaged in a normative exploration of features of a practice within which we, you (the reader) and I, are already participants. I am not talking about something 'out there' which we can examine, as it were, from a distance. We are participants in this practice which I am examining; we must perforce examine it from the internal point of view, for there is no external one.

After these introductory remarks, let me now turn to the matter in hand. My initial thoughts on this matter were contained in a paper entitled 'Global Civil Society: Liberator or Oppressor', which I presented to the British International Studies Association Annual Conference in Southampton in 1995. In that paper, I examined two very different ways in which scholars have considered contemporary global civil society. On the one hand are those who see global civil society as an ethically important but fragile layer of non-state actors sandwiched between states and markets. On this view, civil society is a set of voluntary associations which is vulnerable and in need of nurturing. It is one of the few available defences against the almighty power of states and markets. The salience of civil society from an ethical point of view is that in it valuable non-state and non-market forms of association are preserved. In these associations people come to flourish in ways that can be construed as ethically valuable. A collection of articles along these lines is to be found in Michael Walzer's edited volume *Toward a Global Civil Society*.[4]

On the other hand are scholars like Justin Rosenberg who, in neo-Marxist vein, define global civil society as a social formation that includes the global market. On his view, global civil society has enormous structural power such that even states are subject to it. This civil society is an 'imperial' force with all the negative connotations we usually attach to that word.[5] I argued that Rosenberg's focus on the origins, maintenance and development of the global social system as a whole is a more important enterprise than the narrower concern of Walzer with the relatively powerless social groups wedged between states and markets. Rosenberg's excellent book provides us with an account of the structure of the global social formation looked at as a whole, together with an account of how it works in practice. This is something that those with the narrower view as to what constitutes global civil society do not do.

What Rosenberg does not do, however, is give us a plausible account of the ethical significance of civil society seen in this global way. Throughout his book, there is a tacit ethical evaluation of global civil society. By presenting it as an 'empire' he casts it in an essentially negative light. What he leaves out of account are the positive features of civil society which are fundamental to our flourishing as ethical beings. In particular, he fails to indicate how civil society is the social formation within which we constitute one another as rights holders. Being constituted as a rights holder is an ethical status which most people value highly. What I will do in this chapter is flesh out my analysis of civil society, broadly conceived, in order to indicate the ways in which it is a social form of great ethical value.

I will argue that most people value the ethical standing of being a rights holder and that this standing is achieved (and can only be achieved) within civil society. Beyond this, however, I will be pointing out several extraordinary features of civil society which we generally fail to appreciate and which are of major ethical significance. There is, I believe, a widespread misunderstanding of this social institution, this civil society.

A basic definition

Civil society is that social order within which we constitute one another as first-generation rights holders. In it we recognize one another as bearers of equal packages of rights. The package is normally taken to include such rights as the right to safety of the person, the right to free speech, the right to own property, the rights to the freedoms of association, movement, conscience, and so on.[6] These are rights which we take one another to have simply as people: we do not accord them only to people of a certain race, family, religion or ethnic group.

To claim a right is to specify one's standing within a normative practice. It is to claim a domain within which one is free to act and with regard to which others have a duty not to infringe the area of freedom in question. A rights claim is a property claim, in the sense that only the owner of the right may waive the duties which those on the perimeter of the domain of freedom owe to her.[7] Rights do not feature prominently in all social practices. For example, in slave-owning societies slaves have no rights, in some societies women are considered to be without rights, and in many societies children have only limited rights.

I focus on civil society defined as the practice of first-generation rights holders because this practice is an extended one. Indeed, nowadays it is hardly possible to imagine that there are people who would not claim for themselves most of these rights, to imagine, that is, people who would not claim for themselves at least the right not to be killed, tortured or maimed, the right to free speech, the right to freedom of association, the right to freedom of conscience, the right to hold property, and so on. It is difficult to imagine the counterfactual case which would be provided by someone who made some or all of the following ethical claims for herself: 'I have no rights', 'I am the slave of X', 'I am the chattel of Y', 'I am merely an object, you may do with me as you wish'. Most people are not like this, but claim at least a core of first-generation rights for themselves.[8] This minimum is common to the practice of people across the range of political persuasions, cultures and nations. In contrast to this, it is not at all plausible to suggest that second- and third-generation rights enjoy such wide currency. These are hotly contested at every point, even within homogeneous political groupings.

As evidence that civil society thus defined is widely accepted I put forward the following facts: most states belong to the United Nations Organization, which has built into its basic Charter a concern with human rights; a concern with human rights is now well established in international law; the world economy is now organized on market principles and basic rights are fundamental to these; all states either are or profess to be moving towards democracy, the basic idea of which depends on notions of human rights; the constitutions of many states embody a bill of rights, and since the founding of the UN a series of further rights-based conventions has been produced.

It should be noted that the rights-holding society within which we currently find ourselves did not always exist. It is a modern social formation. For long periods of history there were no such societies. Indeed, for much of history it was considered quite proper for some people to own others as slaves. Until recently, of course, many white South Africans regarded blacks as without rights. An ongoing project for social historians is the tracing of the stages of the slow emergence of this modern social form.[9]

Crucial to my argument is the contention that the rights we hold as members of civil society are not granted to us by the state within which we live, or by the system of sovereign states, or by some international organization. This is not to deny that states and other institutions clearly play an important part in protecting our rights. If anyone were to abuse my rights I would, no doubt, call on the British state apparatus for a remedy. If the state failed me, I might turn to the European Commission on Human Rights. However, if there were no state ready and willing to help me (if the state I was in had collapsed, as has often happened to states in Africa, most recently in Zaire), I might call on a private protection agency for help in asserting my rights. However, admitting that I might turn to the state or to other agencies for a remedy when my rights are abused *in no way detracts from my central point, which is that the notion of being a rights holder in civil society is not conceptually tied to the idea of being a member of a state or a protection association (or any other institution).* In support of this contention consider the following points. First, we can easily imagine a society of rights holders existing in circumstances in which there was no state. Second, were our state to collapse (as happened to the people of Mozambique in the 1980s and in Zaire in the 1990s) we would not consider that we had, therefore, ceased to be rights holders. We would not say: 'We have no functioning state, therefore, we have no rights'; instead, we would say, as people do in such circumstances: 'the rights which we have are not being protected by this government'. Third, and most importantly, we use our first-generation rights to make claims against states and other institutions which abuse them. Far from these institutions conferring rights upon us, we judge the merit of these institutions by determining the extent to which they protect our pre-existing rights, which we hold in civil society. Again, the language we use supports the case I am making. We typically judge a new constitution (such as the one in South Africa, for example) by saying: 'It is a good constitution in that it guarantees the basic rights of all South Africans'. We do not say: 'It is a good constitution because it creates (or gives) South Africans basic rights'; nor do we say that 'the new constitution has turned South Africans into rights holders'. Rather, our claim is that the constitution protects the rights South Africans already had. Finally, when we travel abroad we consider ourselves to be rights holders throughout our travels. We do not, as it were, consider ourselves to be rights holders only in those states with rights-protecting mechanisms and to be rightsless as we move out of such states into areas under tyrannical or authoritarian rule. What we say is that in some places our rights are well protected, whereas in others they are not. We consider ourselves to be rights holders all the way.

My claim, then, is that we are rights holders, that we are such by virtue of our membership of civil society, and that this society includes all rights holders everywhere and is not restricted by the other associations within which we live. In particular, we do not cease to be rights holders at the borders of the states within which we live. Thus, it follows that 'our' civil society is not coterminous with 'our' state.[10] Our language of rights suggests that there is but one civil society. We never ask of someone – indeed, it would not make sense to ask of her – 'which civil society do you belong to?' What would the borders of these be? How would we name this civil society as distinct from that one? If there is but one civil society it follows that the phrases 'civil society' and 'global civil society' are interchangeable terms.[11] In what follows I use them as synonyms.

What I now want to show (and this is the heart of this chapter) is that civil society is an institution with certain features which are extraordinary from an ethical point of view. However, before turning to these I wish to offer a brief explanation as to why these features, for the most part, go unrecognized. I believe that they remain hidden because, in general, our exercises in the ethical evaluation of social institutions are guided by a particularly narrow view of what a social institution is.

The restricted view of social institutions

A major reason for our failure to understand the ethical import of civil society is that we fail to see it as a social institution. We fail to see it as a practice within which people follow a set of rules which could be changed. Indeed civil society, the realm of rights holders, is often presented as the background condition out of which people proceeded to construct institutions such as the state. This background condition is often understood as a pre-institutional state of nature.

Typically, we make ethical judgements about those institutions which are the outcome of the exercise of a common will by a group of people. When we make ethical evaluations of social formations we customarily focus on institutions with clear boundaries, clear memberships and defined authority structures. We focus on those institutions within which members are easily able to distinguish between those who are participants and those who are not (between insiders and outsiders). These are institutions within which members clearly identify themselves as such by saying things like: 'this is my family, my church, my nation, my tribe, my state'. Typically, in making ethical evaluations of such institutions we might consider whether states are just, democratic, protective of individual rights (or group rights), egalitarian, caring, and so on. We might ask similar questions about actual or proposed international organizations. For example, we might ask questions about the justice of the institutional structures governing the relationships between the North and the South. With a view to both the past and the present we might make ethical judgements about religious institutions such as churches. For example, many people are ethically shocked at the activities and structures of the medieval church and the activities and structures of fundamentalist churches today. In like manner, we may evaluate the institution of the family, both as it was and as it is now. Much feminist ethical criticism is targeted at patriarchal family structures. Corporations, too, are the target of our ethical evaluation. With regard to these, criticism is often levelled at the top-down managerial arrangements which hold in companies, and a case is often made for the introduction of more democratic corporate structures and for the introduction of institutional forms which would encourage worker participation in corporate decision-making.

In each of the cases mentioned above, what we evaluate is a social institution which has a specific location, a clear-cut membership, a constitution (in the broad sense of a known set of rules which the members recognize, understand and follow), and in which the constitution spells out the authority relationships which hold within the institution in question. Such institutions are clearly the creation of the people involved in them or their historical forebears. These institutions consist of structures which could be changed by the participants if they so wished.

It seems to me that our failure to provide a proper evaluation of civil society stems from our preoccupation with evaluating the kinds of social formations indicated above; from our preoccupation with evaluating bounded institutions which stem from a common will, with determinate memberships, clear borders and well-articulated authority structures. We judge such institutions in terms of the ethical standards which we hold dear (standards referring to justice, liberty, equality, rights, democracy, the rule of law, constitutionalism, and so on) and where necessary we seek to change the authority structures, moving them towards more ethically acceptable forms.[12]

We generally confine ourselves to making ethical evaluations of the discrete, bounded kind of association mentioned above for the following reasons. First, because we hold that ethical evaluation is closely tied to the possibility of institutional reform and we can easily imagine the reform of such discrete entities as the family, the church, the corporation, the state or an international organization, it is relatively easy to imagine the rules of such associations being rejigged to make them more just, more democratic, more rights protecting, and so on. In particular, it is easy to see why we might spend much of our time evaluating different forms of state. Modern democratic states are self-conscious entities within which there are built-in, self-consciously designed procedures for changing the basic rules of association. These are not simply traditional forms which we have inherited and which we assume will continue in the future as they have done in the past. These associations have mechanisms built in for regulating their own re-creation. A second reason for focusing our ethical evaluation on the kinds of discrete, bounded associations mentioned above is that in such associations we can easily identify the people involved who would be responsible for the reform of the institution in question. These are, of course, the members of the families, the churches, the corporations and the states under consideration. We know who the members of these institutions are. We know who is inside and who is outside the institution under scrutiny.

Civil society: a social institution

In sharp contrast to this kind of bounded institution, civil society hardly seems to be a social institution at all: it is not clear what its boundaries are, who its members are and what its authority structure is. It does not seem to be a good candidate for ethical evaluation for it does not seem amenable to reform and furthermore it is not clear who the parties are who would need to do the reforming. In a number of different ways, civil society is unlike the institutions we normally subject to ethical evaluation.

First, we often make the mistake of thinking that civil society (in the widest sense as 'the society of rights holders') is not a social institution. We make this mistake because our attention is focused on the kind of association which I have been discussing above, within which there is always a group of people who would describe themselves as its members. One might say that in these associations there is a self-conscious common will. In sharp contrast to this, the participants in civil society do not have a clear sense of being members of a rights-conferring institution. We do not say, 'I am a member of civil society and proud of it.' In civil society we think of ourselves as rights holders, but we do not normally consider that to be a rights holder is to be a member of one kind of society rather than another. We talk of 'having rights' as if they were items we possess individually, apart from any society. At first glance, the character of a rights claim might suggest that rights holders are not fellow members of a civil society (or any other kind of society), but are instead in some form of asocial relationship within which they use their rights to keep themselves apart from one another. This is a major misunderstanding, for to be a rights holder is to be a member of a society within which the rights which one claims for oneself are recognized by others within that society. To claim a right against others is to indicate that the others in question are fellow members of a common society, *viz.* civil society. Where no such society exists we might treat others as slaves or mere things and others might treat us as such. Our claims to be the bearers of rights would fall on deaf ears. Thus, although the nature of a rights claim is to 'trump' other kinds of claims, it is nevertheless the kind of claim which can only be deployed within a society of people who conceive of themselves as adhering to rules which legitimate that particular kind of move in the practice of rights. *Rights holding can take place only in a society of rights holders.* It can only take place within a practice or institution of rights holders.

Civil society: an open and borderless institution

Second, the bounded institutions which I discussed above all have more or less clear-cut membership rules, that is to say they have tight borders distinguishing insiders from outsiders. In families, churches, corporations, states and international organizations it is usually quite clear who is and who is not a member. In many such organizations there are set procedures for screening and admitting newcomers into the practice. Churches, clubs, states, and so on have credentials committees of one kind or another with well-defined methods and criteria for determining who might become a member and who should be excluded. Another way of putting this is to say that these institutions either literally or figuratively have determinate 'gatekeepers' and 'border posts', which regulate the admission procedures of the institution in question. *What is remarkable about civil society is that it does not have such gatekeepers and it does not have a clear set of borders.* I believe that it is crucial that we gain a proper understanding of this aspect of civil society. Let us take a closer look at the membership rules of civil society.

How does one join civil society? There is no membership committee to which one can apply. There is no formal procedure for vetting or blackballing would-be members. Civil society is open to all who would enter. One enters it by learning what is involved in claiming rights for oneself and what is involved in respecting basic human rights in others. It is like a game that anyone may join as soon as the person joining has grasped the rules of play. One joins through participating.[13] Most importantly, in civil society existing members have no right of closure; they may not declare civil society full, nor may they specify a policy spelling out which would-be members they are willing to accept or not. None of this means that everybody is automatically a member of civil society. People who do not understand the rules of a rights-holding society are obviously not participants. Thus for example the people of the ex-USSR, who had no experience of being rights holders in civil society (especially with regard to property rights in the marketplace), have gone through (and are still going through) a difficult process of learning the rules of this game.

What follows from this is that one of the questions of ethics which is so difficult to answer with regard to other human associations does not apply with regard to civil society. Ethical questions about what would count as a legitimate reason to exclude a would-be member do not arise. Questions about the granting of citizenship, asylum, the hosting of refugees, and so on, are not on the agenda for civil society. It is a society open to all those who would master its rules.

One feature of the open access entry procedure that I have sketched above is that civil society does not screen possible new members across a whole range of criteria. From an ethical point of view, this is a very problematic aspect of other kinds of human associations. To would-be civilians (that is, to those who would become active in the rights holding practice) civil society poses no questions about present levels of wealth (in other words, it is not elitist in terms of class), ideology, life plans, nationalist commitments, ethnic allegiances, family or clan origins (there is no aristocratic measure hidden in the procedure), educational qualifications (it is not meritocratic) or religious ties. In like manner, there are no checks on grounds of race, ability, gender or geographical location.

It follows from the above that individuals who are members of associational forms which are in conflict with one another (for example John from Nation X and Lea from Nation Y which is in conflict with X) may, nevertheless, join civil society in spite of the conflict between their nations. Thus, suppose that I am a pagan and you are a Jew. From the point of view of civil society this does not matter, since we can both become good civilians, respecters of one another's rights. What this indicates is that civil society can be fundamentally corrosive of existing social borders. Through their cooperation in civil society, members of the rival nations might come to set less store by national borders. Possibly, a better way of putting this would be to say that membership of civil society might enable people to transcend national, religious, tribal and other borders.

Let us consider for a moment the converse of the membership procedures I discussed above: let us consider the procedures for expulsion. An important ethical question for most human associations concerns the criteria that determine when a member should have her membership withdrawn. This question does not arise in civil society, because entry and exit are in the hands of the individual. The individual enters by learning how to claim and respect rights. A person leaves civil society by ceasing to do those things.[14]

There is a final important point that I wish to make about membership of civil society, which is to compare civil society's position *vis-à-vis* non-members with that of most other forms of association. Most human associations specify precisely who is a member and who is not. Once the insider group is defined, there are internal rules which clearly specify what is due to insiders as distinct from outsiders. Thus, members of families are entitled to all kinds of privileges denied to non-members. Similarly, members of a church, a university, a corporation, a state and an inter-state organization are entitled to benefits that are denied to non-members. *In contrast to this, the rules of civil society prescribe an extremely unusual form of conduct towards non-members.* The rules of civil society require that practising rights holders (the members of civil society, like you and me) treat non-members *as if they were fully fledged rights holders in the society.* In other words, from the point of view of insiders, outsiders are to be treated *as if they were already insiders.* What this means is that we rights holders are to treat others as rights holders whether or not they treat us in the same way. Thus, I am required to accord to the outsider the rights to freedom of speech, safety of the person, freedom of association, and so on through the list of first-generation rights, even though she might not grant me this recognition in return.[15] It is this feature of civil society which enables us to talk of 'universal human rights'. I take this phrase to be a form of words which indicates that practising civilians (members of civil society), who claim rights for themselves and respect them in others, are to treat all other people *as if* they were rights holders in good standing. Thus, suppose you as a good civilian, came across someone, somewhere, who had never claimed rights for herself and did not respect them in others and in fact did not know what rights were (in short, someone who was not a practising civilian). As a member of civil society, you would be required to treat her as if she were already a participant in the practice. It is important to notice that by treating her as such you would be both inviting her into civil society and educating her in its ways.[16] This is the process of *Bildung*.

Civil society: an anarchical institution without policies

Civil society is unlike many social institutions which we subject to ethical evaluation in that it has no central authority.[17] In most of the institutions which we subject to ethical scrutiny there is an internal authority structure the form of which is the focus of analysis for those concerned with justice, democracy, liberty, equality, and so on. Families, corporations, states and international organizations all have such structures. As I indicated earlier, in families questions arise about patriarchy versus matriarchy, and about intra-family democracy. In corporations, we are often concerned about worker participation in corporate decision-making; with regard to states the debates about the proper relationship between citizens and government are extremely complex. Similar questions arise with regard to international organizations. However, such considerations are simply not pertinent when it comes to civil society because it is an anarchical society without a determinate authority structure. Civil society is an anarchy. There are some interesting consequences which flow from this. Civil society as a social entity with a determinate history has no policies. Since it has no central authority, questions about what policy civil society should adopt do not arise. It has no corporate position whatsoever on any matter of general policy, whether it concern green issues, redistributive issues or matters of public health, education and welfare. There may be public opinions about such matters within civil society, but there is no mechanism within this institution for the translation of public opinions into official policy positions. Within civil society there is no single public, but there are many publics which shift from time to time and from issue to issue. It is clear that civil society cannot be construed as having imperial policies or aggressive policies (or the converse for that matter).

The expansion of civil society

The members of any social institution may seek to expand or contract that institution. What is singular about the institution of civil society is the way in which expansion occurs. This is best brought out by contrasting it with how expansion generally takes place in other institutions. Because these generally have clear centres of authority, expansion usually happens as a result of a specific decision. This might involve a decision by a government to open the state to immigration, or it might seek expansion through a self-conscious imperial effort. The latter kind of expansion takes place against opposition and typically involves the use (or the threat of the use) of force. In the latter case, there is a clear idea of pushing boundaries outwards. Imperial expansion involves the defeat of existing political entities.

The expansion of civil society is altogether different. Since civil society has no corporate identity and no central authority there can be no policy of expansion which might evoke a threatened response from outsiders. A possible expansion of civil society does not present outsider states, nations or religious movements with an identifiable authority the policies of which can be opposed as being hostile. Yet, civil society may and does expand. As we have seen, civil society is an open society. It is open to all those who would become members. In so far as it is attractive to outsiders it will have a tendency to grow. Its expansion, though, does not proceed by the defeat of existing institutions in set-piece battles of one kind or another. Instead, outsiders join by being treated as rights holders and learning to behave as such. In the initial phases of the process, rights holding might seem as if it can be accomplished without the actor who is joining civil society having to leave, renounce or distance herself from the existing institutions within which she lives. Thus, initially a member of, for example, a traditional society of one kind or another might learn to be a rights holder without ceasing her membership of the traditional institutions. In the long run, though, what is required of an actor in civil society is likely to come into conflict with the norms of traditional practices and in this way it may threaten the long-term viability of such practices. The expansion of civil society, therefore, can be seen to threaten other societies, but the threat is not located in the policies and actions of a specified authority and it does not manifest itself in set-piece confrontations. Those who are 'conquered' by 'imperial' civil society do not see themselves as having been vanquished. Instead, they understand themselves to have shifted status; from being subjects, they have become rights holders.

Politics in civil society

As mentioned in the previous section, civil society has no central authority. *A fortiori*, it follows that it has no formal constitution, no legislature, no executive and no judiciary. This has implications for how we are to understand the *politics* which takes place in civil society. Many scholars take the subject matter of politics to be the study of narrowly bounded institutions and of the behaviour of people in and around them. They use a variety of methods to compare and contrast different kinds of international organizations, states, legislatures, executives and judiciaries. Beyond these they study parties, pressure groups and social movements. Underpinning such studies is a long-term interest in reforming these political institutions. If the study of politics were confined to a study of such narrowly bounded institutions, then there would be a sense in which there would be no interest in the study of civil society as a political phenomenon and it would not be an object of interest for political scientists.

It would be a mistake, though, to exclude civil society from the field of objects of interest of those who study politics. This is because it provides the very ground for politics, as understood by Bernard Crick and Michael Oakeshott. Crick defined politics as a way of solving disputes through discussion, rather than through war and violence.[18] Oakeshott defined politics as talk about the basic rules of association which govern our lives.[19] These definitions do, indeed, seem plausible. Disputes about the shape of state constitutions, campaigns preceding the election of governments, or the activity of pressure groups towards governments all fall into that broad category of activities which we would name 'political'. Much of what we normally describe as political behaviour presupposes the existence of civil society. One of the things we may do with the rights we hold as a consequence of our participation in civil society is to discuss amongst ourselves the forms of subsequent associations we would like to create. One well-known example of this kind of politics taking place at the moment is the debate about maintaining a narrowly defined sovereignty for Britain, or changing the sovereignty rule to allow for a closer union with the European Union. Another such debate (though much further from fruition) is the North/South debate, which is a variant on the older debate about a new international economic order. Postmodern theorists in international relations are engaged in a more radical discussion questioning the role of states in the future global order. Similar matters are raised by environmentalists. What I wish to stress here, though, is that *the taking place of these debates requires the existence of a civil society between those engaged in it*. The many debates about the appropriate political institutions for the twenty-first century, the proper shape of democracy, the inter-state system as a whole, international organizations and a myriad other institutions, take place from within the security of our rights practice. *From an ethical point of view, the politics (the discussion about the shape of future human associations) which the existence of civil society makes possible is more fundamental than the politics which takes place between citizens of democratic states.* This is so in the sense that the very shape, size, borders and constitutional forms of states (and other structures of authority) is something which members of civil society have to settle before intra-democratic politics can take place.

We are so embedded in civil society, we take our rights so for granted, that we often fail to see how fundamental our membership of civil society is. Consider what would be involved in repudiating its existence. It would involve our denying that we ourselves have any right to a say about the shape of the institutions in which we are to live. It would also involve our denying that right to others, on the grounds that they are mere creatures, barbarians or sub-human in some way. For long periods of history people did, of course, make such claims, most recently in South Africa and Rhodesia. At present the practice within which we find ourselves is not of this kind. Globally, it is recognized that all people have a right to a say about the forms of association within which they are to live. For example, the people in Central Africa may use the rights they are deemed to have as members of global civil society to express their opinion about the number and form of political entities which should be created in the area once known as Zaire. The current burst of feminist debates, post-positivist debates, the neoliberal *vs.* neorealist debates, and all the other major debates taking place in international relations theory today, are political discourses within civil society; they take place amongst civilians, the rights holders of global civil society.

Concluding remarks: the pros and cons of civil society

One way of restating the argument of this chapter would be to say that I have been opposing the view of civil society put forward by Karl Marx:

> The so-called rights of man are simply the rights of a member of civil society, that is, of egoistic man separated from other men and from the community – withdrawn into himself, wholly preoccupied with his private interest. The rights of man fit one for life in a brutal society without any sense of community or citizenship. The declaration is like a Diploma that certifies fitness to serve in a war of each against all.[20]

On the view I have put forward, civil society is not a society 'without any sense of community'. Such a society would be one within which we treated one another as slaves, serfs or things. Civil society is a community within which we recognize one another as rights holders. To do this is to accord to the other a significant measure of autonomy. Were we not members of civil society we might well regard the 'other' as sub-human, barbaric, and so on, but as members of civil society we are committed to dealing with others as already participant in the practice of rights holders. The practice demands of us that we invite others in by treating them as if they were already members.

In this chapter, I have outlined the more remarkable features of that form of ethical life (*Sittlichkeit*) known as civil society. These are:

- In terms of the rules internal to this practice those not yet participant in it are to be treated *as if they were rights holders*, they are not to be treated as enemies.
- Individuals come to participate in civil society not through their being *incorporated* into it after they or their polity have been *conquered* by some entity called 'civil society', nor because they were vetted by some admissions committee, but simply by being treated as rights holders and by beginning to act as such.
- Because membership is not exclusive, no wars against 'civil society' need be fought by outsiders seeking to gain admission.
- Any entity such as a state seeking to block participation in civil society is itself contravening the norms of civil society.
- The advance of a rights-holding society is achieved through the actions of individual rights holders and does not logically depend on the actions of greater political wholes, such as churches, states and empires (although these may hinder or facilitate the advance).

There are two further points that I wish to make. First, civil society has a strength that is analogous to the strength of the World Wide Web. Just as the latter has no central component the destruction of which would signify the destruction of the whole, so too civil society, lacking any central authority or determinate geographical boundaries, cannot be defeated through the capture of any particular site or the breaching of any specific boundary. Second, it follows from the fact that membership of civil society is open to all, and from the fact that members are required to treat others *as if* they were rights holders, that the *identity* of rights holders does not depend on the drawing of a sharp distinction between insiders and outsiders (who are branded as hostile 'others'). The maintenance of civil society, therefore, does not depend on the loyalty, commitment, fervour and courage of a community (however defined) fighting against external enemies. For civil society there is no equivalent of a 'national security issue'.

What this chapter has not dealt with are the shortcomings of this form of ethical life. First, although in civil society we constitute one another as rights holders (thus securing for ourselves a measure of autonomy in a society which allows for diversity), civil society is a limited ethical whole in that in it we have not yet constituted ourselves as citizens who determine for ourselves the general rules under which we live. Second, and related to the first point, the operation of civil society over time necessarily produces inequalities in power, which seem to make a mockery of the 'autonomy' that civil society supposedly preserves. Historically, the democratic state is an institutional form which, when superimposed upon civil society, remedies some of the flaws found in the latter. In the democratic state, rights holders gain the superior status of being citizens, and as such they may institute a government which through the tax system institutes welfare policies to iron out the inequalities of civil society, if only to a degree. Crucially, though, the state operates on top of (or in addition to) the institution of civil society. It does not replace it. The freedoms which rights holders in civil society enjoy are not taken away or eradicated when the democratic state comes into being.

The account which I have given as to how the democratic state remedies the flaws encountered in civil society seems plausible, if we presume that the reach of civil society is coterminous with the reach of the democratic state. *The problem nowadays is that civil society is global and democratic states are territorially restricted.* Any particular democratic state cannot counteract the ethical shortcomings of civil society seen as a whole. Similarly, the total set of democratic states are not coordinated enough to achieve this result through joint action. Much work needs to be done on the ethical significance of our existing system of sovereign states, and on possible ways of reforming our political institutions to counteract the ethical shortcomings of global civil society. A fully fledged theory of justice is required in order to determine the limits regarding what a democratic state might legitimately do to remedy the ethical shortcomings of civil society. Offering such a theory is, of course, beyond the scope of this chapter. The work of this chapter has been to argue that in doing this important task we ought not to lose sight of the important ethical role which civil society plays in constituting us as free people. We need to devise and move towards the establishment of institutions which remedy the shortcomings of global civil society without eradicating its achievements.

Notes

1. Justin Rosenberg, *The Empire of Civil Society: A Critique of the Realist Theory of International Relations* (London: Verso, 1994).
2. I have made a start on this larger project in *Ethics in International Relations: A Constitutive Theory* (Cambridge: Cambridge University Press, 1996).
3. See, for example, Stephen Gill's and Tom Young's chapters in this book, as well as Andrew Hurrell and Ngaire Woods, 'Globalization and Inequality',

in *Millennium: Journal of International Studies*, Vol. 24, No. 3 (1995), pp. 447–70.

4. Michael Walzer (ed.), *Toward a Global Civil Society* (Oxford: Berghahn Books, 1994).

5. See Rosenberg, *The Empire of Civil Society*.

6. There are, of course, arguments about what rights ought to be included in the list, but there is broad agreement on a basic core of rights.

7. For an analysis of rights along these lines, see Hillel Steiner, *An Essay on Rights* (Oxford: Blackwell, 1994), Chapter 3.

8. There are some people who would deny the claim I am making here. Some members of fundamentalist religious orders deny, for example, that women have the rights I have mentioned. It is worth noting though that those who argue the case for rightlessness are usually claiming that status for others, not for themselves. Thus, it is more often than not learned religious men who claim that women lack these rights. In some tribal societies, it is men of chiefly rank who deny that women have such rights. It is rare for the category of people identified as without rights to demand this status for themselves.

9. In this vein, see, for example, A. Claire Cutler's discussion of the phases of the emergence of the law merchant in 'Global Capitalism and Liberal Myths: Dispute Settlement in Private International Trade Relations', *Millennium*, Vol. 24, No. 3 (1995), pp. 377–97.

10. It may be useful here to think of the Roman Catholic Church, which is global in its reach. Its members consider themselves to be members of a single church. Although the units of its organizational structure may in large measure be organized in units with boundaries coterminous with the boundaries of states, this is a purely practical matter: the existence of the church and its authority in any given geographical area is not conceptually tied to the existence of a particular state.

11. The point I have made in this paragraph may be illustrated by considering another increasingly global practice: the practice of speaking English. This global practice has regional variations, in the sense that there are any number of differences with regard to grammar and dialect. Yet, the basic rules are sufficiently similar for all English speakers everywhere to understand one another. Although the total population of English speakers is spread about the world and members of it are to be found in all the states of the world, and although different states may have different policies vis-à-vis the practice of English speakers (some might nurture it, some might seek to suppress it), the practice itself is independent of states in the sense that the basic rules governing the grammar and syntax of English are independent of state authority. If all states were to wither away, the practice of speaking English could survive. The same is true of civil society.

12. Here I am not wanting to specify what justice is, what rights ought to be protected, and so on. I am not engaged here in advancing a substantive ethical position, rather I am making a general point about the kinds of social institutions about which we customarily make ethical judgements.

13. A parallel which strikes me as significant here is that the entry procedures of civil society are similar to those which pertain in the Christian church. I am not talking of entry into any specific Christian church but of entry to

the wider Christian fraternity. As I understand it, membership is open to anyone who is prepared to follow Jesus. There are no application procedures. Would-be Christians choose to follow Christ. It is as simple as that. What exactly is to count as 'following Christ' is of course a highly contentious question.

14. A political implication of what I have been saying is that, because in civil society there are no 'gatekeeper' sites, no such places are available to become sites of political struggle.

15. Again there seems to me to be an interesting parallel here between civil society and Christianity. Christians are enjoined to love their brothers and sisters whether or not those brothers and sisters love them in return.

16. Again this is similar to the Christian injunction 'love thy neighbour as thyself'.

17. This point is closely related to one I made earlier indicating that in civil society we do not have a sense of 'we the people of civil society', where 'we' refers to a defined, geographically bounded set of people, with a sense of themselves forming a social whole. The outer borders of civil society simply expand as more people join. Indeed, they are not 'borders' in the conventional sense at all, if the word is taken to refer to a line that is policed against outsiders. The outer limits of civil society are open to outsiders. They are borders which envelop rather than exclude.

18. Bernard Crick, *In Defence of Politics* (Harmondsworth: Pelican, 1971), pp. 15–34.

19. Michael Oakeshott, 'The Language of the Modern European State', *Political Studies*, Vol. 23, Nos. 2 & 3 (1975), pp. 319–41 and 409–14.

20. K. Marx, 'On the Jewish Question', in K. Marx, *Early Writings*, trans. R. Livingstone and G. Benton (Harmondsworth: Penguin Books, 1975), pp. 229–30.

8
'A Project to be Realized': Global Liberalism and a New World Order

Tom Young

> Why should we not attempt a campaign also against our great domestic foe, I mean the hitherto unconquered sterility of so large a proportion of the surface of the kingdom? ... let us not be satisfied with the liberation of Egypt, or the subjugation of Malta, but let us subdue Finchley Common; let us conquer Hounslow Heath; let us compel Epping Forest to submit to the yoke of improvement.[1]

> Westernness constitutes only a final preparation for true humanity.[2]

Liberalism is the armed wing of Enlightenment. It has 'never been an account of the world but a project to be realised'.[3] Although it has conventionally been understood as a matter of the domestic politics of some states, it has always been about globalization. What is different about the current phase of that globalization is the more rapid erosion of the obstacles that have hitherto confronted it. Some of these developments have already been examined from this perspective, but connecting discursive logics to political action remains notoriously difficult.[4] For many, of course, even to start with 'ideas' is heresy. Traditionally, international relations has conceived of relations between states as driven by 'interests'; though the precise scope of this notion has always remained rather opaque it clearly forms part of a family of positions and standpoints in the social sciences which construe political activity as in practice reducible to such 'interests'. In these views, political discourse becomes a kind of froth resting on action inspired by interests. To quote more or less at random, but I hope not unfairly, 'national interests overpower morality'.[5] It tends to follow that where states do articulate their positions in terms other than interest (as, for example, currently with reference to governance, democracy and human rights) then we are witness to some form of higher deception and the analytical trick is to decipher such deceptions and reveal what interests *really are* in play.

None of this is wholly implausible. However, the position taken here is that it is impossible to make any sense of either domestic politics or relations between states without taking account of 'ideas', though that term must be understood more broadly than as the texts conventionally constituted by political theory. If the element of 'ideas' is accentuated in the following account, the least that can be said is that there is no shortage of other approaches. There are, of course, many excellent accounts of political liberalism considered as ideas in the rather narrow, essentially textual sense. There are far fewer accounts of its intense desire to transform people and communities and the practices it has devised to do so: in brief, its 'project'. It is the connection between the two which is central to understanding contemporary liberalism and its place in the world. What is required to explore better the connection between liberal ideas and political action is not the marginalization of the ideas into the ghetto of texts but a more detailed analysis of how liberal ideology 'works', the role of intellectuals and state functionaries in its production and dissemination, its reshaping of forms of social and political power, and the effects of all this on relations between states.

Enlightenment and the liberal project

The claim to be able to reveal the 'universal standpoint', the 'view from nowhere', the 'point of view of the universe' has always lain at the heart of Enlightenment.[6] This weighty task, modestly assumed by intellectuals for the benefit of the rest of mankind, can be achieved only by abstraction from the concrete characteristics of human communities and societies, by reference to a 'natural' level of human existence which is accessible to 'reason'. Whatever its plausibility, such a stance on nature and reason has two inevitable consequences. The first is that it not merely abstracts from, but is massively subversive of, all actual human cultures and practices.[7] This is surely its purpose. In the face of Enlightenment no actual practices have any but a contingent right to exist; all may legitimately be subjected to demands which form no part of their own life and understandings. Secondly, such a stance aspires to place itself beyond the realm of belief while condemning all beliefs to hopeless inadequacy, the products at best of wretched self-interest or pig-headed superstition. To hold unreasoned beliefs is to be somehow subhuman.

These features of Enlightenment developed in philosophical and literary texts were greatly reinforced by its association with science and 'social science'.[8] Enlightenment constituted itself not only in the form of moral or philosophical knowledge, but also in the form of social science claims to knowledge, closely linked to practices of expertise which have insinuated themselves into all aspects of social life. Thus, it not only uncovers universal truths but in its social science form it also understands how societies and communities *really* work, better than their members. Yet, the form of this understanding is always shaped by the 'universal standpoint'. If we already know how Man is by Nature, what is there to say about how he is in fact except how his nature may be restored to him? This is why so much of western thought and social science has characterized existing social forms in negatives, categories of what is *not there*, from 'history-less' peoples to 'undeveloped' societies.

Rendered as political thought and a political project liberalism has faithfully followed its Enlightenment trajectory. The actual facts of social and communal life in particular places and at particular times, considered in themselves, have always been marginal to its thinking. Thus, liberal political thought from Hobbes onwards has proliferated devices (states of nature; veils of ignorance; original positions) which 'strip out' such features. The crucial strategic move has always been to go behind the apparent social realities to a 'deeper' reality. In its claims to universal social and political truths, liberalism is not *an* ideology, it is *the* ideology. Other modern so-called ideologies are, like socialism or feminism, derivative from it and eventually absorbed into it or condemned to permanent critique; or, like 'conservatism', parasitic on it and reduced to little more than plaintive grumbling about its current phase. What is distinctive about this ideology (what arguably makes it ideology) is that, in the way it works, it does not require formal assent to particular propositions or faith. It is in this sense that it is true that the liberal state is neutral as between, for example, different forms of religious belief (though not, of course, their consequences). In their historical development liberal states did not, by and large, try to replace religious belief with some other sets of beliefs. Generally speaking, individuals within liberal societies are free to hold virtually any opinions however bizarre or eccentric. In a sense, the whole purpose of liberal ideology is to present itself as above the level of (necessarily partial) political beliefs. Other *mere* beliefs or ideologies (the latter has a more 'scientific' ring) are then reducible to interests or (variants of) false consciousness.

Nevertheless, even if Enlightenment and liberalism are not about beliefs they must still have believers. Historically, liberalism is peculiarly associated with the modern 'middle class'. That term lent and still lends a false air of familiarity to what was a fundamentally new phenomenon. Doubtless all societies have had thinkers, seers, bards or men of wisdom, but they lived in relationships, however complex and cantankerous, with communities of which they were part. Only modernity has produced a stratum of functionaries and intellectuals (often, of course, the same person was both) who had neither social standing apart from their association with the state (hence their hatred of hierarchy and custom) nor interests in the social sense, and were peculiarly defined by the possession of 'expertise' and later by indirect democratic ratification.[9] A universal standpoint requires, as it were, a universal class. The 'view from nowhere' is voiced by the men from nowhere who desperately long to be at home everywhere: at the very least to keep everyone's home under surveillance. Enlightenment was and is not 'in their interests' as they have no interests, but they were and are the bearers of the Enlightenment project.

The conviction of a superior standpoint, the disdain for cultural diversity and the heady temptations of social engineering have all generated an unease with the world, an incurable restlessness, a profound need to urge the deliriums of liberation on everyone else. From masters of the 'universal standpoint' to masters of the universe is but a short step. Yet, if liberalism has faithfully followed its Enlightenment origins it carries in its soul a fateful tension. Its deepest longings require that *all* societies *really* consist of free reasoning individuals engaging in projects the value of which only they can judge. Once these individuals are 'liberated' from 'oppression' all that remains is to ensure that they cooperate to mutual advantage. The essential institutions for this purpose are civil society and the state. Civil society consists of that sphere of interactions, especially but not only economic ones, that free individuals engage in. These transactions are regulated by a single political authority: the state. The state does not concern itself with the content of individual activities and, since it is neutral as to competing visions of the good, it is able to protect this realm as a realm of freedom and tolerance.

However, this lofty vision of human nature freed from all 'oppressions' also grounds choice, otherwise what value is there in freedom?

This in turn raises the spectre even in theory that individuals and communities may not choose the 'natural' arrangements, a theoretical difficulty that is conspicuously confirmed in real life. Much liberal theory (arguably the most ingenious parts of it) is concerned to offer extremely elaborate constructions whereby actual choices are aligned with 'real' preferences. Ideally choices align with 'nature', however that is understood; in real life they often do not.[10] It is the distance between the two that shapes the liberal project.

Thus, liberalism's political project has not been to inculcate new beliefs, but 'to deconstruct old customary ways of life and to produce new ones'.[11] Liberal social practice is about those disciplines that interiorize new forms of social behaviour characteristic of the 'free individual'. As Charles Taylor puts it, 'radical disengagement opens the prospect of self-remaking'.[12] Such emancipated individuals are, of course, much easier to weld into collectivities and to subject to various kinds of social discipline. Indeed, what accounts for much of the political success of the liberal project is the new forms of power made possible by such disciplines. The potential of these was not lost on established economic and political elites. Part of this is clearly, as Marxists have long stressed, about producing the conditions for industrial capitalism, but it is not only about that. As students of war have often noted, 'by revolutionising society, the state was able as never before to exploit the energies of society for war'.[13]

In fact, no one has understood better than liberals themselves the sheer distance between social realities and the dream of liberation. This understanding informs liberal practice and grounds all its dilemmas. Faced with real resistance, that practice has been forced to rework 'customary ways' or remain partially dependent on or in tension with them. Thus, until recently, the armed forces in modern liberal states have remained to an important degree pre-modern institutions emphasizing values of heroism and combat almost entirely at odds with liberal ideology. Only recently have they been subject to 'liberalization', not only of the obvious kinds, the abolition of special units for women, tolerance of homosexuality, and so on, but in the individualization of the soldier's role. Likewise with the family, an institution which for radicals has long been an institution of 'oppression'. Again, only relatively recently have liberal states moved to 'emancipate' people from the family by individualizing and contractualizing it, and still with considerable misgivings as to the impact of such interference on the role of the family as an agent of moral socialization. As these examples show, liberalism remains endlessly dynamic, a moving though cumulative agenda. Thus, currently part of the function of liberal academia is to explore the as yet 'politically unrealistic' options which may later become part of such an agenda, whether this be world government, the destruction of the nation-state, or the elimination of the differences between men and women.[14]

It is thus both its own discursive logic and endlessly recalcitrant social realities that make liberalism a form of permanent revolution, in certain circumstances indeed permanent terror, constantly seeking new objects of 'liberation'.[15] This generates a logic of modernization that is, and has always been, both domestic and transnational. Some of the most important features of the modern liberal state are best exhibited in its colonial form, where the non-West is seen as essentially empty. In such circumstances, the state is quite clearly the instrument of an enlightened group imposing 'progress' from above on an essentially subject population irrespective of the nature of the 'natives', with at most minor adjustments for local variations.[16] Thus, British colonial rule in India 'represented the great conquering discourse of Enlightenment rationalism, entering into India precisely at the moment of its greatest unchecked arrogance'.[17] Note that the natives are not required to change their overt beliefs, indeed these may even be protected on the model of metropolitan norms. They are, however, required to change their practices and behaviours. 'Modernization' involved the extirpation of 'barbarous' practices, as much by the manufacture of a local 'middle class' as by direct legal proscription.[18] Yet, 'modernization' was something done to western societies before it was done to others. The imposition of 'enlightened' practices on colonial populations precisely paralleled their earlier imposition on domestic western populations.

Civil society and nation-state

The examples of the colonial state and domestic Enlightenment, while they illuminate aspects of the liberal project, omit perhaps the most central feature of political modernity: the mobilization of consent. Colonial forms proved historically transitory. Indeed, liberal colonialism could be said to have dug its own grave. Within a liberal order the very real power of state functionaries cannot simply be a power of subjection and compliance, but must be grounded in some 'rational' instruments, such as public purpose and legal regulation, not least for their own reassurance. The transition to modern political orders *is* a genuine shift. The objects of 'emancipation' cannot simply be coerced;

they must also be brought to 'consent' to the changes being visited upon them. All citizens are to be included within a single political space based on feelings of consent rather than mere compliance. This new political space was subject to two principles of organization. The first, as already noted, is civil society, a concept which forms an important part of liberal theorizing, sustaining such notions as autonomy and pluralism. The picture as presented by liberal orthodoxy tends, however, to ignore central features of the historical experience which created civil society. First, that those groups and organizations which did not fit the emerging liberal order (guilds, communal groups, clans, etc.) were marginalized or coerced out of existence. Second, those new forms of association that did flourish in this new order, far from being 'autonomous', were heavily shaped or regulated by legal norms buttressed by state power. It is not accidental that the constitution of civil society is historically concomitant with the final construction of state sovereignty. Third, this emerging civil society was actively formed by state-driven techniques of cultural homogenization, such as the cultural disaster of mass compulsory education and the promotion of individualism. Finally, it is worth noting that all this in turn occurred in an historical context of incessant war-making, which fuelled increasing taxation, surveillance and standardization.[19]

Contemporary liberal and social scientific understandings of 'democracy', 'civil society' and related terms are massively shaped by this historical experience. 'Democracy' has never meant people ruling themselves, or societies electing representatives which actually represent that society. Nor can representative democracy be seen simply as a device, for overcoming the problems of size in the democratic polity.[20] Rather, it has always been rooted in a fear that 'the people' would not necessarily respect liberal notions of 'reason' and 'justice'. The 'representative' was not to represent the views of 'society', but rather that part of it that guaranteed the protection of the liberal constraints on the democratic process. Once the rest of society had become 'educated' to the point at which it no longer posed a threat to these liberal constraints, then access to the democratic process might follow. Virtually all contemporary liberal theory takes as its *starting point* various 'rights' which are not amenable to democratic change.

However, there was a second principle of reorganization of modern political space that is almost entirely ignored in the official canon of liberal 'political thought', though not its political practice, namely nationalism.[21] The transition to modern political forms involved more than the imposition of a new kind of political machinery (the state), a new form of social order and a new kind of individualism, but took place within the framework of something called the 'nation'. It seems implausible to imagine that before 'modernity' people did not form groups which had identities but, following Sudipta Kaviraj, these were 'fuzzy' rather than 'enumerated'.[22] Political identities have always existed, but there is much about modern nationalism as a political practice that was fundamentally new. Modernizing elites and modern nationalism claimed, of course, to emancipate individuals, but this remained and remains an extremely abstract and, as it were, emotionally cold business. Thus, and to put it rather crudely, the project of liberal modernity draped itself in reworked particular group identities. As a matter of political practicalities, and in order to give some emotional warmth to the process, the 'nation' had to draw on particular attachments such as kin, people and place (or at least the language of such attachments), but to mobilize them in a different way around a different broader identity. The long historical connection between liberalism and nationalism reflected the importance of the latter in assisting in the break-up of older political structures and ensured that, at least until the second half of the twentieth century, most liberals regarded nationalism as a 'progressive' force.

A liberal international order, the Cold War and new states

The emergence of nation-states finally generated a system of such states which itself embodied tensions between the universal and the particular. The concepts and assumptions of the new order required and assumed a language of equality of nations and states, namely national 'self-determination'. However, these characteristics belonged only to 'civilized' nations. Until they had proved their capacity for civilization, 'uncivilized' nations remained outside the magic circle. Conceptually, this precisely paralleled domestic developments; just as citizens must be educated to see themselves and act as individuals before they could participate in civil society, so states also must be brought to Enlightenment before they could be considered equals. In the first phase of the extension of this system, considerable care was taken as to the viability of the new members, at least where the Great Powers could exercise decisive influence. The post-1919 new states, for example, were subject to detailed scrutiny as to their internal political arrangements before they were allowed into the hallowed ranks.

By the early twentieth century, however, the ideas that had sustained clear understandings of 'more and less developed' were becoming discredited. Much of this work was carried out by colonial elites formed in the Western image. It was hardly difficult to emphasize the universal elements in liberalism, and to press the point that the nation-state was not the better form of socio-political organization possessed by *some* peoples but the only form of socio-political organization appropriate for *all* peoples. The nation-state logic could be squared only with the colonial legacy by massive conceptual rigging of the notion of self-determination so that self came to mean 'the people' (whoever they might be) currently living within colonially demarcated boundaries. As Holsti puts it, 'decolonisation *was* the act of self-determination'.[23] This was, of course, a rigged game in which both the western powers and Third World élites were complicit. It had its cynical and self-interested side, but it marked the triumph of Enlightenment and the real beginnings of contemporary globalization.

However, those beginnings were obscured because the reshaping of this liberal international order by the dynamics of the Cold War paradoxically strengthened the elements of pluralism within the system. Universalism was constrained by superpower rivalry, except in rather odd cases where their ideological agendas overlapped, most obviously South Africa. The 'standard of civilization' having been abandoned, states were equal and sovereign and could choose their own economic and political systems. Yet, in practice the new elites appropriated all the assumptions of Western modernity in both their national and international forms. While the need to 'catch up' often legitimated socialist versions of modernization, everywhere the new state was seen as central to bringing about rapid progress. These elites took to heart the imperatives of modernization and mobilization, and were arguably rather more sociologically realistic than their later self-appointed mentors in realizing that these processes, involving such massive transformations of their societies, were barely compatible with liberal democracy. Mobilization, both economic and political, often by overtly authoritarian means, became the order of the day.

Two processes clearly constrained the implementation of these visions in many states. First, such states had to function within concrete social settings often deeply antagonistic to the modernizing project. Some minimal effectiveness made it necessary to deal with social forces which were not congruent with western state models, which in turn led to various forms of patron clientalism and ethnic or regional coalition-building. In many cases, the accumulating difficulties and the shortage of material resources eroded the modernizing impulses of elites and reduced their politics to little more than group aggrandizement. Second, society, as it were, seeped into the state. Lower-level functionaries upon whom elites relied to implement the visions of progress had often only very imperfectly internalized the relevant conceptual vocabulary. Their political 'operational code' could in practice be quite different. In large parts of Africa, but not only there, it has proved impossible to sustain the central institutions of states: armies and bureaucracies. Rather, armies have split along ethnic lines and bureaucracies have failed to administer. Domestic sovereignty has proved highly elusive.[24] Some states threaten to disappear altogether and many are sustained by little more than the requirements of the contemporary world order.

New world order?

The intellectual and political collapse of colonialism and the dynamics of superpower rivalry had sustained a shaky but genuine political pluralism at the international level. The demise of the Soviet bloc removed that shelter. We can now see the postwar period as a deviant phase. Since the end of the Cold War the universal elements of the liberal project have come to the fore. The scope and forms of intervention remain unclear and disputed and are shaped by all sorts of 'pragmatic' considerations, including the domestic political institutions of the Great Powers, traditional state rivalries and the logistical problems thrown up by new kinds of 'humanitarian' intervention. Nevertheless, the outlines of an agenda are clear even if to placate certain political forces this is dressed up in the language of 'interests'.

   This development has taken place not only against the background of the end of the Cold War but also processes of globalization which, although not fundamentally new, are on a much greater scale. A whole range of developments, including technological ones, are making production and markets increasingly global and difficult to subject to national control. Conjoined with this are the forms of an emerging global civil society characterized by the imperative spread of western values (masquerading, it hardly need be said, as 'universal' values) and culture more broadly, in both sophisticated and popular forms. Because these phenomena are not overtly political in the narrow sense it is common to regard them as in some sense natural or as mysterious 'processes', as though they were not in fact considerably shaped by strategic and tactical calculation.[25] The core dynamic of these processes lies, however, in the West.

These tendencies are posing difficult political questions because his-torically the liberal project has been grounded in the nation-state form along with all the attendant paraphernalia of international relations between such states. There are two fundamental dilemmas. For the Great Powers (or rather their élites) there is the question as to whether the liberal project can break with the vehicle of the nation-state and fulfil its global aspirations. Are there sufficient elements of a genuinely global order which would not merely dispense with the need for a hegemonic power or powers but with nation-states as such? Put as starkly as this the question remains very abstract and well beyond the terrain of current politics, but sub-instances of that question are already being posed. Not surprisingly, in the light of the domestic history of liberal states, these questions are posed first in relation to the 'autonomous' sphere of the economy as reflected in demands for the global management of trade or 'independent' central banks, but they are also being posed at the political level. It may be premature, but not wholly fanciful, to suggest that 'the historical pattern of successive "hegemons" has come to an end, and that the hegemonic baton will not be passed from the United States to a new hegemonic nation-state. Instead the baton will be passed in the twenty first century to a transnational configuration'.[26]

The second dilemma concerns the forms of intervention that may be appropriate and functionally effective against those states, and indeed non-state communities, that have failed to fully accept and promote 'modernization' or 'international standards' within their boundaries. This question has most definitely been posed, and new kinds of inter-vention against states have been practised and justified in novel, even if awkward and not very conceptually coherent, ways given the exist-ing language of sovereignty. There have been two notable features of this intervention: a high politics and a low politics, as it were. The first concerns the grounds for explicit political interference in the internal affairs of states; the second the grounds for a whole range of what might be called techniques of microsocial engineering.

As to the first, it will doubtless be widely asserted that the limited history of 'humanitarian' intervention so far shows it to have been riddled with inconsistency, self-serving rhetoric, hypocrisy and selec-tive moralizing.[27] This is undoubtedly the case, but that should not be allowed to obscure a certain emerging direction. The UN Security Council has stretched the formula 'threat to the peace' and its variants to sanction interventions in countries on various 'humanitarian' grounds, certainly on grounds that cannot conceivably be explained by reference to states', or indeed anyone else's, 'interests'.[28] These grounds include starvation in Somalia and a military coup in Haiti.[29] Interestingly, as they progressed, both these interventions became linked to practices to impose democracy on these states, an aspiration, as is widely recognized even in liberal circles, that is fraught with hazards. As with globalization, there is room for real doubt about current trends, but arguably such high-political interventions will be reflected on and in certain contexts will continue, with their operation becoming more efficient.

It is true that real political difficulties attach to them, not least the fickle nature of (an often manipulated) 'public opinion' in western states. It is such difficulties that, in part at least, explain a preference for rather different logics of social transformation, which I have dubbed microsocial engineering. Unlike intervention – which is high profile, high risk and uses military personnel for quasi-political tasks – the social engineering is behind-the-scenes, 'technical' and draws on a large pool of largely western 'experts' who feel committed to the new civilizing mission. It is in this context that 'governance' and 'civil society' have come to be central operational concepts in the policies of both western governments and multilateral bodies. Such considerations are clearly at work in a variety of initiatives from capacity-enhancement programmes to the funding of political parties, but there is also an emphasis that goes beyond the restructuring of governance (in the narrower sense of technical capabilities, and so on) to the restructuring of civil society. There is an implicit recognition that there will be no liberal states until there are liberal persons.[30] This is clear as much in the 'economic' sphere, which in the liberal sense is still largely to be constructed, as in the political.

Not surprisingly the 'civil society' aspect of this project has been colonized by Non-Governmental Organizations (NGOs). Despite a surface hostility towards the international financial institutions and western interests and power, NGOs' loudly proclaimed emphasis on 'grassroots' participation in the development process is to be understood entirely within western preconceptions about the state and the person. The agenda is known in advance; 'progressive' 'grassroots' organizations are simply to be 'mobilized' around it. For their part international financial institutions, though in a formal sense controlled by western states, have a vision of economic order which is rooted in standard liberal conceptions and is not simply the plaything of particular western interests. Both forces are inclined to deny the sovereignty of states, both increasingly stress the creation of 'civil society' and both make no secret of their contempt for cultural traditions that do not square with western notions of rights and justice.

Or disorder?

None of these strategies and interventions is without its contradictions, the largest of which concerns globalization itself. While there is no consensus about these processes, it seems clear that contemporary states, even strong, well-established ones, now face unprecedented pressures from agencies and developments increasingly outside their control. In the past, nation-state building included the construction of a largely national economy that could deliver at least some material benefits to citizens, as well as a national identity that could monopolize their communal and emotional loyalties. These capacities (and possibly these identities) are now being eroded in long-established states. In countries barely formed, historically speaking, it is hard to see how they can ever be acquired. In any case, for many liberals the national state and nationalism have long since ceased to be progressive and globalization is welcomed as an alternative.[31]

More concretely, there is a contradiction at the heart of the current strategy. Liberal society and liberal democracy are forms of social and political order which require citizens who think of themselves as individuals, characterized by material interests between which there can be trade-offs. Markets and civil society constitute spheres of interaction for such individuals. Yet, far from 'the' market and civil society being 'spontaneous' social developments, as liberal myth requires, to be effective they must be penetrated and shaped by a modernizing state, a modernizing state moreover which is driven by a ruling elite armed with new forms of expertise, and motivated by more than just a desire for self-aggrandizement and self-enrichment but also with a vision of how 'to deconstruct old customary ways of life and to produce new ones'.[32] It is arguable that even now the World Bank and others are hobbled by an inability to see that 'free individuals' and the rest of the liberal agenda do not emerge 'naturally' but are the result of political and social processes, often coercive and violent ones.[33] The governance/civil society strategy in many ways undermines the capacities of states while in fact continuing to need strong states. Liberal discourse in its more applied forms to some extent reflects these contradictions.

What, finally, are the prospects for these strategies? It should be noted first that it is widely argued that the recent global wave of democratization can be ascribed to an indigenous explosion of civil society.[34] Space prevents a fuller discussion, but it is possible to be sceptical about this. There are voices and ventriloquized voices, and the latter rarely provide any challenge to the standard western prescriptions for development and governance. Western triumphalism notwithstanding, there would seem to be a range of possible outcomes from the encounter between non-western social and political practices and the liberal project. Certainly, some elites in countries endowed with certain advantages of wealth and/or location will continue a carefully managed but temporary coexistence of the two, aiming in the medium term at the erosion of traditional understandings by liberal democratic norms.[35] As I have already suggested, the more astute amongst them may emphasize the traditional elements in their societies in order to kick-start this process. Gradual improvements in the democratic 'performance' of states will then ensure that democracy becomes a permanent feature of their political systems. The great apparatus of both public and 'private' monitoring institutions that has now been set up in the West (and is busily finding local allies for itself in the South) is, of course, part of a common effort to sustain this process, the essential component of which, as is recognized by the more candid western analysts, is a 'civil society' which will marginalize and if necessary pulverize groups whose modes of existence and values are not compatible with liberal democracy. Certainly, it is clear that the West is prepared to pay dearly for the theatre of democracy.

However, it would be premature to write off other possibilities, including possibilities of resistance. Although a façade of agreement has hitherto been maintained at international gatherings about the supposed universality of western values, some mutterings of dissent were to be heard at the Vienna conference on human rights and at subsequent United Nations meetings.[36] The dissenters were Asian states whose economic weight is growing, whereas African states remain supplicants. Yet, if the successful Asian states feel their societies being corroded by western individualism such dissent may amplify and legitimate dissent amongst others. It is not impossible that, as in recent circumstances where economic turmoil in some Asian countries has been quite brutally exploited by western interests to secure control of those economies, such dissent will be fuelled by economic nationalism.[37] There remain possibilities of resistance in polities where Islam is a potent force. We cannot assume that forms of political living together which are not premised on western egalitarian and other assumptions will necessarily disappear.

More likely, though also more complex and more difficult to make sense of, are what might be called the effects of the 'unbundling' of the liberal project. That is to say that various features of political modernity may be adopted (elections, parties, a language of majoritarianism, etc.), but in a context of a refusal to be bound by the liberal agenda and its understandings of civil society and democracy (individualism, secularism, and so on). Far from being marginalized by civil society, communal groups may find certain institutional features of liberal democracy useful as a means to reinforce or indeed develop their identities. Elections, for example, make people aware of numbers, their numbers, in a way they often were not before. The venomous hatred now evinced for nationalism and communalism by large sections of the western intelligentsia bears witness to these possibilities. Finally, we cannot ignore the possibilities that the refusal of the liberal agenda may enable some countries/communities to extend notions of democracy into spheres from which liberal understanding excludes it. As my argument suggests, it is only superficially paradoxical that those who are most vehement in foisting the liberal project on the peoples of Asia and Africa are also most insistent that they be subjected to the rigours of the international economy. You are free to choose, provided you make the right choice.[38] Yet, when the current illusions about the 'free market' wear off, democracy may well incline people to think again about the distribution of and accountability for economic as well as political power, indeed the very notion of the 'economic' itself. This must fly in the face of current forms of globalization in which the international economy is the mailed fist of the liberal project.

Notes

1. Sir John Sinclair (1803), quoted in J. M. Neeson, *Commoners: Common Right, Enclosure and Social Change in England 1700–1820* (Cambridge: Cambridge University Press, 1993), p. 31.
2. Auguste Comte, cited in Tzvetan Todorov, *On Human Diversity Nationalism Racism and Exoticism in French Thought* (Cambridge, MA: Harvard University Press, 1993), p. 30.
3. Margaret Canovan, 'On Being Economical with the Truth: Some Liberal Reflections', *Political Studies*, Vol. 38, No. 1 (1990), p. 16.
4. See David Williams and Tom Young, 'Governance, the World Bank and Liberal Theory', *Political Studies*, Vol. 42, No. 1 (1994), pp. 84–100.
5. Werner Levi, 'The Relative Irrelevance of Moral Norms in International Politics', in James Rosenau (ed.), *International Politics and Foreign Policy*, second edition (New York: Free Press, 1969), p. 197.

6. See, respectively, Peter Singer, *Practical Ethics* (Cambridge: Cambridge University Press, 1979); Thomas Nagel, *The View from Nowhere* (New York: Oxford University Press, 1986); and, for Sidgwick, Bernard Williams, *Ethics and the Limits of Philosophy* (London: Fontana Press/Collins, 1985).
7. Liberals are often careful not to restrict the possession of reason to human agents.
8. In the eighteenth century, the distinction between these as practices was much less clearly drawn.
9. For historical evidence on the close relationships between eighteenth-century Enlightenment intellectuals and the state, see Robert Wuthnow, *Communities of Discourse: Ideology and Social Structure in the Reformation, the Enlightenment and European Socialism* (Cambridge, MA: Harvard University Press, 1989), especially Chapter 6.
10. Sometimes they do, of course; then even liberals are not averse to citing such evidence though usually only rhetorically. 'Do we not lock our doors when we go out?', Hobbes asks. He is not of course interested in societies where 'we' do not. I draw here on an unpublished paper by David Williams, 'Liberalism and the Liberal Self'.
11. James Tully, 'Governing Conduct', in Edmund Leites (ed.), *Conscience and Casuistry in Early Modern Europe* (Cambridge: Cambridge University Press, 1988), p. 68.
12. Charles Taylor, *Sources of the Self* (Cambridge: Cambridge University Press, 1989), p. 171.
13. Peter Paret, *Clausewitz and the State* (Oxford: Clarendon Press, 1976), p. 32.
14. For examples see, respectively, David Held, 'Democracy: From City-States to a Cosmopolitan Order?', in Held (ed.), *Prospects for Democracy* (Oxford: Polity Press, 1993), pp. 13–52; Veit Bader, 'Citizenship and Exclusion', *Political Theory*, Vol. 23, No. 2 (1995), pp. 211–46; Nancy Fraser, 'After the Family Wage: Gender Equity and the Welfare State', *Political Theory*, Vol. 22, No. 4 (1994), pp. 591–618.
15. So, recently, Robert E. Goodin, Carole Pateman and Roy Pateman, 'Simian Sovereignty', *Political Theory*, Vol. 25, No. 6 (1997), pp. 821–49.
16. See the discussion of land law in James Tully, 'Aboriginal Property and Western Theory: Recovering a Middle Ground', *Social Philosophy and Policy*, Vol. 11, No. 2 (1994), pp. 153–80. I note here the strong parallels with the agrarian reformers of eighteenth-century England, who saw common land as barbaric and in a sense empty. Forms of social and political order other than the state and the market become (literally) invisible. See generally the fascinating account in J. M. Neeson, *Commoners*.
17. Sudipta Kaviraj, 'On State, Society and Discourse in India', in James Manor (ed.), *Rethinking Third World Politics* (London: Longmans, 1991), p. 78.
18. For a nice example, see Geoffrey A. Oddie, 'The Impact of British Rule on Religious Community: The Debate over the Hook-swinging Issue in Bengal and Madras, c. 1830–1894', in Peter Robb (ed.), *Society and Ideology Essays in South Asian History* (Delhi: Oxford University Press, 1993), pp. 177–95.
19. This is, of course, well documented in the writings of Charles Tilly and others. See, for example, Tilly (ed.), *The Formation of National States in Western Europe* (Princeton, NJ: Princeton University Press, 1975).

20. See the opening remarks of Robin Osborne, 'The *Demos* and its Divisions in Classical Athens', in Oswyn Murray and Simon Price, *The Greek City From Homer to Alexander* (Oxford: Clarendon Press, 1990).
21. For some evidence on this, see Margaret Canovan, 'The Skeleton in the Cupboard: Nationhood, Patriotism and Limited Loyalties', in Simon Caney, David George and Peter Jones (eds.), *National Rights, International Obligation* (Oxford: Westview Press, 1996). Intriguingly, Canovan suggests that liberals should continue to keep quiet about such matters.
22. Kaviraj, 'On State, Society and Discourse in India'.
23. Kal Holsti, *The State, War and the State of War* (Cambridge: Cambridge University Press, 1996), p. 76, and generally Chapters 3 and 4. Holsti greatly underestimates the extent to which colonialism was a modernizing project.
24. See Robert Jackson, *Quasi-States: Sovereignty, International Relations and the Third World* (Cambridge: Cambridge University Press, 1990).
25. Thus, Laurence Whitehead talks of the emergence of 'international society' and a 'global economic system' as 'structural characteristics' and 'processes' and 'underlying trends'. See Whitehead, 'Concerning International Support for Democracy in the South', in Robin Luckham and Gordon White (eds.), *Democratisation in the South: The Jagged Wave* (Manchester: Manchester University Press, 1996).
26. William I. Robinson, *Promoting Polyarchy: Globalization, US Intervention and Hegemony* (Cambridge: Cambridge University Press, 1996), p. 365. One cannot help noticing that Robinson's cure for this ailment is a globalization from below (see p. 383). Indeed, he already knows what the stance of such a movement must be which seems oddly undemocratic. The cure for the disease is more of the disease.
27. Anyone who doubts it should read a beautiful little essay by Gerard Prunier, 'The Experience of European Armies in Operation Restore Hope', in Walter Clarke and Jeffrey Herbst (eds.), *Learning from Somalia The Lessons of Armed Humanitarian Intervention* (Oxford: Westview Press, 1997). In the context of a flood of ponderous Anglo-Saxon moralizing and formalism it is a joy to read. For the latter, one might try Oliver Ramsbotham, 'Humanitarian Intervention 1990–95: A Need to Reconceptualize?', *Review of International Studies*, Vol. 23, No. 4 (1997), pp. 445–68, which explains nothing but nicely illustrates how 'social science' can be used to shape agendas. With the greatest respect, Prunier can explain the endless bad faith but not the will to intervene.
28. I recall asking a senior British government official what conceivable interest(s) Britain had in Rwanda. He replied rather impatiently that we had an interest in keeping the peace. Whether this is so or not it is to use interest in a way quite different from those forms of social science and popular discourse that see 'interests' as generative of political (and other) behaviour.
29. Security Council Resolutions 794 and 940 respectively.
30. The two are often conjoined in the concern to bolster westernized professional classes. On this see M. Pinto-Duschinsky, 'Nations in Transition to Democracy: The Management of Radical Transformation', *Ditchley Conference Report*, No. D 97/1. I have not used them systematically here, but such reports provide a useful way of listening in to the thinking aloud of

the international 'chattering classes': see, for instance, the International Crisis Group and the International Institute for Democracy and Electoral Assistance.

31. Bader, 'Citizenship and Exclusion', offers a useful guide to this thinking, which is pervasive in the academic literature.

32. Tully, 'Governing Conduct'.

33. Allan MacInnes suggests that English policy in Scotland after 1745 was 'marked by systematic state terrorism, characterised by a genocidal intent that verged on ethnic cleansing'. See MacInnes, *Clanship, Commerce and the House of Stuart, 1603–1788* (East Linton: Tuckwell Press, 1996), p. 211. His comments are, of course, quite outrageous. Liberal state terrorism and ethnic cleansing are called nation-building.

34. See, for example, Samuel Decalo, 'The Process, Prospects and Constraints of Democratisation in Africa', *African Affairs*, Vol. 91, No. 1 (1992), pp. 7–37, and Stephen Riley, 'The Democratic Transition in Africa', *Conflict Studies*, No. 257 (1992).

35. See Roger Charlton, 'The Politics of Elections in Botswana', *Africa*, Vol. 63, No. 3 (1993), pp. 330–70. Senegal is another interesting African case: see Leonardo Alfonso Villalon, *Islamic Society and State Power in Senegal* (Cambridge: Cambridge University Press, 1995).

36. The Conference did reassert the universal nature of rights as 'beyond question' (UN DocA/CONF.157/23), a delightfully tolerant sentiment, though it should be said that much liberal argument, especially of the born-again variety, operates at this level of intellectual profundity. See Fred Halliday, *Sleepwalking through History: The New World and its Discontents* (Centre for the Study of Global Governance, London School of Economics, 1993).

37. There is more to be said here of course and it may well be that with the disappearance of the Soviet bloc non-liberal capitalism becomes part of 'the enemy'. This is not, I think, racial. Cf. the growing hostility to France (accusations of 'archaism' and so on) in certain Anglo-American circles.

38. For a literal example, see National Democratic Institute for International Affairs, 'The October 31, 1991 Elections in Zambia' (Carter Center of Emory University).

Part III

International Relations beyond Europe

9
China and Global Liberalism

Christopher Hughes

In recent years, some East Asian states have enjoyed rapid economic development, even though they are governed by regimes which are difficult to characterize as 'liberal'. It has proved hard to reconcile this with the thesis that a 'globalization of liberalism' is occurring. Confronted by the rise of East Asian power, analysts looking at the globalization of liberalism have tended to start out by leaving caveats in their work.[1] Then, they develop their theories through *ad hoc* modifications which dilute the original thesis by bringing elements of cultural diversity back into the equation.[2] Alternatively, after an initial post-Cold War enthusiasm for the idea, albeit with minor qualifications when it comes to East Asian cases,[3] they have been forced by more recent events to revive the importance of culture to arrive at pessimistic conclusions which appear to nullify the initial thesis altogether.[4]

Instead of rejecting the globalization thesis altogether, this chapter argues that events in East Asia call for a new understanding of what liberalism's globalization really implies. This amounts to seeing the transmigration of liberalism not so much as a process of liberalism globalizing the world, but rather as a process of liberalism itself being globalized by the world. What is meant by this shift of focus will be explained by focusing on the position of China in globalization theories. By examining the globalization of liberalism from the perspective of Chinese attempts to enter the system of liberal states, it can be shown that the Chinese revolution has involved the articulation of liberal categories and imperatives in specific ways. The result has been an exploitation of ambiguities in the language of liberalism when it is applied to anthropomorphized states, rather than to individual human beings. Thus, a defence of highly illiberal domestic regimes is presented in terms of an international society of free states. For political philosophy, this development is reflected in the much-debated crisis of the Enlightenment project of constructing a universal civilization. For international relations, the transformation of liberalism points to the need to put more resources into understanding how ideas and institutions are adapted as they transmigrate across space and time, through a process of what David Armstrong has called 'socialization' into international society.[5]

Globalization as socialization

For a number of reasons, the People's Republic of China (PRC) represents a particularly problematic case for the globalization of liberalism thesis. It is a Leninist party-state presiding over one of the most rapidly growing of the world's economies, governing the world's largest population, it is a nuclear power that possesses growing conventional forces, it is expected to form the world's biggest market early in the new millennium, and it is a Permanent Member of the Security Council. One possible approach to understanding the role of the PRC in the globalization of liberalism would be to ask how its socio-political system measures up to a standard of liberalism. This is the kind of method adopted by theorists such as Fukuyama and Huntington, who measure the growth of aspects of liberalism in societies against standards such as the American Bill of Rights,[6] or Schumpeter's definition of democracy.[7]

Although such an approach has certainly been valuable in provoking debate, it does raise methodological problems. First of all, can 'liberalism' be measured by the sorts of standards used by Fukuyama and Huntington? The notion of liberalism is itself the subject of a dispute within Anglo-American political philosophy, and this raises issues that are highly relevant for coming to terms with a world of diverse cultures. Many of the communitarian critics of liberalism emphasize that contemporary (Rawlsian) liberalism is embedded in particular traditions of the Enlightenment.[8] This relativization of liberalism allows us to question the assumption that the Enlightenment project is part of a universal civilization founded on the rationality of individuals 'unencumbered' by parochial values.

One of the most interesting things about this debate, however, is that much of the ammunition of the critics comes from a wider field which embraces the territory of international relations. Recently, for example, John Gray has used the apparently successful illiberal models of development in East Asia, including the PRC, as part of his critique of the Enlightenment project, which goes beyond the attacks of the communitarians and calls for an 'agonistic liberalism'.[9] This involves such a degree of tolerance that even the search for the good conceived in terms of the ideal community must be discarded in favour of value-pluralism: 'the theory that there is an irreducible diversity of human values (goods, excellences, options, reasons for action, and so forth) and that when these values come into conflict or competition with one another there is no overarching standard or principle, no common currency or measure, whereby such conflicts can be arbitrated or resolved.'[10]

With the nature of liberalism itself thus under question, and with political philosophy increasingly drawing on the territory of international relations on this issue, we need to ask how international relations itself can both inform and accommodate this wider debate. Looking to the inventory of theory and evidence that has been accumulated from the study of existing relationships between communities, what will be proposed here is that one way of looking at liberalism's globalization can be found in a development of the 'English School' concept of an 'international society'.[11] This approach is useful primarily because it focuses analysis on how the *external* dimensions of liberal states have impacted on politics between communities, under the expansion of the 'Westphalian system of states'.[12] As various communities have transformed into states, there has gradually arisen the need to develop a better understanding of how this also entails the transformation of domestic politics, through a process of 'socialization'.

By looking at China's entry into international society, this chapter will demonstrate how the notion of 'socialization' might be developed, to arrive at an approach to globalization somewhat different from the exercises in measurement found in Huntington and Fukuyama. Central to this will be an understanding of how the impact of liberalism has taken place through a process of adaptation. This process has been determined largely by the need to build a political organization that possesses the minimum characteristics necessary for entry into international society. This has entailed not so much the rejection of liberal notions of the individual, the economy and the state, but more their reinterpretation. Most prominent in this reinterpretation has been a master narrative of national salvation. This narrative enables liberalism to be presented not so much as an argument privileging the liberty of individual human beings, but rather to be converted into an argument for the freedom of the community in a system of world politics conceived as a 'society' of states.

Learning liberalism from the outside

The problems that arise from trying to measure the spread of liberalism according to a given standard can be seen by looking at the transmigration across space and time of 'possessive individualism': the principle that the individual human being ought to enjoy a sphere of private activity within which other individuals and the state have no right to interfere.[13] Although this principle has been central to Anglo-American liberal discourse from John Locke to John Rawls, the variety that arises when it is applied in different contexts is evident in all the creative developments of utilitarianism, socialism and conservatism. Faced with such a range, it is not surprising that a historian of political thought like George Sabine prefers the woolly definition of liberalism as 'the secular form of Western civilization'.[14] When we understand the transformation of this principle in the context of the emergence of the Chinese nation-state, it is hardly surprising that an even greater degree of divergence is to be found. However, we should not see this process as either a Chinese acceptance or rejection of the Enlightenment project. Instead, the emergence of the Chinese nation-state involved a redefinition of possessive individualism which was determined largely by the requirements of socialization into the society of states.

Why the political dispensations that resulted from the impact of liberalism in Europe and North America on the one hand, and China on the other, are so different, can be understood as arising from the opposite ways in which liberalism has impacted on their respective cultures. In the European tradition, the indigenous questioning of the authority of the Church during the Reformation made possible the 'law of Christian nations', the 'public law of Europe' and the 'law of "civilized" nations' after Westphalia. For the Qing dynasty, however, liberalism was first perceived through the medium of the exogenous impact of the European states-system on the hierarchical world order of the Sinocentric system.[15] When the messenger of liberalism is the imperial state, it is not surprising that the subject of liberal discourse in China has not been the nature of human beings, but more how to create the personality of the liberal state as characterized by its external qualities. According to liberal states' own definition of international law, these qualities include, at a minimum, no superior authority beyond the state, the ability to exert supreme authority within a defined territory and the exercise of control over a certain number of people.[16]

One of the primary themes of China's long revolution has been the concern with creating the kind of political organization that can maintain the life, liberty and property of the state as an actor in a metaphorical 'society' of states. Rather than being a rejection of liberalism, this is in fact a development of the implications of liberalism for relations between communities, which can be found in the European tradition itself. From the attempts by post-Reformation jurists to develop a conception of order between sovereign states by drawing analogies with municipal law,[17] to the conception of world politics as an international society as restated more recently in Hedley Bull's *The Anarchical Society*,[18] an anthropomorphization of the state as actor has become embedded in the language of international relations.[19]

What is significant about much of the language of international relations is that it would make little sense without the kind of semantic shift that took place in the European tradition, when states came to be conceived in terms of a macrocosm of the human being, possessing all the attributes of a soul, body and rights that this entails.[20] If that shift was a radical one in the context of Reformation Europe, it was equally revolutionary for the hierarchical order of the Qing dynasty. Yet, the acceptance of this anthropomorphization of the state allows the elite in Beijing to argue that the right of the state to its own sphere of private activity is the fundamental principle of world order. As a PRC spokesperson approvingly put it concerning human rights:

> Hedley Bull said: 'The reluctance evident in the international community even to experiment with the conception of a right of humanitarian intervention reflects not only an unwillingness to jeopardize the rules of sovereignty and non-intervention by conceding such a right to individual states, but also the lack of any agreed doctrine as to what human rights are.'[21]

This recipe for reconciling highly illiberal domestic politics with a liberal international order of states must be understood as a consequence of the order in which the expansion of international society has taken place for different communities. In Anglo-American liberalism, which arises from largely endogenous developments, the discourse over the distinction between a public and a private sphere, the democratic organization of the political sphere and the minimalization of political intervention in the workings of the market are privileged. In

China, on the other hand, the prior necessity has been for a pro-gramme of nation-building, in which the value of individual liberties is assessed in terms of their compatibility with the task of achieving freedom for the state as an actor in international society. The resulting tension that arises from the unresolved ambiguities between individual and collective rights in liberal thinking lies behind what the Marxist historian, Li Zehou, calls China's 'Enlightenment and National Salvation Variations'.[22]

What is meant by this can best be demonstrated by understanding how the freedom of the individual has been defined with reference to the freedom of the state through a process of learning from four different sources. The first three of these sources, the imperial-liberal states of nineteenth-century Europe, Japan and the Soviet Union, will be covered briefly below, to show how the liberty of the individual has come to be subordinated to the needs of nation-building legitimized by a master narrative of national salvation. This will lead up to the question as to where the source of learning about socialization will lie in the post-Cold War era. Liberal democracy may not take a very high priority among the range of models the Chinese will consider.

Learning and the socialization of individualism

Looking, then, at early attempts to learn from the liberal states of Europe, the nineteenth-century exemplars of statehood, Qing reform-ers looked in particular to English liberalism, especially after the defeats of the Opium Wars. What can be seen from this early stage of learning, however, is that what such students wanted to know about liberalism was not how to realize the freedom of individuals. Rather, they were interested in what Benjamin Schwartz, looking at the life of Yen Fu (the first great translator of English political texts into Chinese), has called 'the Faustian element of Western civilization':[23] the secret of how to unlock and harness wealth and power for the state. It is there-fore not surprising that Yen Fu found Spencer's Social Darwinism more interesting than John Stuart Mill's concern with the threat to individ-ual liberty posed by the tyranny of the majority. 'Precisely because his [Yen Fu's] gaze is ultimately focused not on the individual per se, but on the presumed results of individualism, the sharp antitheses between the individual and society, individual initiative and social organiza-tion, and so on, do not penetrate to the heart of his perception.'[24] The resulting effect, as Schwartz sums it up, was that 'what has *not* come through in Yen Fu's perception is precisely that which is often considered to be the ultimate spiritual core of liberalism, the concept of the worth of persons within society as an end in itself, joined to the determination to shape social and political institutions to promote this value'.[25]

This initial bias in favour of liberalism as instrumental to enhancing the strength of the state was reinforced when the search for wealth and power shifted towards the second source of learning about liberalism: the neighbouring community that had made the most successful transformation to statehood, namely Japan. After the defeat of the Qing forces in the Sino-Japanese War (1894–5), students flocked to Japan to learn the secrets of modernity. Yet, in Japan too, liberalism had come through the medium of envoys sent abroad to discover the secrets of nation-building from Europe and the United States, rather than through the European struggle by entrepreneurs to protect themselves against the adverse affects of mercantilism. In the process, the Japanese had learned that entrance into international society meant more than just meeting a standard of civilization, it also meant converting available resources into a force that could meet the liberal powers on their own terms.[26]

However, despite the subjection of individual freedom to the search for freedom for the state in international society in Japan's encounter with the Enlightenment, many of the students from the Qing empire who had gone to Japan still tended to favour radical individualism (expressed in terms of democracy, rights and feminism) over putting liberalism to the service of nation-building.[27] When the Qing dynasty collapsed in 1911, however, and these reformers tried to replace the *ancien régime* with a constitution embracing the ideas of Locke, Montesquieu and Rousseau, a vacuum of authority resulted. This created the conditions for an attempt at imperial restoration and the disintegration of the new Republic of China into warlord fiefdoms. In this context of social and political disintegration the third source of learning about the Enlightenment emerged, in the shape of the Russian revolution.

The institution of Leninist Party dictatorship offered a new model with which to hold together what Sun Yat-sen described as the 'plate of loose sand'[28] that was supposed to constitute the Chinese nation. Under Bolshevik influence, Sun Yat-sen explained the relationship between the new concepts of individual, state and society by reinterpreting Lincoln's government 'of the people, for the people and by the people' and the watchwords of the French Revolution, 'Liberty, Equality, Fraternity', as the Three Principles of 'Nationalism, People's

Rights and People's Livelihood'.[29] This formula privileged the fate of
the nation over the freedom of the individual, providing the ideological foundation for the first blueprint for party dictatorship in China,
legitimized by the need for a period of nation-building (or 'tutelage')
by the Nationalist Party (*Kuomintang*). The linkage between Party dictatorship and national salvation was thus already established in the early
1920s, and was to be inherited as the master narrative of Chinese political discourse by the Communists when they came to power in 1949.
This is why, shortly after consolidating his leadership position and
crushing the outbreak of dissent in the 'Peking Spring' of 1979, Deng
Xiaoping reminded the people of China that, before the Chinese
Communist Party (CCP) enforced its rule and unified the nation,
China used to be seen as 'a heap of loose sand'.[30]

　With the Soviet influence on Chinese politics only ever having
played a supporting role to the earlier established mission of national
salvation, the CCP was in a good position to deal with the crisis of
world communism of the 1980s: it progressively emphasized the
imperatives of nationalist salvation over Marxist egalitarianism. This
also allowed people in China to begin to search for a fourth model of
nation-building. In the late 1980s, however, rather than looking to
the Western liberal democracies, many Chinese turned their eyes to
the examples of rapid economic growth displayed by neighbouring
economies, particularly the Four Dragons (Singapore, Hong Kong,
Taiwan, South Korea). These appeared to offer a solution to the old
problem that was first raised by Confucian reformers in the nineteenth century:[31] to achieve 'modernization' without 'westerniza-
tion'.[32] Such a trajectory becomes quite clear when we look at the
nature of dissent during the period leading up to Tiananmen, when
solutions to the problems of inflation and corruption were debated
within a discourse on what has been called 'neo-authoritarianism' (*xin
quanwei zhuyi*). This looked to the examples of China's neighbours for
an alternative path to economic development, and especially to
strong, authoritative leaders like Chiang Kai-shek in Taiwan and Park
Chung-Hee in South Korea.

The narrative of national salvation in contemporary China

The learning about liberalism that has been going on in China since
the mid-nineteenth century shows how liberalism has been interpreted
according to China's particular requirements as a socializing community. Looking at recent debates on modernity and development in

China, what becomes evident is that the theme of national salvation presents a real problem for the legitimization of political dissent after Marxism. This can be seen by a brief look at the nature of recent debates on modernity and development in China.

Third wave or fourth model?

Although the arguments on neo-authoritarianism have been complex and varied, what is interesting about the doctrine and its critics is that all continue the discourse on liberalism within the narrative of national salvation.[33] Advocates of neo-authoritarianism and their democratizing opponents agree on the need to depart from Marxist doctrine. Both favour the assumption that the institution of private property and the building of markets will lead to political liberalization through the formation of a middle class. They disagree, however, over how to get from a state-owned economy to a society in which there is a dualism between economics and politics, without bringing about national disintegration. As one of the main proponents of neo-authoritarianism, Wu Jiaxiang, puts it:

> We can observe, from the modern history of China, that the political pluralization that comes in advance of the building of markets often leads to fragmentation and chaos, to rule by gangs and cliques, or the partitioning of the government by warlords. If future practice belies this, I would be happy at any time to revise this viewpoint.[34]

With the narrative of national salvation thus re-established, the argument of the neo-authoritarians is fundamentally the same as that of Sun Yat-sen's nationalist revolution: national disintegration needs to be avoided by a concentration of power while reform takes place.

The evidence for the success of this strategy is found in various places throughout the world, but most significantly in the economic success of the Four Dragons under authoritarian governments which appear to have created conditions for recent political liberalization. Again, nation-building has taken precedence over individual liberty. It is highly significant that, in opposing this view, democrats do not take issue with the doctrine of neo-authoritarianism on the grounds that all authoritarianism is incompatible with individualism on principle. Instead, they argue that authoritarianism does not make sense as a solution to the political obstructions put in the way of Deng Xiaoping's economic reforms.[35] In this debate it becomes almost beside the point to advocate the value of political liberty as an end in itself, as the realization of the nature of Aristotle's 'political animal'. The character of the argument is still much more that of Yen Fu's Faustian searchings for national wealth and power, in which democracy is seen as 'the only plausible form through which we can reform and reestablish authority'.[36]

The sad fate of the proponents of democratization in June 1989 is well known. What is not so clear is the influence of the doctrine of 'neo-authoritarianism' after Tiananmen. Although the doctrine has been suppressed by the state, it can be seen as not far removed from the general thrust of the Party's attempts to re-legitimate its dictatorship through economic growth presided over by an increasingly authoritarian state. Deng Xiaoping calls this policy 'grabbing with two hands': '[o]ne hand opening and reforming, one hand suppressing all kinds of criminal activities'.[37] The nationalistic streak of the ideological offensive entailed here is made quite clear in key Party documents, such as the statement issued by the Third Plenum of the CCP's 14th Central Committee on 14 November 1993:

> The Party and government must widen with depth and vigour the development of patriotism, collectivism, socialist education; develop education in Chinese history, especially recent and contemporary history and the fine tradition of the Chinese nation, raising the self-respect of the nation, self-confidence and pride, developing the spirit of bitter and bold struggle, concentrating the great creative force of a billion people in the great task of building socialism with Chinese characteristics.[38]

Whether or not the CCP will succeed in this task of re-establishing its legitimacy is something of a moot point for the globalization of liberalism, when seen in the broader discourse on national salvation within which the CCP must legitimate its activities. What is more significant for liberalism's globalization is the Party's awareness that its leadership is more likely to be consolidated by looking not to the 'third wave' of democracy, but to the 'fourth model' for development offered by the booming economies of East Asia before their recent experiments with political liberalization. It is not surprising that Beijing's officials are more attentive to the example set by Singapore, than to that set by Taiwan. In the former case, capitalism is lauded, but liberal democracy is seen to be a block to economic development;[39] in the latter, divisions and conflict have become increasingly central to politics in the elections that have been held since 1991.[40] As Deng Xiaoping put it in January 1992, while the province of Guangdong is in the business of catching up with the Four Dragons, it should study Singapore's authoritarian methods for maintaining social order.[41] Again, then, liberal ideas can be seen to have been taken up very selectively and only in so far as they work within the narrative of national salvation. Rather than the type of democracy that Huntington avers to being the outcome of this process, Party dictatorship continues to be legitimized in terms of maintaining integrity and the strength of the Chinese state.

Democracy minus civil society

So far, we have seen how individual interests are subordinated to the destiny of the collective as a result of the interpretation of the Enlightenment in terms of national salvation. However, from the earliest years of the twentieth century, a faith in radical individualism and rationality did take root in Chinese thinking, and has flowered in a variety of forms over the decades. The student reformers and revolutionaries in Japan have already been mentioned, yet their failure after 1911 was not the end of attempts to reconcile individualism with national salvation. This continued in the attempt to establish constitutional democracy that rose and fell between 1911 and the establishment of the PRC in 1949. At another extreme, individualism can be seen as manifested in the passion for anarchism that was an important element of politics in the 1920s and 1930s.

It may seem that this was a straightforward appropriation of ideas from the Western Enlightenment. However, all these understandings of liberty were underpinned by the faith that 'Mr Science and Mr Democracy' would 'save the country'. This was the clarion call of the May Fourth Movement of 1919, when students demonstrated in Beijing to express their patriotic outrage over the transfer of the former German concessions in China to Japan at Versailles. It was this May Fourth Movement that the student demonstrators in Tiananmen Square in the spring of 1989 identified themselves with most strongly.[42] As the proclamation of the 'Coalition of Students' Self-Governing Councils of Beijing Higher Educational Institutes' put it in a declaration of 4 May 1989:

> Fellow students and countrymen, what the spirit of democracy means is that people should pool their ideas and think together, and

that every person's abilities should be fully developed and his or her interests protected. What the spirit of science means is that people should respect rationality and build the nation through science. Now more than ever, we need to sum up the experience and lessons of the many student movements since the May 4 Movement, to turn democracy and rationality into a kind of system and procedure. Only thus can the ideas first raised by the May 4 Movement become further institutionalised, the spirit of the movement develop, and the hope of a strong and prosperous Chinese nation become a reality.[43]

The domination of the discourse on democracy by the narrative of national salvation that is displayed in this statement is a reflection of the dilemma faced by dissidents, who must articulate their dissent with reference to the mission of national salvation monopolized by the Party. In times of political reform, such as the late 1980s, not being able to organize beyond the control of the Party-state becomes a secondary problem. The more pressing issue is how to present dissent as a legitimate activity, rather than as a traitorous movement to derail the process of nation-building.[44] This is why the demonstrators in Tiananmen Square had to go to such lengths to emphasize that theirs was a patriotic movement; it was not aimed at overthrowing the Party, but at making the Party more efficient in its nation-building activities through reform of the system of socialist democracy. It hardly needs to be stated that such a system pays little more than lip-service to notions of possessive individualism. Perhaps the role of the national salvation narrative in this is best indicated by the definition of socialist democracy found in an internal document circulated by the Military Science Academy of the People's Liberation Army shortly after the crisis in world communism had erupted: '[i]t is precisely because the people have seized national political rights, are masters of the nation, that they use the spirit of being masters when building their own country. Because of this, socialist democracy greatly mobilises the people's enthusiasm and creativity.'[45]

With the theme of national salvation dominating the discourse on democracy, the penetration of the authority of the state into the life of the individual can be legitimated to such a degree that outside observers are reduced to wondering whether it might be better to generate new categories for analysis, rather than look for a 'civil society' that does not appear to be there.[46] Where, for example, is the dividing line in this story from the front page of a recent issue of the *People's Daily*?

In Changqing Village, to facilitate a good social climate, good customs of domestic harmony, unity of in-laws, and respect for elders, on every twelfth moon there are held activities to appraise daughters-in-law. At the beginning of the first lunar month they announce a list of good daughters-in-law and give out certificates of merit. At the same time, the village branch of the Party gives the daughters-in-law a letter of merit to take home to their parents, thanking them for sending a good daughter-in-law to Changqing village. Last year, because Wei Dongmei did not treat her father-in-law well, she was dropped from the list. Unexpectedly, on returning to her parents, her mother opened the box of gifts and, seeing that there was no certificate of merit, asked why there was something missing and gave her daughter a good telling off. Wei Dongmei hung her head in shame. That day, Wei Dongmei hurried back to her matrimonial home and apologised to her father-in-law. After a few months she even specially bought a television for her father-in-law.

This time, when Wei Dongmei returned to her parents' house, her mother smiled and her son quickly brought out the certificate of merit and shouted, 'My mum has brought a certificate of merit'.

Wei Dongmei went into the sitting room and took a look. The table was full of fruit and sweets ... Dongmei's mother said, 'Dongmei, you have given our family face and won glory, I will look after you well.'[47]

Of course, the *People's Daily*, as the organ of the CCP, would not be expected to trumpet the formation of organizations such as the independent workers' and students' unions that arose in the late 1980s. Nevertheless, the above quote does give some idea of how the Party tries to break down barriers between culture and state ideology to make them one and the same. When that ideology is intimately linked with the cause of nation-building, little space is left for social groups to develop opposition to the state, without this opposition being seen as either anti-social or destabilizing. In this context, post-Marxist dissent needs to be presented more in terms of the rectification of economic problems caused by central planning and corruption, rather than as a movement towards placing the kind of value on the liberty of the individual that is necessary for the development of liberal democracy.

Thus, the narrative of national salvation and the achievement of a position of equality in international society under the leadership of the nation-building Party threaten to make the promotion of the kind of democratic system envisaged by Huntington and Fukuyama something of an irrelevance in contemporary Chinese politics.

Liberalism: national or global?

If the authoritarian paths to development followed by China's neighbours are seen by many inside China as offering a model for progress that is more suitable than liberal democracy, this poses the question of how the wider East Asian experience of socialization is now feeding back into and transforming the nature of international society. Will the learning process about liberalism that is taking place between new members be so successful in its rejection of liberal democracy that it will change the nature of the members who originally constituted the international club? This is something that troubles even the most optimistic of the analysts of the globalization of liberalism, such as Fukuyama, when he states:

> If Asians become convinced that their success was due more to their own faith than to borrowed cultures, if economic growth in America and Europe falters relative to that in the Far East, if Western societies continue to experience the progressive breakdown of basic social institutions like the family, and if they themselves treat Asia with distrust or hostility, then a systematic illiberal and non-democratic alternative combining technocratic economic rationalism with paternalistic authoritarianism may gain ground in the Far East.[48]

Faced by the phenomenon of East Asian-style reform, Huntington is also pessimistic about the development of democracy in East Asia and ponders the possibility of an authoritarian 'third reverse wave'. He identifies a number of conditions that could pose a threat to the 'third wave' of global democratization, most of which appear to be present in East Asia today.[49] These include a perception of decline in the power and social integrity of the United States, a move towards authoritarianism in Russia (which many people in Europe forget is an East Asian state), and the emergence of the PRC as a powerful authoritarian state that is perceived as a threat to the security of many of its reforming neighbours. Although he sees no reason why there should not be a 'fourth wave' of democratization in the future,[50] in his recent article,

'The Clash of Civilizations', this optimism seems to have dissipated altogether.[51]

In his later work, Huntington has offered a vision of the world in which conflict will take place primarily along cultural lines. Echoes are thus present of the wider sense of foreboding that has been growing in North America and Europe since the rise of East Asian economic power in the late 1970s. Faced by growing trade deficits, there has been much fretting over whether the region's success is due to neomercantilist practices or to factors such as the high value attached to education and frugality, the resulting productivity of the workforce, advanced management practices and high rates of saving and investment.[52] Aside from noting the infusion of Japanese management practices into the United States and Europe, some commentators have gone further and argue that Americans might do well to study Japanese educational and family ethics as well.[53]

This poses the perennial question of just how illiberal liberals are prepared to be if they perceive their own way of life to be at stake. As John Rawls recognizes, 'not all regimes can reasonably be required to be liberal, otherwise the law of peoples itself would not express liberalism's own principle of toleration for other reasonable ways of ordering society nor further its attempt to find a shared basis of agreement among reasonable peoples.'[54] Yet, if this is understood within the context of the growing power of illiberal states, does this mean that the implications of globalization must amount to the kind of toleration of diversity advocated by John Gray's 'agonistic liberalism'? Washington's unilateral actions directed at altering the domestic societies of its trade partners through measures such as the US–Japanese Structural Impediments Initiative talks, indicate that the liberal democracies are in fact facing a dilemma when it comes to choosing between tolerance of other regimes and the promotion of liberal democracy and free market economics.[55]

Faced with the possibility of an 'Asianisation of Asia',[56] the liberal democracies have shown an increasing inability to present a clear scale of priorities between political and economic concerns in foreign policy. A potent symbol of this has been the delinking of the renewal of China's MFN status from its human rights record in May 1994, by an administration that had come to power on a platform of not doing business with Beijing. Following this delinking, enthusiastic US 'commercial diplomacy' in the PRC has only underlined the fact that, if there are priorities for Washington, they are increasingly presented in terms of promoting liberal economics rather than liberal politics.[57]

The recent preference of both the United States and the European Union for developing political and commercial links with China can perhaps be seen as a tacit acknowledgement that external pressure has shown poor results in bringing about political liberalization. The rationale behind this is that integrating China into international society, through a process of what has come to be referred to as 'constructive engagement', will 'promote a responsible and constructive Chinese role'.[58] To understand that the outcome of interdependence will not necessarily be political and economic liberalization, however, one need look no further than Singapore. It is hard to think of any other territory that is more integrated into the global economy (apart from the colony of Hong Kong perhaps).[59] As for the impact of the information revolution, the assumption that the spread of images and data will lead to liberal change hardly seems justified in the light of world history since the development of print capitalism,[60] and even less likely when states may possess the technology of control and manipulation thanks to the collaboration of media magnates.[61] In fact, as Samuel S. Kim has pointed out, the assumptions that opening out to the world capitalist system will move China towards economic and political liberalization need to be balanced by an awareness of Beijing's ability to manage asymmetrical interdependence. The result 'seems to have turned dependency theory on its head' through a policy of development based on 'a neo-mercantilist, state-centred, and state-empowering model'.[62] That this can be seen from a broader perspective as a continuation of using science and technology to facilitate China's attainment of great-power status in a Darwinian world of competing nations,[63] brings us back to the central theme of this chapter: the whole process of China's socialization and interaction with liberalism continues to be dominated by the narrative of national salvation.

Conclusion

This chapter has argued that, rather than understanding the spread of liberalism as a process of the imposition of Anglo-American ideas on a supine world, it does more justice to the historical record to see globalization as a process involving different communities adapting ideas and institutions to their respective needs. From this perspective, although the relationship between highly authoritarian regimes and liberalism might seem to be a distant one, links can be seen when we realize how the revolutionary ideas of the state, the private sphere, the market, democracy and civil society have been recast in the furnace of nation-building, civil war, western colonialism, Japanese imperialism and the Cold War. Although the resulting understanding of liberalism within the narrative of national salvation may not have led to any cumulative increase in the liberty of individuals with regard to the state, the concept of liberty is still central to the legitimization of dictatorship, in so far as dictatorship is held to achieve freedom for the collective in a system of states that is built on a metaphor of human society. The resulting dispensation might not be attractive to western liberal democracies, but Beijing can always quote Hedley Bull to retort that the one drawback of liberalism is that one has to put up with the irritating habits of one's neighbours. More significantly, as an indication of the multi-directional nature of socialization, Beijing can also point to a growing swell of support for the transformation of liberalism in world politics in favour of the liberty of states. This can be seen in the promotion by East Asian spokespersons of the idea of 'Asian values', and in more concrete form in events such as the Bangkok Declaration on Human Rights.[64] Issued to clarify a common position for Asian states (including Middle Eastern and South Asian, as well as East Asian) at the Vienna Conference on Human Rights, this document can be seen as an example of liberalism's globalization in that it does not reject the idea of human rights altogether; rather, it sets an agenda in which cultural diversity, economic, social and cultural rights, as well as respect for national sovereignty, are paramount. East Asian spokespersons thus increasingly argue that the rejection of norms derived from the Enlightenment tradition is not a rejection of liberalism altogether, but is a form of greater toleration than that shown by the liberal democracies themselves. Kishore Mahbubani, Singapore's Deputy Secretary of Foreign Affairs, for example, points out that, while authoritative voices such as *The Economist* insist that Islamic countries cannot progress unless they become more 'western', nobody in East Asia says that the world's most populous Islamic state (Indonesia), or its most economically successful Islamic state (Malaysia), should be reshaped in some other mould.[65] Such statements point to the possibility that the PRC may gain increasing support for its version of liberalism as non-intervention and a tolerance of diversity when relations between states are concerned.

The position increasingly advocated by East Asian elites may not be far removed from the views of some of the main participants in the debate on the nature of liberalism itself. There are obvious parallels with the thinking of communitarians and, as pointed out above, Rawls himself has noted the paradox that arises when liberalism is extended to relationships between communities. Is it consistent to go as far as John Gray, who insists that the liberal democracies will have to adopt an 'agonistic' liberal attitude towards non-liberal democratic societies which,

> if they continue to perform well without converging on Western forms of life, may be regarded as the most radical empirical falsification of the Enlightenment project hitherto and so of traditional liberalism, since they are examples of the successful adoption of Western technologies by flourishing non-Occidental cultures that remain deeply resistant to Western values.[66]

That Rawls appears to run into trouble when he attempts to extend his theories to the international arena might seem to provide grounds for sympathy with Gray's position. Why, for example, should a dictatorial regime such as that in China be 'outlawed'[67] when many in that country might see such a regime as the best available option for stable development. To treat China as a community suffering from 'unfavourable conditions', on the other hand, which should be assisted to rise out of its 'political traditions and the background institutions of law, property, and class structure, with their sustaining beliefs and culture',[68] not only harks back to the nineteenth-century 'standard of civilization', it also assumes that somebody has a better solution to China's problems than the Chinese themselves.

That this inability to square the liberal project with developments in East Asia raises uncomfortable questions about the future of liberalism itself becomes more salient when the debate is taken up in the mass media. Here, there is a real danger that what is truly entailed in liberalism's globalization may be lost in the tide of polemics that is resulting in the erection of straw men for the pursuit of political agendas. This is especially apparent when conservative journalists characterize the rise of East Asian power as proof of the redundancy of social democracy,[69] and go so far as to call for a response to East Asia through developing a 'truly modern, elitist democracy of the future', and dismantling 'the increasingly anachronistic egalitarian, populist, permissive and undeferential kind to which we have become dangerously addicted'.[70]

Perhaps what international relations can contribute to this kind of debate is to step back a bit from political philosophy and journalism, and ask whether any of these commentators are basing their arguments on accurate information. Their arguments may indeed be valid, but there is no way to know this until the crude comparisons of stereotypes gives way to a better understanding of how the interaction between communities really takes place. When viewed from the perspective of China's socialization into international society, for example, not only do Rawls' prescriptions appear to be rather irrelevant to the problems being faced, but Gray's approach to cultural relativism also fails to do justice to the fact that cultures are not hermetically sealed units, but are composed of people who do engage in rational dialogue across communal boundaries, even if their conclusions are not always what liberals like.

It is here that the development of the notion of socialization may be useful in providing a better understanding of the mechanics and implications that are involved when ideas and institutions transmigrate. There is, of course, a danger that understanding world politics in terms of the expansion of international society can take on something of a Eurocentric sheen. This is no doubt due to the fact that 'it is not our perspective but the historical record itself that can be called Eurocentric'.[71] The resulting appearance of Eurocentricity tends to have been strengthened by the fact that much of the work carried out on the expansion of international society has focused on the earlier stages of the process, in which the spread of a European 'standard of civilization' can appear to have taken place as a unidirectional flow.[72] That this standard amounted to the spread of norms such as the protection of basic rights, a certain kind of legal-political organization, adherence to international law, the maintenance of permanent diplomatic relations and the demand that other communities respect the various cultural and ethical mores considered necessary to uphold these institutions[73] attests to its origins in the liberalism of the Enlightenment. What this means is that, if the international society model is to continue to be useful for understanding how Enlightenment concepts are transformed when that project itself may have failed, the idea of socialization must be developed adequately to accommodate what may be an increasing variety within the liberal discourse, as ideas and institutions are adapted by communities.

While, within the international society school of thinking, work has begun on developing an understanding of socialization as a two-way process,[74] this project will require a great deal of further empirical and textual analysis if it is to do justice to the complexity of the processes of transmigration. Unfortunately, in international relations there is still a tendency to confine to specialists the study of areas outside Europe and North America. Although much valuable work is carried out on the international relations of such areas, there is little effort put into understanding the wider implications of the results of this work for the normative assumptions upon which the notion of rational relationships between different communities rests. If international relations is to avoid both the Manichean vision of history as the struggle between liberals and authoritarians, as well as overpopulation by the 'pale-faced atheists' of anti-foundationalism,[75] this will require the ability to live dangerously. We must not only engage in more fruitful collaboration between international relations theorists and area studies specialists, but also show a greater willingness to draw on the sophisticated understanding of how transmigration takes place across cultures that has become central to fields such as literary theory and cultural studies.[76] If nothing else, it is to be hoped that what has been presented here is some idea of the nature of the tasks that this may involve.

Notes

1. See, for example, Francis Fukuyama, *The End of History and the Last Man* (London: Penguin, 1992), p. 243.
2. Francis Fukuyama, *Trust: The Social Virtues and the Creation of Prosperity* (London: Hamish Hamilton, 1995).
3. Samuel P. Huntington, *The Third Wave: Democratization in the Late Twentieth Century* (London: University of Oklahoma Press, 1991), p. 304.
4. Samuel P. Huntington, 'The Clash of Civilizations?', *Foreign Affairs*, Vol. 72, No. 3 (1993), pp. 22–49.
5. See especially David Armstrong, *Revolution and World Order: The Revolutionary State in International Society* (Oxford: Clarendon Press, 1993).
6. Fukuyama, *The End of History*, p. 43.
7. Huntington, *The Third Wave*, p. 7.
8. John Rawls, *A Theory of Justice* (Oxford: Clarendon Press, 1972); Michael Sandel, *Liberalism and the Limits of Justice* (Cambridge: Cambridge University Press, 1982); and Alasdair Macintyre, *After Virtue* (London: Duckworth, 1985). For a good general survey, see Stephen Mulhall and Adam Swift, *Liberals and Communitarians* (Oxford: Blackwell, 1992).
9. The term 'agonistic', Gray explains, comes from the Greek term *agon*; which has the meaning both of a contest, competition or rivalrous encounter, and of the conflict of characters in a tragic drama. John Gray, *Enlightenment's Wake* (New York: Routledge, 1995), p. 68.
10. *Ibid.*, pp. 68–9.
11. The seminal work in this school is, of course, Hedley Bull, *The Anarchical Society: A Study of Order in World Politics* (London: Macmillan, 1977). For a (critical) definition of the school, see Roy Jones, 'The "English School" of International Relations: A Case for Closure', *Review of International Studies*, Vol. 7, No. 1 (1981), pp. 1–13. For more recent work on the school, see

Sheila Grader, 'The English School of International Relations: Evidence and Evaluation', *Review of International Studies*, Vol. 14, No. 1 (1988); Peter Wilson, 'The English School of International Relations: A Reply to Sheila Grader', *Review of International Studies*, Vol. 15, No. 1 (1989); and Timothy Dunne, *Inventing International Society: A History of the English School* (London: Macmillan, 1998).

12. Valuable work which has developed this model to understand the expansion of international society includes Gerrit W. Gong, *The Standard of 'Civilization' in International Society* (Oxford: Clarendon Press, 1984), and Hedley Bull and Adam Watson (eds.), *The Expansion of International Society* (Oxford: Clarendon Press, 1985).

13. For a classic introduction to this idea, see C. B. Macpherson, *The Political Theory of Possessive Individualism: Hobbes to Locke* (Oxford: Clarendon Press, 1962).

14. George H. Sabine, *A History of Political Theory* (London: Harrap, 1952), p. 620.

15. For the Sinocentric world order, see John K. Fairbank (ed.), *The Chinese World Order: Traditional China's Foreign Relations* (Cambridge, MA: Harvard University Press, 1968). For a more recent application and development of this model, see Kim Key-Hiuk, *The Last Phase of the East Asian World Order: Korea, Japan and the Chinese Empire, 1860–1882* (London and Los Angeles, CA: University of California Press, 1980). Gerrit W. Gong illustrates the process of transformation involved through an analysis of the entry of Japan, China and Siam into international society, in *The Standard of 'Civilization' in International Society* (Oxford: Clarendon Press, 1984). See also Bull and Watson (eds.), *The Expansion of International Society*.

16. Such are the minimum requirements as commonly understood by international lawyers, see George Schwarzenberger, *A Manual of International Law* (London: Stevens and Sons, 1967), p. 55.

17. Edwin D. Dickinson, 'The Analogy between Natural Persons and International Persons in the Law of Nations', *Yale Law Journal*, Vol. 26, No. 7 (1916–17), pp. 564–91.

18. Bull, *The Anarchical Society*.

19. This should not be confused with what Hidemi Suganami refers to as the 'domestic analogy', which involves the upgrading of the level of management from the domestic to the international. Suganami gives the example of the argument that because domestic society requires institutions such as a police force and an agency to coordinate economic policies, so should international society. Suganami rightly points out that this argument is rejected by Bull. See Hidemi Suganami, *The Domestic Analogy and World Order Proposals* (Cambridge: Cambridge University Press, 1989), pp. 28–9.

20. See Jean Bodin, *Six Books of the Commonwealth*, trans. M. J. Tooley (Oxford: Basil Blackwell, 1967), Book One.

21. Yi Ding, 'Upholding the Five Principles of Peaceful Coexistence', *Beijing Review*, Vol. 33, No. 9 (1990), p. 12.

22. Li Zehou, '*Qimeng yu jiu guo de shuang zhong bian zou*' ('Variations on National Salvation and Enlightenment'), in *Zhongguo xiandai sixiang shi lun* ('On the History of Chinese Contemporary Thought') (Taipei: Feng Yun Shidai Chuban Gongsi, 1991).

23. Benjamin Schwartz, *In Search of Wealth and Power: Yen Fu and the West* (Cambridge, MA: Harvard University Press, 1964), p. 242.

24. *Ibid.*, pp. 239–40.

25. *Ibid.*, p. 240, emphasis original.

26. For an historical account of the rise of Japanese nationalism, see Delmer Brown, *Nationalism in Japan* (Berkeley and Los Angeles, CA: University of California Press, 1955).

27. A good recent account of the interaction with liberalism in this period is Lin Qiyan, *Buxiang minzhu: Zhongguo zhishi fenzi yu jindai minzhu sixiang* ('Towards Democracy: Chinese Intellectuals and Modern Democratic Thought') (Hong Kong: Zhonghua Shu Ju, 1989).

28. Sun Yat-sen, *Sanmin zhuyi* ('Three Principles of the People') (Taipei: Da zhongguo tu shu youxian gongsi, 1969), p. 1.

29. Shao Chuan Leng and Norman D. Palmer, *Sun Yat-sen and Communism* (London: Thames and Hudson, 1961), p. 26.

30. Deng Xiaoping, 'The Present Situation and the Tasks Before Us', in Deng Xiaoping, *Selected Works 1975–1982* (Beijing: Foreign Languages Press, 1984), p. 252.

31. The formula of separating essence from function (*ti-yong*), taking Western technology to save the Chinese essence, was formulated by the Confucian reformer Zhang Zhidong (1837–1909). See Joseph Levenson, *Confucian China and Its Modern Fate* (Berkeley and Los Angeles: University of California, 1965), pp. 59–79. It has remained a sub-theme in the development of Chinese politics down to the Special Economic Zones of today's PRC.

32. Fareed Zakaria, 'Culture is Destiny: A Conversation with Lee Kuan Yew', *Foreign Affairs*, Vol. 73, No. 2 (1994), pp. 116–18.

33. For the debate on neo-authoritarianism, see the four volumes of translations in *Chinese Sociology and Anthropology*, Vol. 23, No. 2 (1990–91) and Vol. 24, No. 1 (1991).

34. Wu Jiaxiang, 'The New Authoritarianism: An Express Train Toward Democracy by Building Markets', *Chinese Sociology and Anthropology*, Vol. 23, No. 2 (1990–91), p. 45.

35. Rong Jian, 'Does China Need an Authoritarian Political System in the Course of Modernization?', *Chinese Sociology and Anthropology*, Vol. 23, No. 2 (1990–91), p. 55.

36. *Ibid.*, p. 64.

37. Deng Xiaoping, '*Zai Wuchang, Shenzhen, Zhuhai, Shanghai deng di de tanhua yaodian*' ('Essentials of Talks in Wuchang, Shenzhen, Zhuhai and Shanghai'), *Renmin ribao* (People's Daily), overseas edition (6 November 1993), p. 1.

38. *Zhonggong zhongyang guanyu jianli shehui zhuyi shichang jingji tizhi ruogan wenti jueding* ('Resolution of the Central Committee of the Chinese Communist Party Concerning Various Problems in Building a Socialist Market Economy System'), complete text in *Renmin ribao*, overseas edition (17 November 1993), pp. 1 and 3.

39. Kishore Mahbubani, 'The Pacific Way', *Foreign Affairs*, Vol. 74, No. 1 (1995), pp. 103–4.

40. As the PRC's Xinhua news agency put it in a domestic service announcement, 'the so-called Taiwan's "democratic politics" is nothing but a show of

strange spectacle in which men and women in respectable suits and dresses are seen punching and kicking each other and letting out unprintable swearing words in the "Legislative Yuan" [parliament]. Money, power-abuse, out-of-control gangsters, vote-buyers "gaining [the] upper hand", and other scandals run rampant in all levels of elections.' Beijing Xinhua Domestic Service in Chinese, 6 August 1995 (FBIS-CHI-95-151, 7 August 1995).

41. *Zai Wuhan, Shenzhen, Zhuhai, Shanghai deng di de tanhua yaodian* ('Essential Points of Talks in Wuhan, Shenzhen, Zhuhai, Shanghai'), *Deng Xiaoping Wenxuan, Vol. 3* (Beijing: Renmin chubanshe, 1993), pp. 378–9.
42. On the parallels between 1919 and 1989, see Vera Schwarcz, 'Memory and Commemoration: The Chinese Search for a Livable Past', in Jeffrey N. Wasserstrom and Elizabeth J. Perry (eds.), *Popular Protest and Political Culture in Modern China* (Boulder, CO: Westview Press, 1994), pp. 109–23.
43. 'Let Our Cries Awaken Our Young Republic!', *Chinese Sociology and Anthropology*, Vol. 23, No. 1 (1990), p. 16.
44. This point is made in more detail by David Kelly and He Baogang, 'Emergent Civil Society and the Intellectuals in China', in Robert F. Miller (ed.), *The Developments of Civil Societies in Communist Systems* (Sydney: Allen and Unwin, 1992), pp. 33–4.
45. Military Science Academy of the PLA, *Renquan he minzhu wenti de bianxi* ('The Distinction Between Human Democracy and Human Rights'), *Neibu wengao* (Internal Documents) (1990): 10, p. 26.
46. Perry, *Popular Protest*, p. 2.
47. *Renmin ribao* (People's Daily) overseas edition (8 February 1995).
48. Fukuyama, *The End of History*, p. 243.
49. Huntington, *The Third Wave*, pp. 292–4.
50. *Ibid.*, pp. 315–16.
51. Huntington, 'The Clash of Civilisations', pp. 22–49.
52. Perhaps the first shot fired in this broadside was Ezra Vogel, *Japan as Number One: Lessons for America* (New York: Harper Colophon, 1979), followed up more recently with *The Four Little Dragons* (Cambridge, MA: Harvard University Press, 1991). Chalmers Johnson also made a huge impact on this debate with *MITI and the Japanese Miracle* (Stanford: Stanford University Press, 1982). See also James Fallows, *Looking at the Sun: The Rise of the New East Asian Economic and Political System* (New York: Pantheon Books, 1994), and James E. Auer, 'The Imperative US–Japanese Bond', *Orbis*, Vol. 39, No. 1 (1995), pp. 37–54.
53. Auer, *ibid.*, p. 51.
54. John Rawls, 'The Law of Peoples', in Stephen Shute and Suran Hurley (eds.), *On Human Rights* (New York: Basic Books, 1993), pp. 42–3.
55. The PRC was prevented by the United States from being a founding member of the WTO due to disputes over intellectual property copyrights. Some commentators attributed this to the underlying problem of the US trade deficit with the PRC. See, for example, David Roche, 'How China Can Secure its Future', *Financial Times* (11–12 February 1995). For a critique of US trade policy towards Japan, see Jagdish Bhagwati, 'Samurai's No More', *Foreign Affairs*, Vol. 73, No. 3 (1994), pp. 7–12. The latest in a long series of attempts to alter the structure of Japan's economy, going back to the

Structural Impediments Initiative of the Bush administration, has been the Clinton administration's unilateral imposition of tariffs on Japanese luxury cars in June 1995, which was almost universally criticized. The tariffs failed to achieve the main US demand for numerical quotas to be used to assess Japan's level of openness to US exports. 'Mr Clinton and Japan', *Financial Times* (9 May 1995).

56. Yoichi Funabashi, 'The Asianization of Asia', *Foreign Affairs*, Vol. 72, No. 5 (1993), pp. 75–85.

57. A US trade mission to the PRC led by Commerce Secretary Ron Brown at the end of August 1994 opened a new era of 'commercial diplomacy' with the signing of $5 bn worth of agreements, while Brown announced the determination of the United States to get its 'fair share' of the $250 billion worth of infrastructure projects before the end of the century. For Brown, 'China's importance – strategically and economically – demands that we construct a more comprehensive relationship.' His thinking was made clear when he told a meeting of the US–China Business Council that US exports to the PRC were growing at four times the rate of exports to the rest of the world, and that 150,000 Americans earned their living from these exports. 'Sino–US Relations enter New Phase', *Financial Times* (31 August 1994), p. 4. See also *International Herald Tribune* (30 August 1994).

58. Commission of the European Communities, *A Long Term Policy for China-Europe Relations* (COM(9)279, Brussels, 5 July 1995), p. 3.

59. With a population of only 3 million, Singapore posted US$ 74 bn in exports and US$ 85 bn of imports of merchandise trade in 1993, and US$ 11.5 bn of imports and US$ 20.7 bn of exports of commercial services in 1993. The figures for Hong Kong, with a population of 6 million, are merchandise exports US$ 135.4 bn, merchandise imports US$ 141.3 bn, imports of commercial services US$ 12.4 bn (1992), exports of commercial services US$ 28.9 bn (1992). *1994 Trends and Statistics: International Trade* (GATT).

60. On the relationship between print capitalism and the rise of nationalism, see Benedict Anderson, *Imagined Communities* (London: Verso, 1991).

61. 'Murdoch Cultivates his Asian Contacts', *Financial Times* (13 February 1995), p. 3.

62. Samuel S. Kim, 'China and the World in Theory and Practice', in Samuel S. Kim (ed.), *China and the World: Chinese Foreign Relations in the Post-Cold War Era* (Boulder, CO: Westview, 1994), p. 29.

63. *Ibid.*, p. 28.

64. 'Report of the Regional Meeting for Asia of the World Conference on Human Rights, Bangkok, 29 March–2 April 1993' (United Nations General Assembly, A/CONF.157/ASRM/8, 7 April 1993).

65. Mahbubani, 'The Pacific Way', p. 105.

66. Gray, *Enlightenment's Wake*, p. 83.

67. Rawls, 'The Law of Peoples', p. 78.

68. *Ibid.*, p. 75.

69. 'A Warning to the West', *The Sunday Times* (22 October 1995), Editorial.

70. Peregrine Worsthorne, 'The Right-Wing Path to Oppression', *Sunday Telegraph* (21 May 1995). For an interesting critique of the use of the Asian stereotype of the minimalist state in the politics of the British Conservative Party, see Will Hutton, 'Tory Fantasy of Far Eastern Promise', and Andrew

Higgins, 'Life and Death on the Landing', both in *The Guardian* (*Outlook* section) (28–29 October 1995).
71. Bull and Watson, *The Expansion of International Society*, p. 2.
72. Gerrit W. Gong, *The Standard of 'Civilization' in International Society* (Oxford: Clarendon Press, 1984), and Gong, 'China's Entry into International Society', in Bull and Watson (eds.), *The Expansion of International Society*, pp. 171–84.
73. Gong, *The Standard of 'Civilization'*, pp. 14–21.
74. Armstrong, *Revolution and World Order*.
75. This image of anti-foundationalists is raised by Chris Brown, who draws it from Nietzsche's idea of the 'pale' atheist who, 'while rejecting belief in God, thinks it possible to carry on living much as before'. Chris Brown, *International Relations Theory: New Normative Approaches* (London: Harvester Wheatsheaf, 1992), p. 198.
76. Since Edward Said's *Orientalism* (London: Penguin Books, 1991), a whole genre has arisen in these fields to approach the task of understanding the nature of perception across cultural-political barriers. A particularly interesting approach that may be of use to international relations is the development of the concept of 'hybridity': see Robert Young, *Colonial Desire: Hybridity in Theory, Culture and Race* (London: Routledge, 1995).

10
International Human Rights Norms and the State in Egypt and Tunisia: Globalization, Liberalism and Culture

Katerina Dalacoura

This chapter will examine the issue of the internationalization of human rights norms by focusing on two Middle Eastern countries.[1] It has three aims. First, to assess the extent to which human rights, as concept and value, are becoming increasingly important and legitimate in the Middle East. Second, to show that this process, in so far as it is taking place, does not involve a straightforward growing acceptance of international human rights norms by disparate cultures and societies. On the contrary, it results in enormous strains and frequent setbacks, which may ultimately cause its reversal. Third, to argue that our attempt to understand the process of the internationalization of human rights norms can be successful only if we concentrate on the profoundly ambiguous role of the state: the state is the source of both the violation and protection of human rights, it is the entity against which culture defines and redefines itself, and it is the link and mediator between the international environment and domestic society.

This brief study provides a comment on the concept of, and debate about, globalization in international relations theory.[2] The definition of the term 'globalization' is wide and not all its aspects will be discussed here. The objective of this chapter is to trace the emergence of political norms (relating to human rights) as they develop in global interaction between various societies and cultures. In one very basic sense, globalization in this chapter therefore refers to the internationalization of human rights norms. However, the spread of human rights ideas is only one feature of the wider process of 'globalization'. This chapter will therefore attempt to situate the internationalization of human rights within this broader phenomenon and examine how the various economic, political and ideational strands within the globalization process interact. It is very difficult, of course, to draw general conclusions about global processes on the basis of the study of only two societies, and my comments are necessarily limited. None the less, as I will show, these processes are so complex that it is only through the meticulous analysis of particular situations that we can avoid the generalities into which discussions of globalization often tend to degenerate.

The approaches towards globalization can be divided into two broad categories. One, represented in this volume by Stephen Gill, focuses on globalization as the spread of market structures and neoliberal economics and is explicitly or implicitly critical of its impact, which reinforces power structures and causes the erosion of the prospects for democratization. The liberal view, on the other hand, views the spread of liberal economics as a positive phenomenon in so far as it increases wealth and erodes state boundaries and nationalist sentiments.[3] This chapter occupies a third position which is, for want of a better word, state-centric, though not in the realist or communitarian sense. In this view globalization – of both economic and ideational forces – leads to a growing homogenization of disparate societies and states.[4] It has not as yet undermined the position of the state as a powerful institution; questions of political organization and culture are still being worked out primarily between citizens within its boundaries. In other words, my position here is that the state is going strong and that calls for its demise are still premature. It is plausible that globalization of economic forces will in the long run reduce the hold of the state on society, but this is not an immediate concern which we can meaningfully discuss (at least in the Middle East).[5] Further, a global civil society (as described by Mervyn Frost in this volume) is still embryonic, barely emerging from the shadow of the state.[6]

The chapter is organized as follows. The first section will define human rights and briefly set out the normative problems surrounding their validity in a global multicultural context. The second will focus on Egypt and Tunisia and demonstrate that human rights have become an increasingly visible and contentious issue since the 1970s. It will introduce the question of culture and Islam, and discuss various attempts to construct specifically Islamic conceptions of human rights. The third section – the crux of the chapter – will concentrate on the position and policies of the states in those two societies, as regards human rights, and juxtapose them with those of Islamist opposition movements. The conclusion will summarize the findings and bring out their relevance to the debate on globalization.

The meaning and validity of human rights norms

Human rights are the rights people have by virtue of their humanity.[7] The definition is straightforward enough and it can be argued that, during the twentieth century, this simple idea became increasingly acceptable internationally, even if only as a declaration of intent. The problems surrounding human rights begin when this principle is translated into a list of specific rights. For example, almost 50 years after the proclamation of the Universal Declaration of Human Rights, there is still considerable controversy and disagreement over even this supposedly definitive document. In recent years, furthermore, problems have also arisen concerning the introduction of new 'third' and 'fourth' generation rights.[8]

The controversy centres on the issue of cultural relativism and relativism in general. It is not the main purpose of this chapter to discuss the philosophical aspects of the problem of relativism, but a clarification of my views on human rights is essential as on it depends the cohesion of the argument. I take the conception of human rights and the 'list' of rights provided in the Universal Declaration and the International Covenants on Civil and Political Rights (1966) and on Economic, Social and Cultural Rights (1966) to be morally authoritative. Women's rights, as expounded in the Convention on the Elimination of All Forms of Discrimination against Women (1979), are also central to the conception of human rights as they are understood here.[9]

My view, which I will not elaborate on, is that only a liberal philosophical position can ensure respect for human rights and that relativism and cultural relativism, despite their frequent liberal intention, would entail the abandonment of the concept of human rights. Communitarian theories, similarly, would not allow for the defence of human rights.[10] I also posit that human rights and liberalism refer to the individual, not to the state. Chris Hughes shows elsewhere in this volume how the failure to assert this distinction with regard to the 'morality of states' can be a source of legitimation for authoritarian regimes which violate human rights and defend their right to do so, without interference, in the name of liberalism.

Human rights, therefore, are taken in this discussion to be individual rights the most authoritative formulation of which is contained in the instruments of international law mentioned above. Group or collective rights in this perspective are legitimate only if they are an expression of these individual rights. This understanding of human rights will be used as the standard against which their internationalization can be assessed.

From this starting point, it is a fairly safe generalization to assert that, since the 1960s, there has been a growing world-wide consensus that human rights must be respected. The growth of human rights NGOs is one sign of this development, as salience of human rights in the concerns of international organizations is another.[11] Within widely divergent societies, however, human rights have also become a central issue in political debates. Ordinary people exhibit greater awareness of them, and they have ceased to be an elite issue. Increasingly, over the last 20–30 years, the argument that political and civil rights must await the realization of development projects (and that therefore social or economic rights must take precedence over political and civil rights) has been sidelined.[12] The obverse argument, that economic and social rights are not of equal stature to political and civil rights, has been marginalized, at least in academic debate.[13] There is, it seems, a growing consensus and convergence of opinion on both making human rights a central issue in any political context, and on the belief that the pertinent 'list' of rights must involve basic political and civil rights and at least some rudimentary economic and social rights.

The problem is that, despite this seeming convergence and growing salience of human rights issues world-wide, the increasing acceptance of the list of rights as given in the Universal Declaration in *form*, has been accompanied by greater contention over the *content* and *substance* of those rights. More specifically, whereas countries or individuals accept that human rights are a good and worthwhile cause, they put forward culturally-specific interpretations of the term as an alternative to supposedly western understandings. This was evident at the United Nations Conference on Human Rights in Vienna in September 1993, during which some countries proposed an Asian understanding of human rights, it has also been manifested in debates on African conceptions of rights; and the growing literature on human rights in the Muslim world, which gives an Islamic content and justification to rights principles.[14] The second section of this chapter will show in some detail how, in the case of the latter, the conceptions of rights put forward by *some* Islamist groups have resulted in a perversion of their meaning.

The contention over what human rights mean and how they should be pursued in political and social life is cultural, or rather it is presented as such. Its first and most immediate result is to sustain the outdated and crude distinction between western and non-western cultures, which ignores the fact that the debate on human rights rages even more pressingly within, rather than *between*, cultures. To challenge this picture of international relations, the remainder of this chapter will show that culture is *not* a central explanatory medium for any proper analysis of human rights issues in our time. To argue otherwise would be to fall hostage to a questionable culturally essentialist thesis.[15] 'Culture' is a malleable and vague concept, open to rival interpretations and even manipulations.[16] In thinking about the links between culture and human rights – an eminently political issue – we must turn to the question of political agency. In other words, because culture does not have a political existence independent of those who seek to employ it as a political instrument, it is to the state and its rivals that we must turn for a proper analysis. For it is often states that uphold and champion the alternative Islamic, Asian or African understandings of human rights. Furthermore, in the cases of Egypt and Tunisia, among other countries in the Middle East, it is political opposition groups wishing to capture the state which propose alternative 'Islamic' human rights. These political opposition groups, as section 3 will show, are not the media of expression of authentic popular culture, but political movements which have emerged and developed out of a dialectical relationship with the state they battle and the society they wish to dominate.

Islamist conceptions of human rights in Egypt and Tunisia

Egypt and Tunisia are useful cases for the examination of the issues raised in this chapter. In the first place, both countries have been subject to international political, economic and cultural influences to a considerable degree, making them fruitful objects of study for the impact of globalization. The process was initiated in the colonial times of the nineteenth century, with British involvement in Egypt and French involvement in Algeria followed by the colonization of Tunisia proper in 1881. Integration in the world market and political domination, direct or indirect, was coupled with a remarkable degree of cultural penetration. The ideas of nineteenth-century liberalism – progress, representative democracy, individual freedom and secularism – impacted powerfully on Egyptian and Tunisian societies, and contributed to the rise of nationalist and reformist movements, which ultimately turned against the colonizers who upheld them in principle while violating them in practice.

Upon independence, the openness of Egypt and Tunisia to international forces did not diminish. The former's strategic position in the Middle East and alignment to the USSR from 1956 onwards, and the latter's close links to France and the Western world generally (which were not eliminated by the 'socialist' experiment of the 1960s), ensured that they have always remained permeable by international forces. This openness has increased since the 1970s for domestic as well as international reasons. The two countries have, since that time, undertaken a tortuous liberalization of their economies and, more relevant to our purposes, of their political systems.

In the second place, because of their openness to global forces on a political, economic and security level, the two countries are good cases for the study of the interaction of the various strands of the globalization process. In both Egypt and Tunisia, since the 1970s, and even more so since the 1980s, human rights have become central in political discourse, and are upheld, debated and appropriated by every major actor in the domestic political arena. This is evident in the emergence of human rights organizations, but also in the pronouncements of government and opposition.[17] As Islamist[18] movements rose to prominence during the same period, they also took up human rights. They were compelled to do so, as I will show later in this chapter, because human rights had become a growing concern in their respective societies and could not be ignored by any serious political contender. In order to incorporate human rights in their ideology, Islamist movements had to work out ways in which such rights could be harmonized with their understanding of Islam. In the process, the meaning of human rights underwent considerable reinterpretation and, in some cases, perversion.[19] In sum, international influences and pressures had a strong impact, and human rights norms thus became increasingly acceptable in the Egyptian and Tunisian societies. However, on the other hand, they caused a major cultural reaction.

I am equating, in this context, 'cultural reaction' with 'Islamist reaction'. There are major problems in identifying the two, given both the indefinable nature of the term 'culture' and the similarly indeterminate and controversial nature of Islam and what it means in any given society in any given historical period. It is therefore necessary to clarify two issues. First, it is by no means my intention to argue that Islam is an objective, clearly defined entity with permanent characteristics. On the contrary, as many studies have shown, Islam is shaped and transformed by the societies in which it spreads.[20] My argument in the next section will reinforce this. Second, I do not claim that there is something in Muslim societies that renders Islamism a more genuinely popular option than other ideologies. To claim that would be to deny the long periods during which the majority of the people of Egypt and Tunisia have endorsed and identified with secular ideologies and world-views.[21] Instead, I am simply positing that during a specific historical period, from the 1970s onwards and increasingly from the 1980s, and for particular social, political and economic reasons, the major opposition to the established regimes in Egypt and Tunisia has come from Islamist movements.

In the eyes of the majority of Egyptians and Tunisians, and throughout the Arab world, culture and Islam are perceived as being two sides of the same coin. For this reason, the Egyptian Muslim Brotherhood and the Tunisian Nahda movements have attempted, and to an extent succeeded, in arguing that culture must be equated with their own, particular interpretation of Islam: that is, Islam as an illiberal political ideology.[22] In other words, Islamist movements, by posing as the sole representatives of the 'authentic' popular spirit, have tried to appropriate both Islam and culture and impose on them their own interpretation. It is within the confines of this Islamist world-view that I propose to examine their definition of human rights. Initially, the Islamists adopted human rights as protection against state repression, because the Egyptian and Tunisian regimes which at first had nurtured them quickly realized that the Islamists had slipped from their control and turned against them. However, the opposition movements also attempted to construct a *synthesis* between human rights and Islam. Eventually, the Muslim Brotherhood and the Nahda were arguing that their understanding of human rights was the sole genuine one and that universal human rights are a western imperialist plot. The Koran can be read in a humanist light and offers considerable potential for a reconciliation with human rights principles. To deny that would be an affront to the many liberal Islamist intellectuals who have worked out such a meaningful reconciliation, or indeed to many ordinary people who take the view that Islam is or must be an open and tolerant religion. It would also imply that it is only a Christian or a secular system of ideas that is hospitable to human rights principles, which is not the case. However, having said that, even a cursory examination of their pronouncements indicates that the two major Islamist opposition movements in Egypt and Tunisia have failed, to date, to provide a liberal interpretation of Islam and a concomitant understanding of human rights, in the proper spirit of the term.

A few examples will illustrate the point.[23] There are three major problems with a reconciliation of the Islamic religion with human rights principles: freedom of conscience (the freedom of a Muslim to renounce his or her religion), the position of women, and the position of non-Muslims in a Muslim society. In all three areas the contradictions between Islamic law, traditionally conceived, and the principles of equality and freedom of conscience are glossed over rather than resolved in the discourses of the Egyptian Muslim Brotherhood and the Tunisian Nahda.[24] In the case of the first problem, they declare, on the basis of some Koranic injunctions, primarily the one which asserts that 'there is no compulsion in religion',[25] that Islam allows freedom of conscience. However, Islamist thinkers and politicians make this vague assertion without confronting the difficulties it entails. In particular, they are averse to being open about their belief that apostates in Islam must be executed. Alternatively, they claim, without explanation, that this rule does not violate freedom of conscience. On the second issue, they assert that there is absolute equality between the sexes and that Islam prescribes a difference in role between men and women, not an unequal status. In this way, issues such as polygamy and inequality in inheritance laws are explained away and it is argued that Islam, more than any other religion, respects women. Alternatively, another argument is employed, pointing out that men and women are, according to Islam, 'equal before the law' while failing to clarify that the Islamic law, traditionally understood, is profoundly discriminatory against women.[26] On the third question, of non-Muslims within a Muslim society, similar arguments are used: non-Muslims must be 'protected' and 'respected'; their autonomy is secured. But in fact their separate standing is just a cloak for unequal status and their autonomy a means of rendering them second-class citizens.

There are further problems with the Muslim Brotherhood's and Nahda's ideas on basic rights and freedoms: for example, their ambiguous views on multi-partyism and democratic representation generally. It must be noted, however, that there is considerable disagreement within those movements with regard to all the aforementioned issues and, furthermore, that there is considerable discrepancy between leaders and followers.[27] Many female followers, for example, see the Islamist movement as a means of enabling them to participate in political and social life, involving their liberation, not their restriction.

They either ignore their leaders' pronouncements on sexual inequality or accept them in name only.[28]

There is also, within Egyptian and Tunisian societies, a number of alternative Islamist groups which put forward more liberal interpretations of Islam. These are looser movements, mostly of intellectuals, but their influence far exceeds their number. They have attempted to resolve the three thorny issues of reconciliation between Islam and human rights discussed above in a more satisfactory manner, by concentrating on the historicity of the Koran and on its progressive spirit. They are therefore able to suggest that the letter of the *sharia* (Islamic) law need not be observed in our time – indeed that the *sharia*, far from immutable, is obsolete and that the method of *ijtihad* (reinterpretation of the religious text) must be continued in order to develop social and political rules emanating from the Koran in accordance with the requirements of modern times. The liberal Islamists, therefore, are able to accommodate human rights principles with regard to freedom of conscience, women, non-Muslims and democratic norms, without arguing for a separation between religion and politics.[29]

The alternative views of their followers and pressure from liberal Islamists create tensions within the dominant Islamist movements in Egypt and Tunisia. These tensions, however, have not as yet led to a serious transformation of their ideas, although such a development is not inconceivable. On the level of political discourse, the conclusion must be that both the Tunisian and Egyptian Islamist movements have failed to arrive at satisfactory reconciliations between their understandings of Islam and the principles of human rights. They have taken on board the agenda of the Universal Declaration, often literally matching each right elaborated in this document with their rival Islamic interpretation. However, they have not come up with a meaningful Islamic alternative. In this sense, although these groups have been affected by the spread of global human rights norms, have felt compelled to respond to the challenge they present, and have retained their form, they have interpreted them in a way that denies their very substance and purpose.

It could be argued that the development described above signifies a gradual convergence of positions, and that it is a transitionary phase towards full acceptance of human rights norms by Islamist movements. There is, in my view, no cause for such optimism at this juncture, because of state repression and the confrontational environment in which the groups operate.[30] Rather, the tentative conclusion to date must be that globalizing forces and international human rights norms, by their very impact, have had a reverse outcome to the one expected or intended by human rights supporters within and outside the two countries in question. These norms have been seen, by large numbers of Egyptians and Tunisians, as an affront to Muslim cultural specificity, not as the means for its protection. The reasons for this development will be explored in the following section.

Understanding the relationship between human rights and Islamism

The third and final argument in this chapter has two components. The first is that the Islamist interpretation of human rights principles described above has been the outcome of international inputs, as mediated by the Egyptian and Tunisian states. The second, concomitant point is that it is state policies and choices in the domestic realm which have also determined the Islamist ideological positions in relation to Islam, culture and human rights. I posit, on the basis of the historical experience of the two countries, that it is only by concentrating on the state and its relationship with the international environment, on the one hand, and society, on the other, that we can assess the prospects for the globalization of human rights norms in our time. If the process described below is not replicated in other countries or regions of the world in its exact form, it nevertheless points towards a direction of enquiry about human rights and globalization which may be generally useful.

State and liberal policies

During the 1970s and the 1980s the Egyptian and Tunisian regimes initiated a process of political liberalization in their respective countries. In the 1970s, President Sadat proclaimed the return of democracy to Egypt, an end to arbitrary rule and respect for human rights. He took cautious steps towards multi-partyism, the culmination of which was the legalization of a number of political parties. After the popular riots of 1977, however, democratization was arrested. It resumed after the assassination of Sadat and the coming into office of Hosni Mubarak in 1981. During the 1980s, freedom of speech and association were enhanced and a semi-democratic electoral process was institutionalized. Under Mubarak, however, the Muslim Brotherhood (which had initially been nurtured by Sadat) provided a growing challenge to the Egyptian regime. The crackdown on the radical Islamists, and also on the more moderate Muslim Brothers, which became ferocious from

1992 and 1995 respectively, signalled a second major reversal of liberalizing policies and a return to the restriction of freedoms.[31]

Tunisia liberalized at a later stage. During the 1970s, the proclaimed democratization of the political system failed to materialize. Prime Minister Hedi Nouira ruled with an iron fist, while President Habib Bourguiba continued to retain a grip on the political process. Nevertheless, even during that time and more so in the 1980s, there was a renewed interest in, and popular pressure for, civil and political rights. The Tunisian Organization of Human Rights was founded in 1977. Tunisia's traditionally powerful trade union movement exerted pressure on the government in support of social and economic rights. Such activism involved a widening realization that those rights could only be effectively secured within a democratic framework. The crackdowns suffered by the General Union of Tunisian Workers in 1978 and 1984 indicated a return to authoritarianism and exacerbated the sense of stagnation in Tunisian political life. The overthrow of Bourguiba in 1987 and his replacement by President Zine El Abidine Ben Ali led to a brief liberalization period, which was, however, soon reversed as the Islamists grew in popularity. Similarly to Egypt, Tunisia is currently undergoing a repressive phase.[32]

How are we to make sense of these developments and fits and starts as regards the respect of human rights in Egypt and Tunisia? The impetus for liberalization in both societies arose partly from domestic conditions, but international forces played a crucial role in two ways. First, influences on political and economic thinking began to change as grand modernization projects were abandoned in the late 1960s and 1970s in many parts of the world (and especially in Latin America). This was accompanied by a partial recoil from the 'full-belly' thesis and a realization that human rights and development go hand in hand. The impact of non-governmental organizations such as Amnesty International also added to the shift away from authoritarian or at least state-centric policies and towards more emphasis on individual rights.[33] The second way in which international factors caused the cautious liberalization was through the need of those states to secure material western support. This need was most pressing in Egypt following the 1967 war and Nasser's death in 1970. It was met by Sadat's shift of alliance from the Soviet Union to the United States. It also meant, for both Egypt and Tunisia, greater integration in the world market as structural adjustment programmes were introduced.[34] The power of ideas coming from abroad (transmitted through academic writings and NGOs but also through the simple power of example) and economic and security considerations therefore reinforced one another in making the two states liberalize. Yet, the intermingling of human rights norms with western interests had a pernicious effect, in that among segments of the population, human rights, the 'West' and the Egyptian and Tunisian states became identified as one and the same entity. Human rights and the general principles underlying them were therefore perceived as western propositions.

The point that needs to be stressed at this juncture is that the initiative for political liberalization lay with the states in question. International and domestic pressures were considerable, but they did not force the hand of the regimes in question. The option of continuing with authoritarian policies was still available, albeit at increasing costs to the regimes. It was deemed, therefore, a better policy to shift to greater political openness. This policy change was made possible by the institutional development and evolution of the two states. They began to liberalize because they were, to a degree, secure in their hold of society. The Egyptian and Tunisian states are fundamentally strong states, effective in their control, legitimate to a considerable degree in the eyes of their people, and an integral part and institution of society.[35]

The historical development of both states accounts for this. The Egyptian state has been a centralized and powerful institution, which developed gradually since the early nineteenth century. The regime that captured it in 1952 under Nasser strengthened it even further. This regime has undergone transformations, but has shown considerable staying power. Similarly, the Tunisian state has steadily evolved since the nineteenth century into a powerful set of institutions, and the traditional homogeneity of Tunisian society has added to its strength. Bourguiba came to power at independence in 1956 at the head of a nationalist movement which had engulfed Tunisian society as a whole. The regime he installed continues to enjoy considerable legitimacy. Neither the British colonizers in Egypt nor the French in Tunisia arrested the development of state institutions in any major way. On the contrary, they encouraged novel methods of central control and enhanced state authority. Further, neither state currently depends on a *rentier* economy, as the countries are not major oil producers. This may be an economic drawback – particularly in the case of Egypt, which has experienced many periods of economic stagnation since the 1930s – but it has also allowed for social integration.

It is with this background in mind that we need to understand the changes over the last 25 years or so. The Egyptian and Tunisian states were confident enough to allow some political challenge and initiate changes in the legal systems towards respecting basic freedoms. Furthermore, apart from reforms of a strictly political nature, which were admittedly only a hesitant step in the right direction, the two states continued to be guarantors of women's rights and to promote modernist and anti-traditionalist principles. Upon independence, the Bourguiba regime had carried out a reform of Islamic law, the Code of Personal Status of 1956, which had gone further than any other in the Arab world towards securing women's rights. The principles of this family law are still upheld and defended by the Tunisian regime.[36] The Egyptian regime rests on the principle of equality between the sizeable Christian Coptic minority and the Muslim majority of the country. The Sadat regime in 1979 attempted to buttress women's rights and weaken the hold of Islamic law.[37]

Women's rights are not only human rights: they are the cornerstone of any truly liberal system. For it is impossible strictly to separate the private and the public in any society, and the maintenance of traditional hierarchies in family relationships has a pernicious effect on all social and political relationships. It is thus crucial to emphasize the Tunisian and Egyptian states' defence of women's rights which may still be wanting but is, nevertheless, considerable and balance it with their more dismal record in civil and political rights. With this broader picture in mind, it is possible to argue that in many ways it is the state in those two countries that seeks to promote human rights or, indeed, that in the case of women's rights, the regimes presently in power are their best guarantee. In that sense, a strong state (in the sense of a *legitimate state that is capable of upholding the rule of law*) implies a respect for human rights, not their abuse. Even in the case of political rights, the partial liberalization that has taken place in Egypt and Tunisia (for these two countries are a far cry from authoritarian regimes in the Middle East like Iraq or Syria) has been the result of powerful and well-integrated state institutions. The strength of a state is in this case analogous, not obverse, to the vitality of civil society.

I have argued, so far, that the Egyptian and Tunisian states, by upholding modernist principles and partially liberalizing their polities, have adopted and become identified with international human rights norms and Western interests. These norms were introduced primarily through being taken up by the states in question, not through transnational actors and links, although the latter played a part. Therefore, the reaction of Islamist movements against the states they battle includes a rejection of the norms they stand for. The rejection of 'Western' human rights, in other words, is a rejection of the political agency which represents them. The second and related question is why the dominant opposition to these regimes and their policies has come, in the last 20 years or so, from the Islamists. Was there anything inevitable in the rise of religious and 'cultural' opposition? To answer this question we need to examine the domestic political configurations in the two countries.

The emergence of the Islamist opposition

The emergence of the Islamist opposition has been the outcome of the defeat of ideological alternatives in both countries. Regime policies, driven by fears of the secular opposition, were a powerful reason for the emergence of the Islamists. Further, the Islamist movements' ideology is defined by their respective states, in that they occupy the ideological space unappropriated and 'uncontaminated' by the regimes. Specifically, the Egyptian and Tunisian states have at times championed, at least in word if not in deed, both liberal and socialist ideals and have thereby coopted and undermined liberal or socialist opposition movements. The only ideology with which the states have not been associated has been Islamism.

In Egypt, Sadat's fear of Nasserism meant that his regime, in power from 1970, used its clout against the leftist opposition. It undermined the secular liberal opposition of the New Wafd because its political rebirth, in 1978, was too promising.[38] To counterbalance these secular opposition movements Sadat encouraged the Islamists, who seemed compliant and subservient to his will. The persistent political hammering of the left and liberal opposition and the support of the Islamists by the regime are only the partial explanation of the latter's emergence, however. The broader setting of disillusionment in Egyptian politics was caused by the crushing defeat in the Six Day War of 1967. Another source of disillusionment was the failure of the socialist experiment of the 1960s, which was accompanied by widespread hardship and discontent over elite corruption. The war and economic crisis partly delegitimized the regime and the secular world-view for which it stood. Thus, it caused a search for alternative political solutions. Islamism emerged as the only unsullied ideology, with a promise to strengthen the nation against its enemies (mainly Israel) and cure the social and political malaise. It was the perceived failure of alternative ideologies, in other words, not some automatic appeal of Muslims to

Islam as a political religion, that caused the growth of the Islamist movement in the 1980s.

In Tunisia the elimination of alternatives was the result of regime policies rather than outside defeat. Habib Bourguiba, who considered political opposition as a personal affront, persistently sabotaged the liberal opposition, the Movement of Socialist Democrats, from its emergence in 1971. During the 1970s and early 1980s, Bourguiba also saw the leftist opposition as a great threat. Leftists were therefore continuously subjected to persecution and imprisonment. However, it was the Tunisian trade union movement that bore the brunt of the regime's repressive policies, as mentioned above. After political confrontation in 1978 and 1984, the union was crushed and the opportunity for a viable opposition (Labour) party to emerge in Tunisia was lost.[39] The ground was open for the rise of the Islamists who were the only political movement to remain unscathed either by association with or repression by the regime. Economic strains from the late 1970s onwards exacerbated the delegitimation of the regime.

Why is it, however, that the Islamists have not appealed purely to a traditionalist Islam, but have been forced to attempt a synthesis between Islam and human rights? Here the manner in which they emerged – essentially by default – becomes pertinent once again. For if the secular parties descended into political oblivion, the principles for which they stood did not become altogether eclipsed. Political and civil rights had entered political discourse as a demand of the body politic, and had become prominent concerns in the face of regime limitations. The parallel emergence of Islam meant that the two positions had to be somehow fused. Therefore, whereas the Egyptian Muslim Brotherhood and Tunisian Nahda initially rejected human rights as being 'foreign' and irrelevant to their world-views, they gradually reversed their position and adopted human rights as one of their causes. As major political actors aiming at the capture of power, the Islamists were compelled to take into account the concerns of the society they wanted to dominate. Human rights and democracy were issues that could not be ignored, and the evolution of their ideas as regards this matter is a sign of the extent to which Islamism is shaped by the society in which it emerges. The Islamists' ideology evolved in interaction with both state and civil society.

In the light of the above arguments, we can understand the Egyptian and Tunisian experiences more clearly. The states in question are relatively strong and legitimate, and are founded upon a long history of institutional development. They have dominated political practice and ideology, and all opposition movements have emerged in a context created by them. Islam and culture are therefore the latest means of opposition by aspiring counter-élites. The dominant position of the states is also evident in that they have been able to withstand the Islamist attack, and there are those who argue that the Islamist movements do not enjoy the support of the majority of their populations.[40] This is no mean achievement given the repeated failures of the regimes on all counts: economic, political and, in the case of Egypt, in foreign policy. Conversely, the achievement is only partial in that, although state institutions retain their ability to control society, their legitimacy has begun to wane. The strains show in the growing rigour of the Islamist opposition, especially in Egypt. Economic problems induced in turn by economic liberalization and structural adjustment, undertaken in tandem with political liberalization, have enormously added to the difficulties experienced by those states.[41] The result has been that after the initial steps towards liberalization and after being taken aback by the secular and later Islamist opposition that these gave rise to, these states reverted to repressive policies and violations of human rights. The Egyptian and Tunisian states were strong enough to begin the liberalization but not strong enough to sustain it.[42]

As the challenge from Islamists mounted, there was a further development apart from repressive policies. In their attempt to undercut the Islamist movements, the Tunisian and Egyptian states have begun to adopt some of their prescribed policies, at least in a superficial manner. Presidents Mubarak and Ben Ali have gone on pilgrimages to Mecca and invoke Allah in their speeches.[43] Religious programmes have filled the audio-visual media and the religious authorities are often appeased by the regimes. Through such measures they have tried to claim that they are, in fact, the real defenders of the faith and the authentic representatives of popular culture. In this dialectical relationship between states and Islamist movements, it is human rights principles that have suffered, as the states which previously championed women's rights and modernist values have become more reluctant to do so, at least openly, lest they damage their religious credentials.[44]

Conclusion

This chapter has attempted to trace some of the outcomes of the process of globalization by concentrating on the experience of two societies. It has argued that human rights norms are indeed spreading and becoming more relevant in the politics of disparate societies. It has also argued that this process engenders a cultural reaction on the part of these societies, and that, for this reason, it may ultimately come to be reversed.

The conception of human rights against which their internationalization is to be measured is, as was explained in the first section, that contained in the Universal Declaration of Human Rights and the other instruments of international law. This was stated rather than defended because it would otherwise have caused a long digression from the central argument. However, we need to clarify and employ one particular conception of human rights in order to assess their internationalization. There was no implication in this line of argument that it is only a western, Christian or secular understanding of human rights that is valid. Indeed, as Islamist liberals have shown, a harmonization of Islam and human rights principles is feasible. What has occurred, however, in the cases of Egypt and Tunisia is the patent failure of the dominant Islamist opposition movements to achieve such a harmonization.

The second section showed how the prevalent interpretation of Islam by the main Islamist movements in those two countries is very problematic with respect to human rights principles. It noted that three major issues present a direct and obvious conflict between Islam, traditionally conceived, and human rights principles: freedom of conscience, equality of the sexes and relations between Muslims and non-Muslims. The possible reasons why liberal Islamism has not predominated were not addressed. The only point addressed in this part was that the internationalization of human rights has caused a major cultural reaction in the two countries under consideration, and that this reaction has taken the form of the appropriation and perversion of human rights principles.

The third section tried to link the various threads together and connect the domestic phenomenon of cultural reaction with the international environment and globalization by concentrating on the role and position of the state. It argued that international human rights norms had a powerful impact on Egypt and Tunisia, but not through transnational actors or the emergence of a strong civil society. Rather, international human rights norms were an option available in the global 'market of ideas' and they were adopted and introduced by the state. This is not to denigrate the efforts of human rights activists, nor the battles of Egyptian and Tunisian citizens for democratization. It is only to note that such efforts, although important, were not the deciding factor in democratization during the 1970s and 1980s. It was the regimes which chose the option of democratization (and liberalization of the economy) and they did so, I argued, from a position of relative strength, not weakness.

In those two cases, therefore, and possibly in others, it is the state which introduces the international human rights norms into society, for whatever reasons, not civil society picking up those norms and forcing states to respect them. Further, the reaction against those norms is not of a culture against international norms but of a political movement appropriating a set of cultural principles (which can, as we know, be interpreted in a variety of ways) against the state which has adopted these international norms and has become identified with them. This is what the 'Islamist reaction against the West' consists of in our cases.

The exploration of the domestic causes for the emergence of Islamism further unpacked the notion of culture and its connection with human rights principles. Again the analysis of these causes rested on the state, its policy choices and its relation with society. The Islamists emerged as the dominant opposition after the two regimes weakened the secular opposition parties. Also, because the Egyptian and Tunisian states have a long history of institution-building and enjoy some, albeit now dented, legitimacy, they are able to determine the ideological agenda. Islamist movements react against them from the only political space unoccupied by state ideological involvement, that of Islam, which is also conventionally identified with culture. In sum, there was nothing inevitable about the emergence of political Islam and the 'cultural reaction' in those two Muslim societies.

The consequence of these developments is that, for the foreseeable future, the states in question remain a better guarantee for human rights than opposition movements, especially through the policies of protecting some women's rights if not guaranteeing them full equality, treating (in the case of Egypt) Muslims and Copts as equal citizens, and upholding freedom of conscience to some degree against the onslaught of the Islamists. Given the mixed and, during the 1990s, increasingly repressive record of the regimes in terms of civil and political rights, this conclusion is indeed a grim one.

This chapter has attempted to dispel two different yet interrelated pictures of international relations. The first is of globalizing forces bypassing or rendering the state irrelevant in their homogenization of disparate societies.[45] Instead, I have refocused attention on the state and its role as key mediator between the international environment and domestic society. I have also indicated that the various strands in globalization – for example, growing integration in and openness to the world market, on the one hand, and the increasing impact of human rights norms or models of political liberalization, on the other – pull in contradictory directions. The trend towards homogenization is far from unilinear and this may have the impact of reversing globalizing forces, leading, ultimately, to the rejection of international human rights norms.

The second picture of international relations which this chapter has tried to undermine is that of the world being divided into cultural 'regions' or blocs and the related implication that culture may have an impact on international politics. By refocusing attention on the central role of the state as a political actor, I tried to show that culture cannot be an independent variable in our analysis of international politics. To deny this is to fall hostage to cultural essentialism on either side of the supposed cultural divide.

Notes

1. Many of the arguments I make in this chapter are drawn from my work on *Islam, Human Rights and International Relations: Liberalism and the Interpretation of Religion* (London: I. B. Tauris, 1998).
2. On globalization generally see Evan Luard, *The Globalisation of Politics: The Changed Focus of Political Action in the Modern World* (Basingstoke: Macmillan, 1990), and M. J. Peterson, 'Transnational Activity, International Society and World Politics', *Millennium Journal of International Studies*, Vol. 21, No. 3 (1992), pp. 371–88.
3. See, for example, Kenichi Ohmae, *The End of the National State: The Rise of Regional Economies* (New York: Free Press, 1995).
4. For a parallel view of international society, see Fred Halliday,'International Society as Homogeneity: Burke, Marx and Fukuyama', *Millennium*, Vol. 21, No. 3 (1992), pp. 435–61.
5. See comments at the end of this chapter.
6. This is not to say that I disagree with the ethical content of the global civil society as envisaged by Frost. I do not hold that the state or society constitutes the individual, but that the state provides the framework within which individuals work out their rights and duties. This is not in disagreement with liberal principles which, as I assert later, inform this chapter.
7. The literature on human rights is of course vast. For some of the best studies see John Vincent, *Human Rights and International Relations* (Cambridge: Cambridge University Press, 1986); Jack Donnelly, *Universal Human Rights in Theory and Practice* (Ithaca, NY: Cornell University Press, 1989); and Donnelly, *International Human Rights* (Boulder, CO: Westview Press, 1993). For fascinating insights, see Philip Windsor, 'Cultural Dialogue

in Human Rights', in Meghnad Desai and Paul Redfern (eds.), *Global Governance: Ethics and Economics of the World Order* (London: Pinter, 1995), pp. 177–89.

8. See Rosalyn Higgins, *Problems and Process: International Law and How We Use It* (Oxford: Clarendon Press, 1994), Chapter 6.

9. Ian Brownlie (ed.), *Basic Documents on Human Rights* (Oxford: Clarendon Press, 1992).

10. For a discussion on the interpretations of liberalism, see John Rawls, *A Theory of Justice* (Oxford: Oxford University Press, 1972), and *Political Liberalism* (New York: Columbia University Press, 1993); Charles Taylor, *The Ethics of Authenticity* (Cambridge, MA: Harvard University Press, 1991); Jeremy Waldron (ed.), *Theories of Rights* (New York: Oxford University Press, 1984); Stephen Mulhall and Adam Swift, *Liberals and Communitarians* (Oxford: Blackwell, 1992); Michael Sandel (ed.), *Liberalism and its Critics* (Oxford: Blackwell, 1984); and Shlomo Avineri and Avner de-Shalit (eds.), *Communitarianism and Individualism* (Oxford: Oxford University Press, 1992). For a view more directly relevant to international relations, see John Rawls, 'The Law of Peoples', in Stephen Shute and Susan Hurley (eds.), *On Human Rights: The Oxford Amnesty Lectures* (New York: Basic Books, 1993), pp. 41–82.

11. See the Introduction in Philip Alston (ed.), *The United Nations and Human Rights: A Critical Appraisal* (Oxford: Clarendon Press, 1992), especially p. 2, on the 'dramatic increase' of United Nations organs dealing with human rights.

12. See, for example, David P. Forsythe (ed.), *Human Rights and Development: International Views* (Basingstoke: Macmillan, 1989).

13. Compare Maurice Cranston, *What Are Human Rights?* (New York: Taplinger, 1973), with Henry Shue, *Basic Rights: Subsistence, Affluence and US Foreign Policy* (Princeton, NJ: Princeton University Press, 1980).

14. Kevin Boyle, 'Stock-Taking on Human Rights: The World Conference on Human Rights, Vienna 1993', in David Beetham (ed.), *Politics and Human Rights* (Oxford: Blackwell, 1995), pp. 79–95; Rhoda Howard, 'Is There an African Concept of Human Rights?', in John Vincent (ed.), *Foreign Policy and Human Rights* (Cambridge: Cambridge University Press, 1986), pp. 11–32; and Ann Elizabeth Mayer, *Islam and Human Rights: Tradition and Politics* (London and Boulder, CO: Pinter Publishers and Westview Press, 1991). Note however that the African debate on human rights raged particularly in the 1970s and has now subsided (I am grateful to James Mayall for this information).

15. For a different view, see Samuel P. Huntington, 'The Clash of Civilizations?', *Foreign Affairs*, Vol. 72, No. 3 (1993), pp. 22–49.

16. For an excellent exposition of this view, see Sami Zubaida, *Islam, the People and the State: Political Ideas and Movements in the Middle East* (London: I. B. Tauris, 1993).

17. See Susan Waltz, *Human Rights and Reform: Changing the Face of North African Politics* (Berkeley, CA: University of California Press, 1995); Waltz, 'Tunisia's League and the Pursuit of Human Rights', *The Maghreb Review*, Vol. 14, Nos. 3–4 (1989), pp. 214–25; and Kevin Dwyer, *Arab Voices: The Human Rights Debate in the Middle East* (London: Routledge, 1992).

18. The word 'Islamist' is used here to denote individuals and groups who seek the application of Islamic principles – as they interpret them – to political life. Given the broadness of this category, and the range of opinion it includes, the term Islamist is a very useful one because it is sufficiently 'neutral'. It is also useful in that it allows us to distinguish Islamists from 'fundamentalists', the latter being radical and extremist groups. Fundamentalists are Islamists but not all Islamists are fundamentalists.

19. This point is also made by Jack Donnelly, 'Human Rights and Human Dignity: An Analytic Critique of Non-Western Conceptions of Human Rights', *American Political Science Review*, Vol. 76, No. 2 (1982), pp. 303–16.

20. See, for example, Clifford Geertz, *Islam Observed: Religious Development in Morocco and Indonesia* (Chicago, IL: University of Chicago Press, 1968), and Maxime Rodinson, *Islam and Capitalism*, trans. Brian Pearce (London: Allen Lane, 1974).

21. Zubaida, *Islam*, Introduction to second edition, p. xiii.

22. The literature on the Muslim Brotherhood of Egypt is vast. The classic study is Richard P. Mitchell, *The Society of Muslim Brothers* (London: Oxford University Press, 1969). See also John Esposito, *The Islamic Threat: Myth or Reality?* (Oxford: Oxford University Press, 1992); Gilles Kepel, *The Prophet and Pharaoh: Muslim Extremism in Egypt*, trans. Jon Rothschild (London: Al-Saqi Books, 1985); and Nazih Ayubi, *Political Islam: Religion and Politics in the Arab World* (London: Routledge, 1991). The literature on the Tunisian Nahda movement is also extensive. For some of the best analysis, see Abdelkader Zghal, 'Le Retour du Sacré et la Nouvelle Demande Idéologique des Jeunes Scholarisés', in Christiane Souriau (ed.), *Le Maghreb Musulman en 1979* (Paris: CNRS, 1981), pp. 41–64; Zghal, 'The Reactivation of Tradition in a Post-Traditional Society', *Daedalus*, Vol. 102, No. 1 (1973), pp. 225–37; Douglas K. Magnuson, 'Islamic Reform in Contemporary Tunisia: A Comparative Ethnographic Study' (PhD thesis, Brown University, 1987); Elbaki Hermassi, 'La Societé Tunisienne au Miroir Islamiste', *Maghreb-Machrek*, No. 103 (1984), pp. 39–56; and Susan Waltz, 'Islamist Appeal in Tunisia', *Middle East Journal*, Vol. 40, No. 4 (1986), pp. 651–70.

23. This information has been collected by the author during fieldwork in Egypt (October 1992 and April 1997) and Tunisia (April 1993), and in an interview with the leader of the Tunisian Islamist movement, Rashid Ghannoushi, in London (April 1992).

24. Note, however, that the Egyptian and Tunisian Islamists are still more moderate in their views than, for example, the Algerian Islamic Salvation Front or the Saudi or Sudanese regimes. In many ways, as well, the Tunisian Islamists are more moderate than the Egyptian Muslim Brotherhood. In Tunisia, also, there is no equivalent to the Islamist terrorist groups which became so prominent in Egypt in the 1990s.

25. *The Koran*, fifth edition, trans. with notes N. J. Dawood (London: Penguin, 1990), 2:255 (p. 38).

26. Islamic law traditionally has allowed men up to four wives and has given them the rights to divorce without judicial procedure (the utterance of a phrase is sufficient). It also gives men automatic guardianship over the children in case of divorce. Inheritance laws are also discriminatory in that men receive double the inheritance of women. In the judicial process, the

testimony of one male witness is equal to the testimony of two women. See Joseph Schacht, *An Introduction to Islamic Law* (Oxford: Clarendon Press, 1964).

27. The Muslim Brotherhood for example suffered a split with the creation, by some of its younger members, of the Wasat (Centre) Party in 1996. This is now defunct, however.

28. See Souhayr Belhassen, 'Femmes Tunisiennes Islamistes', in Souriau, *Le Maghreb*, pp. 77–94; Sophie Bessis and Belhassen, *Femmes du Maghreb: L'Enjeu* (Tunis: Cérés Productions – Editions J. C. Lattes, 1992), especially pp. 191–275; and Joel Beinin, 'Egyptian Women and the Politics of Protest', review article of Arlene Elowe Macleod, *Accommodating Protest: Working Women, the New Veiling and Change in Cairo* (New York: Columbia University Press, 1990), in *Middle East Report*, Vol. 22, No. 3 (1992), pp. 41–2.

29. In Tunisia, the liberal Islamists centre on the Progressive Islamist group, whose leading figures are Hamid Enneifer and Shaheddine Jourshi. In Egypt this tendency is not represented by a group but by isolated individuals such as Muhammad Said Al-Ashmawi, Kamal Aboulmagd and Muhamniad Siled Al-Awa. For a powerful statement in favour of Islamic liberalism, see Abullah Ahmed An-Naim, *Towards an Islamic Reformation: Civil Liberties, Human Rights and International Law* (Syracuse, NY: Syracuse University Press, 1990).

30. This is also discussed by Mayer, *Islam and Human Rights*, pp. 191–2.

31. On the Egyptian politics of this period, see John Waterbury, *The Egypt of Nasser and Sadat: The Political Economy of Two Regimes* (Princeton, NJ: Princeton University Press, 1983); Mark N. Cooper, *The Transformation of Egypt* (London: Croom Helm, 1982); Leonard Binder, *In A Moment of Enthusiasm: Political Power and the Second Stratum in Egypt* (Chicago, IL: University of Chicago Press, 1978); Hamied Ansari, *Egypt: The Stalled Society* (New York: State University of New York Press, 1986); and Raymond A. Hinnebusch, *Egyptian Politics under Sadat: The Post-Populist Development of an Authoritarian-Modernizing State* (Boulder, CO: Lynne Rienner, 1988).

32. On Tunisian politics, see Clement Henry Moore, *Tunisia since Independence* (Berkeley, CA: University of California Press, 1965); I. William Zartman *et al.* (eds.), *Political Elites in Arab North Africa* (New York: Longman, 1982); Lisa Anderson, *The State and Social Transformation in Tunisia and Libya* (Princeton, NJ: Princeton University Press, 1986); and Elbaki Hermassi, *Leadership and National Development in North Africa* (Berkeley, CA: University of California Press, 1972).

33. International human rights norms had an impact on civil society, which in turn exerted pressure on the state in favour of human rights principles. It was not, however, the deciding factor in bringing about political liberalization. Liberal policies were not instituted mainly as a result of public pressure, although it was a contributory factor.

34. Note, however, that these structural adjustment programmes were introduced in a very piecemeal and hesitant fashion and that, despite early pronouncements, they started having an impact only from the late 1980s onwards. See I. William Zartman (ed.), *Tunisia: The Political Economy of Reform* (Boulder, CO: Lynne Rienner, 1991); Timothy Niblock and Emma

Murphy (eds.), *Economic and Political Liberalization in the Middle East* (London: British Academic Press, 1993); and Alan Richards and John Waterbury, *A Political Economy of the Middle East: State, Class and Economic Development* (Boulder, CO: Westview Press, 1990).

35. I do not wish to exaggerate this point. The limitations of the states under examination here are numerous – and are expressed in their partially repressive nature and in their corruption, evident especially in Egypt – but when placed in a global context and contrasted with, for instance, sub-Saharan African states, their achievements are extensive. Compare, for example, Robert Jackson, *Quasi-States: Sovereignty, International Relations and the Third World* (Cambridge: Cambridge University Press, 1990).

36. On the question of women and the law in Tunisia, see Alya Cherif Chamari, *La Femme et la Loi en Tunisie* (Casablanca: Editions de Fennec, 1991); Bessis and Belhassen, *Femmes du Maghreb,* and Aziza Darghouth Medimegh, *Droits et Vécus de la Femme en Tunisie* (Lyons: L'Hermés-Edilis, 1992).

37. This law was challenged in the courts by Islamists and partly reversed in 1984, however. On the question of women and the law in Egypt, see Earl L. Sullivan, *Women in Egyptian Public Life* (Syracuse, NY: Syracuse University Press, 1986), and on the Coptic minority, J. D. Pennington, 'The Copts in Modern Egypt', *Middle Eastern Studies*, Vol. 18, No. 2 (1982), pp. 158–79, and Saad Eddin Ibrahim *et al., The Copts of Egypt* (London: Minority Rights Group, 1996).

38. See Raymond A. Hinnebusch, 'The Reemergence of the Wafd Party: Glimpses of the Liberal Opposition in Egypt', *International Journal of Middle East Studies*, Vol. 16, No. 1 (1984), pp. 99–121; Donald Malcolm Reid, 'The Return of the Egyptian Wafd', *International Journal of African Historical Studies*, Vol. 12, No. 3 (1979), pp. 389–415; and Hinnebusch, 'The National Progressive Unionist Party: The Nationalist-Left Opposition in Post-Populist Egypt', *Arab Studies Quarterly*, Vol. 3, No. 4 (1981), pp. 325–51. On the Opposition in Egypt generally, see Mona Makram-Ebeid, 'The Role of the Official Opposition', in Charles Tripp and Robert Owen (eds.), *Egypt under Mubarak* (London: Routledge, 1989), pp. 21–51.

39. On the liberal opposition in Tunisia, see Clement Henry Moore, 'Clientelist Ideology and Political Change: Fictitious Networks in Egypt and Tunisia', in Ernest Gellner and John Waterbury (eds.), *Patrons and Clients in Mediterranean Societies* (London: Duckworth, 1977), pp. 255–73. On the trade union movement, see Hachmi Karoui and Mahdi Messaoudi, 'Le Discours Syndical en Tunisie à la Veille du 26 Janvier 1978: L'Elan Suspendu', and Mohsen Toumi, 'Le Discours "Ouvrier" en Tunisie: Usages Syndicaux et Usages Politiques', both in Noureddine Sraieb (ed.), *Le Mouvement Ouvrier Maghrebin* (Paris: CNRS, 1985), pp. 285–304 and 305–17 respectively.

40. There can be no evidence for this, however. We can see that the popularity of the Muslim Brotherhood in Egypt has been eroded after 1992 due to the atrocities committed by radical Islamist groups (which are linked in public opinion to the moderate Muslim Brotherhood). On the Tunisian Islamists not commanding a majority, see Elbaki Hermassi, 'The Islamicist Movement and November 7', in Zartman (ed.), *Tunisia*, pp. 193–204. But all

major commentators and authors agree that exact information on the strength of the Islamist support, as well as on the social composition of this support, is not available.

41. In the 1990s, economic liberalization and structural adjustment policies have survived political liberalism, which is in abeyance. There is perhaps a causal relationship between the two phenomena, although the increasing rigour of the Islamist movements is a second major factor in causing the restriction of political liberties. Note that recent economic indicators for Egypt are good and improving: see the *Economist Intelligence Unit, Egypt: Country Report,* First Quarter 1997 and Country Profile, 1995–96. Tunisia's performance is less impressive, but the country does not suffer from the tremendous income gaps of Egypt: see the *Economist Intelligence Unit,* Tunisia: Country Report, First Quarter 1997 and Country Profile, 1996–97.

42. The current situation regarding human rights and civil liberties is depressing, especially in the case of Tunisia. See *Human Rights Watch, World Report 1997,* pp. 276–81 and 303–7 for Egypt and Tunisia respectively.

43. Fred Halliday, 'The Politics of Islamic Fundamentalism: Iran, Tunisia and the Challenge to the Secular State', in Akbar S. Ahmed and Hastings Donnan (eds.), *Islam, Globalisation and Post-Modernity* (London: Routledge, 1994), pp. 103–4.

44. See, for example, the Egyptian Organisation of Human Rights, *Freedom of Thought and Belief Between the State's 'Anvil' and the Islamic Groups' 'Hammer',* 1 May 1992 (Statement by the Egyptian Organisation of Human Rights).

45. It may be the case, as stated in the introduction, that the further globalization of capitalism will eventually have the effect of reducing the weight of the state and therefore its ability to control society. But this, although plausible, is not necessary and in any case is not an immediate prospect in the societies discussed here.

11
Neoliberalism, Globalization and Resistance: The Case of India

A. K. Ramakrishnan

In the post-Cold War context, liberal international theory appeared to have re-emerged as a powerful explanatory instrument of global change. Traditional liberal international theory had lost ground due to challenges from both Realist and Marxist theories. The inability to account for the configuration and deployment of state power and interest and their mutations in an international framework, on the one hand, and the incapacity to explain structural inequalities within nation-states and at the international level, on the other, kept liberal theory away from the centre-stage of academic international relations for a long period of time. I wish to argue that the return of liberal international theory is not based on any considerable recent advancements in liberalism's conceptual and methodological apparatus. The problems of traditional liberalism continue to mar its explanatory possibilities. It is the contemporary assertion of neoliberalism that is often viewed as the return of liberal internationalism. What we see today is a shift from conventional liberal internationalism to what I call 'neoliberal globalism'.

Neoliberal globalism came into prominence along with the ascendancy of the process of globalization – the accelerated attempt at incorporating every nook and corner and every sector of the world into the capitalist mode and its market logic through the unfettered flow of transnational capital. The march of globalization is not as smooth as has been commonly projected. It encountered resistance of various kinds. One major aspect of contemporary neoliberal globalism is its blindness towards the phenomenon of resistance. The triumphalist nature of neoliberal globalist discourse emanates to a large extent from its refusal to account for resistance movements against globalization. A major task of this essay is to bring to the fore resistance to globalization as a significant element in examining the validity of liberal internationalism and its new variant, neoliberal globalism.

First, this chapter provides a brief discussion on the shift towards, and the assumptions of, neoliberal globalism and its implications for Third World development. Then, it gives an account of resistance movements against globalization in India waged by farmers, traditional fisherfolk and others and led by organizations such as Karnataka Rajya Raitha Sangha (KRRS) and National Fishworkers' Forum (NFF). These movements are then viewed in a revised New Social Movement (NSM) paradigm within the context of varying claims on the nation-state. Finally, the implications of resistance movements to neoliberal globalism are brought forth.

From liberal internationalism to neoliberal globalism

Liberal international theory entertains a conception of linear evolution of international relations towards greater individual freedom through international cooperation and the process of modernization.[1] Liberal philosophy in general and liberal international theory in particular 'fail to assert that meaningful freedom, for the relatively *less* privileged, is possible only within a reasonably *just* and secure social and international order'.[2] This failure is more glaring in neoliberal globalism where privilege and freedom of transnational capital is taken for granted irrespective of the position of people at local and national levels.

The growth of neoliberalism supposedly from liberal foundations also denotes a corresponding shift from liberal internationalism to neoliberal globalism. Neoliberalism has been primarily understood as an economic doctrine with a set of policy prescriptions. In most discussions on neoliberalism, pivotal political questions are relegated to the background. But, recent writings show a considerable improvement in the way of perceiving neoliberalism by bringing back politics. Neoliberalism is now increasingly being portrayed as a political doctrine, a political discourse or as a disciplinary practice.[3] The earlier phenomenon of pushing politics away might have arisen due to the very nature of the neoliberal paradigm which perceives economy and politics – markets and states – as autonomous entities.[4] Neoliberalism's central theme has been that 'interest groups exploit society by means of political system' by siphoning out public funds in the form of subsidies, entitlements and welfare payments.[5] It is argued that political control over economy and resources should, therefore, end. The possibility of powerful economic interests exploiting the less powerful does not figure as a major concern in the neoliberal discourse.

In developing neoliberal globalism as an ideological system, certain historical theses are being mooted: that there is a convergence of history towards the ideas of liberal democracy and free markets, that the world has 'just emerged from a cosmic struggle in which these ideals have been vindicated', and that in the evolving world order 'rule of law will at last prevail under US leadership'.[6]

Richard Gardner writes about the 'comeback of liberal internationalism' in the post-Cold War era by defining it as 'the intellectual and political tradition that believes in the necessity of leadership by liberal democracies in the construction of a peaceful world order through multilateral cooperation and effective international organizations'.[7] To him, 'this meant first and foremost U.S. leadership', even though some other power centres have emerged elsewhere. Organizations like the UN, NATO, World Bank, IMF and GATT, the formations of which were led by the United States, should at present and in future be led by the US 'to promote collective security, economic welfare, and human rights'.[8] To Gardner, President Bush was 'one of the most liberal internationalist presidents of recent years' for he was instrumental in bringing back the US leadership in 'world order politics'. Thus, the unleashing of globalization forces and the heralding of neoliberalism are found to be the essential feature of this comeback of liberal internationalism or reassertion of US leadership. This is the shift towards neoliberal globalism, wherein even the difference between government policies and intellectual pursuits won't matter much.

The way in which neoliberal globalism perceives Third World development is interesting to note. As Scott Burchill points out, Fukuyama's claim 'that political and economic development always terminates at liberal-capitalist democracy assumes that the non-Western world is striving to imitate the Western route to modernization'.[9] Fukuyama thus implicitly recognizes the need for the Third World to catch up with development. But, the liberal school's view, according to Durfee and Rosenau, is just the opposite:

> Their understanding of how world affairs function is such that they would see no need to play catch-up, and, instead, would reason that if publics and governments alike are able to exercise patience, eventually market forces will expand sufficiently to bring about a higher standard of living for all concerned.[10]

Neoliberal globalism, with its uncritical legitimation of globalization, thus finds itself in a dichotomous position with regard to Third World development. The experience of many Third World countries shows that both catching up and free market policies increased marginalization of the vast majority of the people. There is now a greater understanding both within and outside the Third World that 'catching-up development is not possible at all'.[11] It is impossible 'not only because of the limits and inequitable consumption of the resource base, but above all, because this growth model is based on a colonial world order in which the gap between the two poles is increasing, especially as far as economic development is concerned'.[12] Neoliberal policies are found to increase this gap, and neoliberal globalism, with its substantial disregard for the existing structural unevenness of world polity and economy, is finding itself as a justificatory ideology for this 'colonial world order'.

Fukuyama asserts the 'unquestionable relationship between economic development and liberal democracy'.[13] But, there is an indirect prescription from him for the Third World: 'A modernizing dictatorship can in principle be far more effective than a democracy in creating the social conditions that would permit both capitalist economic growth and, over time, the emergence of a stable democracy.'[14] Globalization forces expand their wings by wooing regimes irrespective of whether they are dictatorships or democracies. Neoliberal globalism, with its seemingly ambivalent position on democracy, provides doctrinal support for the undifferentiated globalization to continue and grow. Another author writes about the 'affinity between democracy and the market system' as there is 'diffusion' of power in both these systems.[15] The control of the market system by transnational corporations and its implications for the distribution of power globally and locally do not get any attention in his treatment of this linkage between market and democracy. To Ryrie, 'the most important problem ... is not inequality but poverty',[16] as if poverty and inequality are two divorced issues. He emphasizes that *'the basic development task now consists of creating a successful market economy and that the main challenge to aid donors is to help poor countries achieve this'.*[17] This is because '[t]he worldwide consensus in favour of the market economy is just as relevant for the Third World as it is for the advanced industrial countries'.[18] This strange prescription of a catching-up market economy to the Third World in the name of a self-proclaimed 'world-wide consensus' on free market regimes faces challenges on two counts: one, the globalization policies aimed at creating a liberalized market system in the Third World are faced with local and national resistance; and two, there is no consensus at all on the desirability of the free market model in the Third World. There, of course, exists a vocabulary of globalization referring to the 'Washington consensus', which involves policy prescriptions such as trade liberalization, privatization, balanced budget, removal of subsidies and deregulation of domestic markets. The myth of consensus on these globalization measures has been exposed both theoretically[19] and, as we will see, through movements of various sorts in India. A discussion on various dimensions of globalization as a process is not undertaken here.[20] What follows is an attempt to capture the implications of globalization in certain sectors of Indian economy, especially agriculture and fisheries, and the nature of resistance in these and allied spheres.

Globalization in Indian agriculture and farmers' resistance

Globalization and the injection of 'free trade' in agriculture under the IMF–World Bank–GATT/WTO regime aim at providing 'freedom for transnational corporations (TNCs) to invest, produce and trade in agricultural commodities without restriction, regulation or responsibility'.[21] This 'free market' approach adopted in India under the structural adjustment policies envisages free export–import dynamics whereby the level and structure of domestic prices of agricultural commodities are brought at par with global prices.[22] It is based on a 'quite simple and straightforward' belief that '"setting prices right" sets everything else right',[23] and therefore, goes the argument, price distortions which are basically induced by government regulations and interventions have to be removed by unseating the government from the field. But the reality is that global prices of agricultural products are determined not by the logic of demand and supply alone, but by the power of very few transnational trading companies. Their resources, marketing techniques, networks and brand names determine or 'rig' prices internationally, leaving very less scope for Indian and Third World farmers to have any say in the market.[24] Such a global reality, coupled with innumerable domestic hurdles which Indian farmers have to confront, exposes the baselessness of the globalization argument for price equilibrium in agriculture. Large sections of farmers and experts have been demanding state intervention for the protection of small farmers from international price fluctuation and for meeting domestic societal demands.[25]

Indian farmers have been much concerned about the way in which structural changes were brought about in the domestic sector in tune with transnational interests. The growth of agribusiness corporate ventures, the displacement of food crops with cash crops, environmental degradation and biodiversity loss incurred by monoculture agroindustrial crop patterns, the threat posed to food security, the repercussions on land rights and farmers' rights on procuring and reusing seeds, etc. have been their important concerns in the globalization scenario in India. After a fairly detailed study of such a scenario, Utsa Patnaik writes:

> It is reasonably clear that the new trends will lead to an accentuation of the economic differentiation which already exists strongly in rural society, to a point of sharp dualism between a minority of export-oriented capitalist farmers and companies out for quick profits regardless of social costs on the one hand, and a mass of cultivators whose returns from the domestically consumable crops falls as a direct result of the relative price shifts inherent in the new policies and their active promotion by the government. The livelihood of rural labourers is under threat and irreversible environmental problems are in the making.[26]

Vandana Shiva notes two kinds of liberalization in agriculture: external and internal. External liberalization consists of the neoliberal economic package involving (1) liberalization of fertilizer imports, (2) removal of land ceiling regulation, (3) removal of subsidies on irrigation, electricity and credit, (4) deregulation of the wheat, rice, sugar cane, cotton and edible oil and oil-seed sectors, (5) dismantling of the food security system, (6) removal of controls on markets, traders and processors, (7) abolition of inventory controls, (8) removal of subsidies on cooperatives, and (9) the treating of farmers' cooperatives at par with the private sector. If these measures are intended to remove centralized state control over agriculture, they result in highly centralized agribusiness TNCs like Cargill and Pepsico gaining control over agricultural land, water and seeds. These TNCs emerge as 'new Zamindars' (landlords). Thus, external liberalization 'serves the external interests'.[27]

Internal liberalization means 'liberating agriculture in the direction of ecological sustainability and social justice', which involves, according to Shiva, (1) freeing agriculture from high external inputs like chemical fertilizers and pesticides, (2) freeing farmers from capital-intensive farming methods, (3) removing landlessness of the peasants, (4) removing the fear of dispossession of farmers by monopolies through the latter's control over land, water and biodiversity,

(5) removing the spectre of starvation by ensuring food as a human right, (6) freeing the rural folk from water scarcity by ensuring equitable water rights, (7) freeing knowledge and biodiversity from IPR monopolies, and (8) reinvigorating local markets and rebuilding food security.[28] The farmers' movement against globalization in India by and large has been rejecting the external liberalization and demanding internal liberalization.

It was in the context of the debates on the Dunkel Draft Proposals of the Uruguay Round of GATT negotiations that the farmers' movement became a recognizable force. A major organization at the forefront of anti-globalization struggle was the Karnataka Rajya Raitha Sangha (KRRS). Even though KRRS was formed in 1980, it became famous in the early 1990s by initiating public, political and academic debates on GATT proposals on a national scale.[29] Farmers' resistance grew in Karnataka during 1992–93 against the attempt at gaining monopoly rights on seed and plant material by transnational companies. Farmers were angered by the Trade-Related Intellectual Property Rights (TRIPs) regime of GATT which 'allows seed multinationals monopoly rights on seed either in the form of patents or breeders rights'.[30] The germ plasm of seeds bred traditionally by Third World farmers are utilized by TNC seed monopolies for developing so-called 'high-yielding' or 'improved' varieties through biotechnology. The monopoly rights acquired by TNCs on this basis are seen by the Indian farmers as 'piracy' or 'theft of intellectual property rights on a grand scale',[31] an act sanctified by the IPR regime of GATT and later World Trade Organization (WTO). The farmers were outraged by the prospect of buying seeds every season from TNC monopolies as against the former's practice of unrestricted storage and distribution of seed varieties, and of the eventual dependency on these monopolies.

The farmers' resistance began in a big way on 2 October 1992, Gandhi's birthday, with a 'seed *Satyagraha*' in Bangalore. Farmers belonging to the KRRS stormed the Bangalore office of Cargill, one of the world's largest seed TNCs and the biggest grain trader, in December 1992 and served them notice to quit India. In July 1993, the KRRS physically demolished Cargill's seed unit at Bellary in Karnataka. On 2 October 1993, about 100,000 Indian farmers rallied in Bangalore along with environmental activists, scientists and farmer's leaders from various Third World countries such as Malaysia, Indonesia, Thailand, South Korea, Nicaragua, Brazil, Ethiopia and Zimbabwe to protest against GATT proposals and globalization.[32] Professor Nanjundaswamy, leader of KRRS, said that 'the farmers should not be content with ransacking and demolition of Cargill units but should aim at ousting MNCs from Indian soil'.[33] At another occasion Nanjundaswamy remarked: 'We insist on a free exchange of seed and knowledge across the globe, boycotting and bypassing the enclosures, the landlords, the controllers of a biodiversity, which belongs to the people. The movement, based on resistance, is now becoming a more positive assertion of popular rights.'[34]

The farmers' movement was able to raise major issues related to globalization on a national scale and achieved limited success in resisting TNC operations in seeds and related fields and in obtaining assurance from the Indian government that farmers' rights to grow, exchange and reuse seeds will not be affected by signing the GATT treaty. Resistance also resulted in blocking, at least for the time being, the amendment of the Indian Patent Act of 1970 in tune with GATT/WTO specifications.[35]

Fishworkers' struggle

The globalization policy pursued by the government of India in the fisheries sector included the opening up of marine waters of the Indian Exclusive Economic Zone (EEZ) to joint ventures of Indian and foreign companies. These joint ventures are totally export-oriented and are intended to contribute towards India's foreign exchange earnings.[36] During the first five years of the adoption of the New Economic Policy (NEP) by the Indian government, export of fish and fish products increased by 2.10 times. Globalization measures under NEP also resulted in average annual increase in the value of fish exports going up from 26.1 million US dollars during the ten years of 1980–90 to 147.8 million US dollars during the NEP years of 1990–95.[37]

The export-oriented policy with its stress on intensive exploitation of marine resources put severe pressure on traditional artisan fisherfolk and small-scale producers. The traditional fishing community has been concerned with the ecological consequences of intensive mechanized fishing for quite some time now. They have been organizing movements in different parts of the country, especially in the western coast from late 1970s onwards under the banner of National Fishworkers' Forum (NFF).[38] The NFF was in the forefront of agitations for banning fish trawling during the monsoon months of June and July, the breeding season for marine fish. It has been able to force various provincial governments to ban monsoon trawling. The NFF in the course of their agitations had to confront the government as well as mechanized trawler owners. The confrontation between traditional fisherfolk and mechanized boat operators has been a frequent phenomenon in the western coast for the last two decades. The main thrust of the struggle of the traditional fishing community has been to preserve marine ecology for utilizing it in a sustainable manner for their livelihood and for common good.[39]

The globalization measures under NEP threatened marine resources and fishworkers' livelihood on a big scale. Foreign vessels, in their effort to maximize catches for generating maximum profit, use large-scale technologies which result in the destruction of the marine eco-system.[40] Traditional fisherfolk's resistance to globalization is informed by their commitment to the protection of the very coastal and deep sea environment on which the livelihood of the community is based. The government policy of allowing big foreign vessels and chartered ships to exploit the marine wealth in an indiscriminate way forced the fishworkers to launch new struggles.[41] The NFF took the leadership to bring together various traditionally conflicting sections into an umbrella forum, the National Fisheries Action Committee Against Joint Ventures (NFACAJV). This 'consortium of strange bedfellows'[42] united to fight globalization included traditional artisanal fisherfolk, small mechanized trawler owners and even those involved in the export processing sector. The struggle of NFF and NFACAJV against globalization included nation-wide protests, blockades, demonstrations and hunger strikes. For example, on 23–24 November 1994, the 7,500 km coastline in India came to a virtual standstill with about one million fishworkers keeping away from work at sea, fish markets and processing plants.[43]

The consistent resistance forced the central government to appoint the Murari Committee to review its policy on joint ventures and deepsea fishing. The Murari Committee recommended cancellation of permits to foreign vessels under joint venture, denial of extension of existing licences and adoption of measures to prevent marine pollution and to preserve marine environment.[44] After continued struggle, in August 1996, the Indian government accepted the Murari Committee report, but failed to implement it *in toto*. The government's decision not to allow new foreign vessels in Indian waters itself was a great victory for the fisherfolk. But, the deep sea fishing policy announced by the central government in February 1997 envisages cancelling new licences for foreign fishing vessels but continuing with the existing ones. In this context, the NFF and NFACAJV are engaged in new struggles for complete reversal of globalization measures in the fishing sector.[45]

Further, the NFF with its pioneering struggles against globalization plans to forge a global forum with similar organizations and movements elsewhere.[46] This is especially relevant in the context of increasing globalization of the territorial waters and the marine resources of most Third World countries not only under transnational corporate interests but also under the aegis of Food and Agricultural Organization's (FAO) fisheries management strategy.[47] The NFF has also been active in the struggle for forcing the government to enforce the Coastal Zone Protection Act which was designed to protect coastal environment.

People's resistance has also emerged in a big way against export-oriented intensive shrimp farming in the coastal belt. Shrimp aquaculture has been found to be highly environmentally, socially and economically destructive due to the high rate of water usage, conversion of fertile agricultural lands into aquaculture farms, the introduction of chemical inputs in soil and water, and the erosion of the basis of livelihood for the poor coastal people.[48] The struggle by various organizations like Grama Swaraj Movement against globalized aquaculture resulted in the Supreme Court of India giving a verdict to close down commercial shrimp farms throughout the Indian coast.[49] But the government is now contemplating ways to dilute the judgement.

As in the case of the fishworkers' movement, movements against export-oriented aquaculture also have formed a national network, People's Alliance against Shrimp Industry (PAASI) and they have also initiated joint activities with similar struggles in the Third World. Attempts are also made to generate awareness among shrimp consumers in the West. According to Shiva,

> [t]he new politics of solidarity between Third World communities and northern consumers is part of an emerging citizen politics at the global level that is making visible the social and ecological costs of globalisation and creating new mechanisms for social control and regulation of commerce at the international level.[50]

Globalization has been very rapid in Indian infrastructural sectors like power. Transnational corporations have been able to make great inroads into the power sector as exemplified by the Enron project in Maharashtra and the Cogentrix project in Karnataka.[51] These mega-power projects are also centres of people's resistance; the struggle against Enron being able to catch wide national attention. Apart from these current struggles and movements, there were successful struggles against transnational companies like DuPont in Goa.[52]

Streams of resistance: labour and new social movements

Resistance movements against globalization in India consist of trade union movements and new social movements (NSMs). The farmers' and fishworkers' struggle may be regarded as belonging to the category of new social movements, even though there is a substantial trade union content in National Fishworkers' Forum, etc. There, of course, are certain aspects of these two struggles which do not fit well with traditional NSM paradigms. We shall take up this issue a little later. Organized workers' movements belonging to different mainstream political persuasions played a role, but not up to their potentials, in offering resistance to the onslaught of globalization. The fear of job losses, the chaotic and insecure nature of the labour scene and the de-ideologization of the working class in the context of neoliberal globalization have influenced their activities in a big manner. The trade union movements' struggle against globalization has been centred especially on public sector undertakings facing disinvestment and the insurance and banking sectors. While massive globalization measures have been adopted by the Indian government in the 1990s, the trade union movement was successful in limiting the extent of globalization in certain sectors like insurance and banking but was unable to reverse the process to any considerable level.

World capitalism's 'perpetual moulding of a world labour force'[53] surely involved conflicting claims and resistance by the labour force, or, as Michael Yates puts it, the labour movement has always been 'in the process of becoming'.[54] But the globalization process has been successful to a considerable extent in scattering and restricting the potentials of labour movement through unleashing new tendencies in the labour sphere. As Dave Broad points out, globalization initiated or accelerated such phenomena as 'degradation of labor, feminization of labor, housewifization of labor, informalization of labor, casualization of labor, and peripheralization of labor'.[55] These processes together with 'labour force liquidation'[56] resulting out of transnational operations did have an impact on the Indian labour sector and the trade union movements. It is to an extent true that in India, '[u]norganised labour, peasants and the agrarian work-force at present seem to be showing increased class consciousness, which the trade unions fail to demonstrate'.[57] This does not in any way imply a retreat of the working class altogether. Since the situation demands an active movement from the labour force, they are positively compelled to align with other movements belonging to the NSM stream.

Even though we consider the farmers' and fishworkers' movements as belonging to the NSM fabric, certain issues regarding conventional NSM theorizing need to be addressed. New movements emerged in a context when ecological disruption and market violence have grown to mammoth proportions challenging liberalism's age-old assumptions. As Leslie Thiele puts it,

> [t]he fear of want and the fear of defeat in a competitive market place – motivations once proposed by early liberals as the philosopher's stones of human nature, capable of turning the earth's lead into gold and bringing civilization unending progress and riches – now threaten to turn against us with a vengeance.[58]

Liberalism's failure was very significant especially for the Third World since development projects inspired by its grand vision more or less uniformly marginalized communities of people from resources and power. The new social movements attempt at confronting this reality basically at micro levels. Initially, NSMs stressed micropolitics or the politics of everyday life.[59] But, according to Alberto Meluci, NSMs 'occupy an intermediate space of social life where individual needs and the pressures of political innovation mesh together'.[60] From such an ambivalent position, they have caught the imagination of many as 'the major arena of struggle against globalization'[61] and they have already been transformed into a 'new political factor'[62] in the lives of people, especially in the Third World.

However, most social analysis tried to depict NSMs as cultural phenomena divorcing them from their political economy context and content. This analytical standpoint meant 'denying ways in which the origins, identities, and development of subordinated categories of people remain fully rooted in the dynamics of advanced capitalism'.[63] The analysis in the cultural matrix 'failed to take into account their [NSMs'] ongoing struggles with the state and capital'.[64] This imperative to take note of the political content of NSMs necessitates a redefinition of the very NSM paradigm. To Leslie Thiele, 'social movements are political organisations that attempt to restructure attitudes, values and behaviour; they are composed of and oriented to a relatively nonexclusive population; and they function primarily through communicative rather than coercive means'.[65] This reformed liberal view will not adequately explain all varieties of anti-globalization NSMs, especially the farmers' movement in India. NSMs not only imply an advanced capitalist and globalized context of their emergence and operation, but, more importantly, 'a popular power that is anti-capitalist'.[66] Third World NSMs emerged in the aftermath of what is called 'the debacle of development' or 'maldevelopment'[67] with the understanding that the dominant discourse of development meant marginalization of the majority. The fossilization of traditional politics, the disintegration of established political organizations, the loss of credibility of conventional parties and political processes, and above all, the very obvious shift in the activities of the state in favour of markets provided the space and rationale for their surfacing.[68] The failure of conventional ideologies and institutions to respond to widening inequities and to gender, ecological and social justice concerns also acted as their foregrounding logic. From non-party micro-politics they have started increasingly responding to macro-politics of state, markets and capitalism, while mooring themselves in the local milieu. It should be made clear here that by NSMs we do not mean Non-Governmental Organizations (NGOs) of local or transnational kinds, but rather new movements with mass participation. Some of these NSMs, such as the fishworkers' and farmers' movements in India, are even coming to terms with Samir Amin's thesis that '[a]ctually existing capitalism remain very much an obstacle to advances by people and there is no alternative to popular national transformation'.[69] This is happening simultaneously with these NSMs becoming more aware of the need for local–global linkages of struggles, especially in the globalization context where IMF/World Bank/WTO/TNC regimes themselves are becoming very much a part of local lives of the Third World.

There are, at the same time, fears expressed by the intelligentsia that 'the genuine search for a new vision, a new paradigm of development is pre-empted by the very process of globalization'.[70] The new visions are necessarily rooted in struggles rather than in any prescriptive theorizing forerunning them. As pointed out by Lester Ruiz, 'what is at stake for those committed to the transformation of the planet, as exemplified in struggles for justice and liberation, is the uncovering of the dynamics of capital, especially of global capital'.[71]

Neoliberal globalism, nation-state and resistance movements

Neoliberalism, doctrinally and ideologically, stresses the need for a minimum role for the nation-state not only in commerce and economy but in other human endeavours as well. For neoliberals, the state is 'parasitic' and 'non-productive', making 'little or no positive contribution to society's material well-being'.[72] In their urge to discredit the state and exalt the market, neoliberals often refer back to classical economic theory and Adam Smith. There, they confront much difficulty since Smith considered government as an important instrument in facilitating the operation of the market. Therefore, most contemporary neoliberals base their ideas on those of Friedrick Hayek and Milton Friedman, who stress minimum state intervention.[73] This 'minimum government' doctrine replaced Keynesianism as the economic principle in the Reaganite and the Thatcherite right-wing political (dis)order of the late 1970s and the 1980s.[74] Latin America, especially Chile, was the major Third World site chosen for operationalizing neoliberal principles.

The process of globalization entails the weakening of the nation-state at one level with the ascendancy of transnational corporatism as a colonial power. Global capital flows along with mobility of population, information and technology obviously put the nation-state in a fix. The nation-state, according to Ismail Serageldin of the World Bank, is 'no longer up to the task' due to the fact that it has become 'both too big and too small' – too big internally and too small externally.[75] The inference is that, in such a context, local and transnational authorities increasingly take the place of the nation-state.

The TNCs and other globalization forces including the national bourgeoisies seek a weak nation-state externally and a strong nation-state internally so as to enable smooth capital flows and market operations by regulating, overcoming or suppressing people's resistance and by providing 'safety-nets'. Neoliberal globalism finds it difficult to account for this dual claim of present-day globalization.

In a perceptive article, Aijaz Ahmad notes the significant 'mutation of the nation-states' in the Third World.[76] The nation-state, according to him, 'seems less and less to represent the interests of the nation in world affairs. Increasingly, the nation-state now seems to represent the interests of global finance *to* the nation.'[77] This, to him, does not mean the decline of the nation-state. Simultaneously with the conquest of all available spaces by global capital, Ahmad sees a dialectic process of 'intensification of the nation-state form'.[78] Wallerstein notes that the capitalist world system 'cannot function well without strong states ... within the framework of a strong interstate system'.[79] At the same time, ideologues of capitalism, including neoliberal globalists, cannot air this fact because the legitimacy of their system is derived from unmediated 'economic productivity' and 'general welfare'.[80]

Neoliberal globalists are unable to reconcile the pertinent question: 'if not the nation-state, then what?'[81] Many academics and movements especially in the Third World strongly feel that the state is 'the only collective institution through which redistributive justice, planned development and a comprehensive politics of broad, basic and inalienable entitlements is possible'.[82] In a world of unequal development and of exploitation of resources of the weaker by the powerful, 'the nation-state is the only defence available to the citizens',[83] especially to the subordinated peoples.[84] Authors like Robert Solo believe in the 'positive' power of the state and its uniqueness as an 'answerable', 'responsible' and 'effective' system.[85] For Eric Hobsbawm, in today's world, 'the state, or some form of public authority representing public interest, was more indispensable than ever if the social and environmental inequities of the market economy were to be countered, or even ... if the economic system was to operate satisfactorily'.[86] Hobsbawm thinks that the very fate of humanity rests upon restoring public authorities like the state.[87] Even a committed anarchist like Noam Chomsky considers the defence of state authority as a goal to be pursued in contemporary times since 'rolling back the state' means rolling back the progress made in the realms of human rights and democracy. To him, like many others, this means the immediate task of defending democratic state institutions and public participation with a long-term critical perspective on state power and authority.[88]

Wallerstein points out that it was the movements which played an important role in legitimating and stabilizing nation-state structure, especially in the last century, and that conventional movements find it difficult to perform such a function in the contemporary milieu.[89] Conventional NSMs wanted a less oppressive, uninterfering and weak nation-state in order to realize the potentials of the civil society. These civil society-oriented and mostly NGO-based NSMs were inclined in theory and practice to avoid addressing nation-state politics, an act which contributed to their inability to influence macropolitics.[90] There is a marked shift in emphasis with the emergence of new resistance movements like the KRRS and the NFF. They try to grapple with the dialectic of civil society and state and to engage in macropolitics in their own ways. There is an attempt from various resistance movements to bring back the state as a centre of contestation of power. KRRS's attempts to enter into electoral politics and NFF's efforts to forge a national political alliance of movements alongside their direct confrontation with globalization forces are indicative of such a change.

Neoliberal assumptions on nation-state and politics are thus being increasingly contested by movements of this sort.

Liberal international theory, Stephen Krasner notes, assumes that there are different actors including states, TNCs, NGOs, etc., and that international relations provide opportunities for every actor while each of them is pursuing different objectives.[91] Neoliberal globalism marks its shift by undermining the role of certain actors like the state and by giving greater importance to non-state actors like the TNCs, while each of them has to pursue the common objective of unfettered market access. It believes in the need for an international institutional arrangement for safeguarding a 'liberalized' global economic regime and, at the same time, transnational corporatism. Anti-globalization movements like the KRRS and NFF put into question these very assumptions of neoliberal globalism by their exposing of, and resistance to, globalization under the GATT/WTO 'liberalization' regime and the TNC monopolies. The neoliberal globalist vision of governance through non-state actors is thus thoroughly challenged by Third World resistance movements.

The farmers' movement in India has been trying ideologically to combine nation-state politics with an alternative liberal framework to neoliberal globalism. The fishworkers' movement has been stressing nation-state politics in the sense that it wants the state to protect national and local resources from global exploitation. It is by combining grassroots activism with national and global issues and by attempting to forge global alliances in their opposition to neoliberal globalism that resistance movements try to go beyond the boundaries of conventional politics and movements.

It should be noted that such movements are still not in the centre-stage of nation-state politics. At another level, conventional political organizations and equations in India are undergoing change with the traditionally marginalized communities and groups staking their claim to state power. The political future of resistance movements in India depends largely on their ability to engage and align with such new political forces. Their attempt to traverse from the periphery to the centre of national politics also requires alliances with the labour movement. Any failure in such endeavours will marginalize the resistance movements from nation-state politics in spite of the challenges they offer to neoliberal globalism.

Resistance movements in India envisage a global order within which meaningful local–global linkages are mediated by the nation-state in a communitarian direction. In short, they wish to see the ordering of global politics from a bottom-up perspective, rooting themselves in local and national sites of power and thereby contrasting sharply with the neoliberal globalist top-down approach.

Notes

1. See Mark W. Zacher and Richard A. Matthew, 'Liberal International Theory: Common Threads, Divergent Strands', in C. W. Kegley Jr. (ed.), *Controversies in International Relations Theory* (New York: St. Martin's Press, 1995), pp. 107–50.
2. Christian Bay, 'Conceptions of Security: Individual, National and Global', in Bhikhu Parekh and Thomas Pantham (eds.), *Political Discourse: Explorations in Indian and Western Political Thought* (New Delhi: Sage Publications, 1987), p. 129.
3. See Stephen Gill, 'The Global Panopticon? The Neoliberal State, Economic Life, and Democratic Surveillance', *Alternatives*, Vol. 20, No. 1 (1995), pp. 1–49; Ricardo Trumper and Lynne Phillips, 'Cholera in the Time of Neoliberalism: The Cases of Chile and Ecuador', *Alternatives*, Vol. 20, No. 2, (1995), pp. 165–94; James Petras and Steve Vieux, 'Shrinking Democracy and Expanding Trade: New Shape of the Imperial State', *Economic and Political Weekly*, Vol. 31, No. 30 (1996), pp. 2014–18; James Petras and Steve Vieux, 'Neo-Liberalism and Daily Life', *Economic and Political Weekly*, Vol. 31, No. 38 (1996), pp. 2594–97; and Adrian Leftwich, 'Governance, the State and the Politics of Development', *Development and Change*, Vol. 25, No. 2 (1994), pp. 363–86.
4. See Arthur A. Goldsmith, 'The State, the Market and Economic Development: A Second Look at Adam Smith in Theory and Practice', *Development and Change*, Vol. 26, No. 4 (1995), p. 634.
5. Petras and Vieux, 'Shrinking Democracy and Expanding Trade', p. 2014.
6. Noam Chomsky, 'World Order and its Rules: Variations on Some Themes', *Scandinavian Journal of Development Alternatives*, Vol. 13, No. 3 (1994), p. 5.
7. Richard Gardner, 'The Comeback of Liberal Internationalism', *The Washington Quarterly*, Vol. 13, No. 3 (1990), p. 23.
8. *Ibid.*
9. Scott Burchill, 'Liberal Internationalism', in Burchill, Andrew Linklater *et al.*, *Theories of International Relations* (Basingstoke: Macmillan, 1996), p. 28.
10. Mary Durfee and James N. Rosenau, 'Playing Catch-up: International Relations Theory and Poverty', *Millennium: Journal of International Studies*, Vol. 25, No. 3 (1996), p. 539.
11. Maria Mies, 'The Myth of Catching-up Development', in Maria Mies and Vandana Shiva (eds.), *Ecofeminism* (New Delhi: Kali for Women, 1993), p. 60.
12. *Ibid.*
13. Francis Fukuyama, *The End of History and the Last Man* (London: Penguin, 1992), p. 125.
14. *Ibid.*, p. 119.

15. William Ryrie, *First World, Third World* (Basingstoke: Macmillan, 1995), p. 107.
16. *Ibid.*, p. 104.
17. *Ibid.*, p. 86, emphasis original.
18. *Ibid.*
19. For an exposition and critique of the 'Washington consensus', see T. Krishna Kumar, 'Silent Consensus against Washington Consensus', *Economic and Political Weekly*, Vol. 32, No. 13 (1997), pp. 657–62.
20. For a critical view of globalization, see, for example, various chapters in this volume and M. A. Oommen, 'Anatomy of Globalisation', *Mainstream* (Autumn 1995), pp. 75–83; Dalip S. Swamy, 'Alternative to Globalisation', *Mainstream*, Vol. 33, No. 20 (1995), pp. 15–23; Paul Hirst and Grahame Thompson, 'The Process of "Globalization": International Economic Relations, National Economic Management and the Formation of Trading Blocs', *Economy and Society*, Vol. 21, No. 4 (1992), pp. 351–96; Andrew Hurrell and Ngaire Woods, 'Globalisation and Inequality', *Millennium: Journal of International Studies*, Vol. 24, No. 3 (1995), pp. 447–70; Arthur MacEvan, 'Globalization and Stagnation', *Monthly Review*, Vol. 45, No. 11 (1994), pp. 1–16; and Arif Dirilik, 'The Postcolonial Aura: Third World Criticism in the Age of Global Capitalism', *Critical Inquiry*, Vol. 20, No. 2 (1994), pp. 338–56.
21. Vandana Shiva, 'GATT, Agriculture and Third World Women', in Mies and Shiva, *Ecofeminism*, p. 231.
22. Sukhpal Singh, 'Structural Adjustment Programme and Indian Agriculture: Towards an Assessment of Implications', *Economic and Political Weekly*, Vol. 30, No. 51 (1995), p. 3311.
23. S. N. Mishra, 'Agricultural Liberalisation and Development Strategy in Ninth–Plan', *Economic and Political Weekly*, Vol. 32, No. 13 (1997), p. A-19.
24. Sucha Singh Gill and Jaswinder Singh Brar, 'Global Market and Competitiveness of Indian Agriculture: Some Issues', *Economic and Political Weekly*, Vol. 31, No. 32 (1996), p. 2176.
25. *Ibid.*, pp. 2176–77 and Mishra, 'Agricultural Liberalisation', p. A-25.
26. Utsa Patnaik, 'Export-Oriented Agriculture and Food Security in Developing Countries and India', *Economic and Political Weekly*, Vol. 31, Nos. 35–37 (1996), p. 2448. For further details on the implications of globalization of Indian agriculture, see Singh, 'Structural Adjustment Programme', pp. 3311–14, and D. M. Nachane, 'Intellectual Property Rights in the Uruguay Round: An Indian Perspective', *Economic and Political Weekly*, Vol. 30, No. 5 (1995), pp. 257–68. For a critique of globalization in agriculture in the Third World context, see Priyatosh Maitra, 'Internationalisation of Capitalist Production in Agriculture, Multinationals and the Negation of Nation-States', *Frontier*, Vol. 28, Nos. 8–11 (1995), pp. 30–6; Meera Nanda, 'Transnationalisation of Third World State and Undoing of Green Revolution', *Economic and Political Weekly*, Vol. 30, No. 4 (1995), pp. PE20–PE30; Michel Chossudovsky, 'IMF, World Bank and Famine', *Frontier*, Vol. 28, No. 47 (1996), pp. 7–8; and Franz Broswimmer, 'Botanical Imperialism: The Stewardship of Plant Genetic Resources in the Third World', *Critical Sociology*, Vol. 18, No. 1 (1991), pp. 3–17.

27. Vandana Shiva, 'Globalisation of Agriculture and the Growth of Food Insecurity', *Bija – the Seed*, Nos. 17–18 (1996), pp. 25–6.
28. *Ibid.*, p. 26.
29. Kripa A. P., 'Raitha Sangha's Political Dilemma', *Economic and Political Weekly*, Vol. 30, No. 3 (1995), p. 140.
30. Vandana Shiva, 'Environmental Impact of Economic Globalisation', *Manorama Yearbook 1996* (Kottayam: Malayala Manorama Company, 1996), p. 100.
31. See Jeremy Seabrook, *Notes from Another India* (London: Pluto Press, 1995), p. 75.
32. For details, see Wishvas Rane, 'Farmers' Rally against GATT Proposals', *Economic and Political Weekly*, Vol. 28, No. 44 (1993), p. 2391.
33. *Ibid.*
34. Quoted in Seabrook, *Notes from Another India*, p. 77.
35. See Patnaik, 'Export-oriented Agriculture', p. 2449.
36. John Kurien, 'Impact of Joint Ventures on Fish Economy', *Economic and Political Weekly*, Vol. 30, No. 6 (1995), p. 300.
37. 'Fishworkers Showing the Way', *NAPM Bulletin*, Vol. 1, No. 3 (1996), p. 4. See also Ashish Kothari, 'Environment and New Economic Policies', *Economic and Political Weekly*, Vol. 30, No. 17 (1995), p. 926.
38. For details, see Mukul, 'Traditional Fisherfolk Fight New Economic Policy', *Economic and Political Weekly*, Vol. 29, No. 9 (1994), p. 475.
39. See National Fishworkers' Forum, *National and State Level Unions' Reports* (Thiruvananthapuram, 1991).
40. The impact of market-oriented economic policies on marine ecology and fish economy is discussed in Saritha Acharya and Niru Acharya, 'Structural Adjustment and Small Producers: Reflections from Case Studies', *Economic and Political Weekly*, Vol. 30, No. 1 (1995), pp. 45–52.
41. See A. K. Ramakrishnan, 'The State should be Responsible to our Resources', *Passline*, Vol. 2, Nos. 19–20 (1997), p. 5.
42. Kurien, 'Impact of Joint Ventures on Fish Economy', p. 300.
43. *Ibid.*
44. 'Fishworkers Showing the Way', p. 5.
45. For details on the latest phase of the fishworkers' struggle, see 'Rally Behind the Struggling Fisherfolks', *NAPM Bulletin*, Vol. 1, No. 8 (1997), pp. 2–3, and 'Fishfolk's Move to Save Marine Resources', *Passline*, Vol. 2, Nos. 19–20 (1997), pp. 5–6.
46. For details, see 'Storms in High Seas', *Health Action*, Vol. 10, No. 4 (1997), pp. 4–6.
47. See Ramakrishnan Korakandy, 'Managing World Fisheries: Third World's Loss', *Economic and Political Weekly*, Vol. 31, No. 34 (1996), pp. 2289–91.
48. For details on these impacts, see Vandana Shiva, 'Women, Ecology and Economic Globalisation', Keynote Presentation at VII National Conference of Women's Studies, Jaipur, 27–30 December 1995.
49. On the nature of the struggle against export-oriented aquaculture, see M. Naganathan, K. Jothi Sivagnanam and C. Rajendran, 'Blue Revolution in a Green Belt', *Economic and Political Weekly*, Vol. 30, No. 12 (1995), pp. 607–8, and Mukul, 'Aquaculture Boom: Who Pays?', *Economic and Political Weekly*, Vol. 29, No. 49 (1994), pp. 3075–8.

50. Shiva, 'Women, Ecology and Economic Globalisation'.
51. See Sulabha Brahme and Sharayu Mhatre, 'Enron: Neo-Colonialism in Action', *Frontier*, Vol. 29, No. 3 (1996), pp. 4–8; Amulya K. N. Reddy and Antonette D'Sa, 'Enron and Other Similar Deals vs New Energy Paradigm', *Economic and Political Weekly*, Vol. 30, No. 24 (1995), pp. 1441–8; and Girish Sant, Shantanu Dixit and Subodh Wagle, 'Dabhol Project PPA: Structure and Techno-Economic Implications', *Economic and Political Weekly*, Vol. 30, No. 24 (1995), pp. 1449–55.
52. See Gary Cohen and Satinath Sarangi, 'People's Struggle Against DuPont in Goa', *Economic and Political Weekly*, Vol. 30, No. 13 (1995), pp. 663–4.
53. Immanuel Wallerstein, 'The Inter-State Structure of the Modern World-System', in Steve Smith, Ken Booth and Marysia Zalewski (eds.), *International Theory: Positivism and Beyond* (Cambridge: Cambridge University Press, 1996), p. 89.
54. Michael D. Yates, 'Does the U. S. Labor Movement Have a Future?', *Monthly Review*, Vol. 48, No. 9 (1997), p. 11.
55. See Dave Broad, 'Globalization versus Labor', *Monthly Review*, Vol. 47, No. 7 (1995), pp. 20–31.
56. See Frederick F. Clairmonte, 'Transnational Conglomerates: Reflections on Global Power', in Krishna Ahooja-Patel, Anne Gorden Drabek and Marc Nerfin (eds.), *World Economy in Transition* (Oxford: Pergamon Press, 1986), p. 153.
57. Dinesh Hegde and Sorab Sadri, 'Trade Unions and the Changing Socio-Political Environment: Their Form, Nature and Role', *Man and Development*, Vol. 18, No. 2 (1996), p. 111.
58. Leslie Paul Thiele, 'Making Democracy Safe for the World: Social Movements and Global Politics', *Alternatives*, Vol. 18, No. 3 (1993), p. 278.
59. Muto Ichiyo, 'Alliance of Hope and Challenges of Global Democracy', *Lokayan Bulletin*, Vol. 11, No. 1 (1994), p. 41.
60. Alberto Meluci, 'Liberation or Meaning? Social Movements, Culture and Democracy', *Development and Change*, Vol. 23, No. 3 (1992), p. 75.
61. Gayatri Chakravorty Spivak, 'Imperialism and the US Left', *Frontier*, Vol. 28, No. 44 (1996), p. 5.
62. Raymond Williams, *Towards 2000* (Harmondsworth: Penguin, 1983), p. 249.
63. Barry D. Adam, 'Post-Marxism and the New Social Movements', *Canadian Review of Sociology and Anthropology*, Vol. 30, No. 3 (1993), pp. 316–17.
64. *Ibid.*, p. 317.
65. Thiele, 'Making Democracy Safe', pp. 281–2.
66. Samir Amin, 'Social Movements at the Periphery', in Ponna Wignaraja (ed.), *New Social Movements in the South* (New Delhi: Vistaar Publications, 1993), p. 89.
67. See Vandana Shiva, *Staying Alive* (New Delhi: Kali for Women, 1988), and Arturo Escobar, 'Reflections on "Development": Grassroots Approaches and Alternative Politics in the Third World', *Futures*, Vol. 24, No. 5 (1992), pp. 411–36.
68. See Escobar, *ibid.*, p. 419.
69. Amin, 'Social Movements at the Periphery', p. 87.
70. Swamy, 'Alternative to Globalisation', p. 15.

71. Lester Edwin J. Ruiz, 'After National Democracy: Radical Democratic Politics at the Edge of Modernity', *Alternatives*, Vol. 16, No. 2 (1991), p. 165.
72. Goldsmith, 'The State, the Market and Economic Development', p. 648.
73. For details, see Barry Hindess, *Freedom, Equality, and the Market* (London: Tavistock, 1987).
74. See Burchill, 'Liberal Internationalism', p. 54.
75. Arnaud de Borchgrave, 'Globalization – The Bigger Picture: An Interview with Dr. Ismail Serageldin', *The Washington Quarterly*, Vol. 19, No. 3 (1996), p. 161.
76. Aijaz Ahmad, 'Globalisation and the Nation-State', *Seminar*, No. 437 (January 1996), pp. 43–8.
77. *Ibid.*, p. 43. See also Aijaz Ahmad, 'In the Eye of the Storm: The Left Chooses', *Economic and Political Weekly*, Vol. 31, No. 22 (1996), p. 1330.
78. Ahmad, 'Globalisation and the Nation-State', p. 47 and Aijaz Ahmad, 'The Politics of Literary Postcoloniality', *Race and Class*, Vol. 36, No. 3 (1995), p. 12.
79. Immanuel Wallerstein, 'The ANC and South Africa: Past and Future of Liberation Movements in World-System', *Economic and Political Weekly*, Vol. 31, No. 39 (1996), p. 2699.
80. *Ibid.*
81. Ahmad, 'Globalisation and the Nation-State', p. 48.
82. *Ibid.*
83. Arun Ghosh, 'Capitalism, Nation State and Development in a Globalised World', *Economic and Political Weekly*, Vol. 32, No. 14 (1997), p. 685.
84. See Oliver Mendelsohn and Upendra Baxi, 'Introduction', in Mendelsohn and Baxi (eds.), *The Rights of Subordinated Peoples* (Delhi: Oxford University Press, 1994), p. 10.
85. Robert Solo, 'The Formation and Transformation of States', in W. Ladd Hollist and F. LaMond Tullis (eds.), *An International Political Economy* (Boulder: Westview Press, 1985), p. 83.
86. Eric Hobsbawm, *Age of Extremes: The Short Twentieth Century, 1914–1991* (New Delhi: Penguin, 1995), p. 577.
87. *Ibid.*, p. 578.
88. Noam Chomsky, *Powers and Prospects: Reflections on Human Nature and the Social Order* (Delhi: Madhyam Books, 1996), pp. 73–5.
89. Wallerstein, 'The ANC and South Africa', p. 2699.
90. For details on the linkages between nation-state, civil society and movements in the context of globalization, see Rajni Kothari, 'Under Globalisation: Will Nation State Hold?', *Economic and Political Weekly*, Vol. 30, No. 26 (1995), pp. 1593–1603, and 'Globalisation and Revival of Tradition: Dual Attack on Model of Democratic Nation Building', *Economic and Political Weekly*, Vol. 30, No. 12 (1995), pp. 625–33.
91. Stephen Krasner, 'The Accomplishments of International Political Economy', in Smith, Booth and Zalewski (eds.), *International Theory*, p. 110.

Index

272 *Index*